Religion and Gender

edited by

Ursula King

BLACKWELL
Oxford UK & Cambridge USA

Copyright © Blackwell Publishers Ltd 1995

First published 1995
Reprinted 2000, 2005

Blackwell Publishers Ltd
108 Cowley Road
Oxford OX4 1JF
UK

Blackwell Publishers Inc.
350 Main Street
Malden, Massachusetts 02148
USA

British Library Cataloguing in Publication Data

A CIP catalogue record for this book is available from the British Library.

Library of Congress Cataloging-in-Publication Data

Religion and Gender / edited by Ursula king
   p.   cm
   Includes bibliographical references and index.
   ISBN 0–631–19376–6 (alk. paper). – ISBN 0–631–19377–4 (pbk. alk. paper)
   1. Sex role – Religious aspects. 2. Religion – Study and teaching.
I. King, Ursula.
BL65.S4R44   1995
291.1'78343 – dc20   94–10767
                                   CIP

Typeset in 10½ on 12 pt Sabon Symposia by Apex Products, Singapore
Printed and bound in Great Britain by Marston Book Services Limited, Oxford

This book is printed on acid-free paper

Contents

Part II Empirical Investigations

List of Tables

Contributors

Kari Elisabeth Børresen, Professor in Medieval Studies/Humanistic Women's Studies, Department of Cultural Studies, University of Oslo, and Research Professor, Royal Norwegian Ministry of Culture, Oslo, Norway.

Felicity Edwards, Associate Professor in Systematic Theology, Faculty of Divinity, Rhodes University, Grahamstown, South Africa.

Naomi Goldenberg, Professor, Department of Religious Studies, University of Ottawa, Canada.

Rosalind I. J. Hackett, Associate Professor, Department of Religious Studies, University of Tennessee, Knoxville, USA.

Morny Joy, Associate Professor, Department of Religious Studies, Faculty of Humanities, University of Calgary, Canada and President of the Canadian Society for the Study of Religion.

Ursula King, Professor and Chair, Department of Theology and Religious Studies, University of Bristol, England and former President of the British Association for the Study of Religions (1991–4).

Kim Knott, Senior Lecturer, Department of Theology and Religious Studies, University of Leeds, England.

Penelope Margaret Magee, Lecturer, formerly University of South Australia, now working with the South Asian Women's Study and Support Group, affiliated to the National Centre for South Asian Studies, Melbourne, Australia.

Marilyn F. Nefsky, Associate Professor and Chair, Department of Religious Studies, University of Lethbridge, Alberta, Canada.

June O'Connor, Professor and Chair, Department of Religious Studies, University of California, Riverside, CA, USA.

Donate Pahnke, Assistant Professor, Department of Religious Studies, Faculty of Humanities, University of Bremen, Germany.

Rosalind Shaw, Assistant Professor, Department of Sociology and Anthropology, Tufts University, Medford, MA, USA.

Erin White, Lecturer, School of Studies in Religion, University of Sydney, Australia.

Preface and Acknowledgements

Contemporary gender studies are influencing and transforming many academic disciplines. They have also set a new agenda for the study of religion both in theology and religious studies. For historical and practical reasons gender studies possess at present primarily a woman-centred focus. Yet the angle of gender is larger and includes both women and men. The Introduction to this book discusses how women's studies, men's studies and gender studies are interrelated, each providing new insights, data and questions for research in religion. It also examines current work on women in different religious traditions, questions raised about methodologies, and debates about the paradigm shift in religious studies. The Introduction includes a bibliography of the most significant publications on religion and gender over the last few years.

The essays in this volume present a wide range of examples of current research on religion and gender undertaken by an international group of women scholars from Europe, North America, Australia and South Africa. Together with the Introduction they provide an overview of new theoretical and critical perspectives with special attention to new developments in epistemology, hermeneutics, methodology, feminist anthropology, new religious movements and spirituality as shaped by the insights of contemporary scholarship on gender.

The essays of this volume are new and have not been published before except for two contributions: Naomi Goldenberg's essay, 'The Return of the Goddess: Psychoanalytic Reflections on the Shift from Theology to Thealogy' (chapter 6) is taken from her book *Resurrecting the Body: Feminism, Religion and Psychoanalysis* (1993) and reprinted here by permission of the Crossroad Publishing Company, New York. An earlier version of the chapter by Felicity Edwards (chapter 8) appeared in the *Journal of Theology for Southern Africa*, vol. 66 (March 1989) and its revised form is published here with permission.

The idea of this book originated when I organized a panel on Religion and Gender for the XVIth International Congress of the International Association for the History of Religions, held in Rome 3–8 September 1990. The panel met during three days of the Congress when nineteen women scholars from around the world gave papers which raised lively discussions among the male and female audience. Thirteen of the participants provided chapters for this book, although these are not identical with the papers given at the Rome Congress as all contributions have been revised and in some cases replaced by different ones. My own essay, 'A Question of Identity: Women Scholars and the Study of Religion' (chapter 10), is an enlarged version of a paper first presented at the Women and Religion section of the Annual Meeting of the American Academy of Religion, Chicago, November 1988.

Although the concerns and orientation of the different essays are closely interrelated, the contributions have been grouped into two sections depending on whether the primary emphasis is on theoretical and philosophical issues or, alternatively, on empirical and historical matters. It is my hope that this book will be of interest to a wide academic readership in both religious and gender studies and that it will introduce undergraduate and graduate students to current debates in the study of religion and gender, making them aware of the rich research possibilities in this field.

I would like to thank all contributors for their patience, help and collaboration, and Alison Mudditt of Blackwell Publishers for her cooperation. I would like to express special thanks to Susan Morgan for assisting me in the bibliographical research for the Introduction, to Valerie Farrow and Pam Williams for all their efforts in helping me to prepare the manuscript for publication, and to Tina Beattie for help with the proofreading.

The book owes its existence to the research efforts of women scholars working across national and intellectual frontiers. I would like to dedicate it to all scholars of religion around the world, both female and male, who through their attention to critical gender studies are working towards a thorough transformation of both the study and the practice of religion.

Introduction: Gender and the Study of Religion

Ursula King

Gender issues are of great importance in contemporary society and culture. Although they concern both women and men, at present gender studies are still mainly focused on women because women have been voiceless for so long. Throughout most of human history there has existed an asymmetry in the relations of power, representation, knowledge and scholarship between men and women. Thus there exists a large agenda to be addressed in order to overcome women's invisibility, marginalization and subordination in history and society.

Gender has now become a critical category for the analysis of all data, including those of religion. At present most gender studies are almost identical with women's studies. Many current issues in the debates about women, their experience and self-understanding, status and role, are still influenced by or indirectly related to religious teachings and world-views, even when these are sharply criticized and rejected. At present there is often no recognition of women as agents and participants in their own right in most literature surveys in the field of religious studies. Frequently unexamined androcentric presuppositions underpinning the work of many male scholars cause serious deficiencies at the level of data gathering, model building and theorizing in religious studies. Despite this, many scholars continue to affirm their equally unexamined commitment to 'value neutrality' and 'objectivity'. Much of their sexism is not overt, but rather a 'sexism by omission'. They do not view their subject matter in relation to gender construction and traditional gender roles, both of which create uneven and unjust power structures.

In the past, women's religious roles and statuses have occasionally been an object of inquiry for male scholars but with the growth of critical feminist awareness and women's own scholarly development, women themselves are now both subjects as well as agents of scholarly analysis. The existence of women scholars and the critical transformation of their consciousness means that their research challenges the existing paradigms of religious studies because all phenomena are examined from the perspectives of gender and power. This has introduced an important paradigm shift in the contemporary study of religion, both in theology and in religious studies.

In order to understand what this paradigm shift is about and to position the specific studies of this book within their wider context, a number of clarifications are necessary. The essays gathered here have been grouped under 'Theoretical Reflections' and 'Empirical Investigations' so as to indicate their primary orientation. Theoretical and empirical dimensions are often interlinked and cannot always be divided neatly. Yet for the sake of clarity it is helpful to keep these two areas distinct, even though they are not completely separate. While the purpose of this book is to inform and be useful as a reference work providing research results and up-to-date bibliographies, it also aims to stimulate and advance theoretical debates on religion and gender by clarifying basic concepts and issues and by asking questions about future directions.

Gender and religion are closely interrelated as our perceptions of ourselves are shaped by and deeply rooted in our culturally shared religious and philosophical heritage, even when this is rejected. Religious traditions, beliefs and practices too are shaped by and perceived from the perspective of gender. Initially, this may be an unconscious process but with the contemporary growth of critical gender studies the transmission and perception of religious beliefs and the participation in religious activities have themselves become reflexive activities. Gender studies are beginning to make an impact on the contemporary study of religion and are setting new research agendas for religious studies. However, this is a slow process and the profoundly transformative effect of a basic paradigm shift has so far been less noticeable in religious studies than in other areas of the humanities.

It is the aim of this volume to contribute to further discussion of this development by asking why are gender variables so important, and how do they provide a new orientation for religious studies?

Both religion and gender are widely ramified concepts which can be used in either a general or more specific sense. It is important that this multi-dimensionality is always kept in mind. The following discussion will look at religion and gender in turn, consider the impact of contemporary gender studies on religious studies, and examine the methodological and practical implications of the paradigm shift in religious studies brought about by the attention to gender.

Religion

What understanding of 'religion' is implicitly assumed or explicitly articulated when referring to 'religion and gender'? We are aware of the complexities attached to the definition of 'religion', the difficulties in using such a term cross-culturally, especially in the study of non-Western religions, and the dangers inherent in the reification of the concept 'religion' evident in recent Western history, as Cantwell Smith (1990) has so well demonstrated. But what new problems and difficulties or, alternatively, which new insights occur when the notion of 'religion' is linked to gender-specific inquiries? Is the concept 'religion', then, used as traditionally defined by Western philosophy and theology, or is it arrived at by empirical induction? In other words, do we accept 'religion' as it has been historically and culturally evolved, as primarily a 'cumulative tradition', or is 'religion' rather understood as something experiential and personal, especially in relation to the personal experience of women and the different forms in which that experience finds its historical and contemporary expression? There is also the question of whether religion is mostly seen in terms of its institutional structures and historical-cultural embodiments which would require the investigation of gender-specific issues in very particular ways, or whether we can adopt in our research a much more open-ended, heuristic concept which enables us to investigate and explain particular activities of women (both past and present) as distinct from those of men. How far were women's religious experiences and activities important and meaningful without being recognized as such from the traditional point of view of the dominant religious institution(s)? It seems to me that different studies on women and religion adopt quite different understandings of the concept of 'religion' without necessarily discussing this: not all authors are methodologically critical and self-aware. I would like to underline the importance of the polysemic nature of the concept 'religion', especially in relation to gender issues. There is much talk today about the social, cultural and historical construction of gender, but such construction applies equally to the concept of 'religion'. Religion cannot be understood without its history and the multi-layered pluralism through which it has found complex social and cultural expression.

Religion is more than an object of study. It has been described as a core concern, as expressing and addressing the sacred, or as disclosing a transcendent focus linked to ultimate value. Religion has not only been the matrix of cultures and civilizations, but it structures reality -- all reality, including that of gender – and encompasses the deepest level of what it means to be human. Thus the study of religion, as the study of all creative activities of human beings, involves one's own subjectivity and reflexivity. It therefore raises complex questions for methodology, i.e. *how* it can be most appropriately studied and known. From a perspective of critical gender analysis, established methodologies prove inadequate, as will be discussed below.

Both the deconstruction and reconstruction of religious studies as an established discipline and of 'religion' as a concept – a lived and shared reality, a humanly meaningful activity, associated with both very specific and also more general, universal meanings for women – are important intellectual goals to be arrived at in reflecting on the study of religion in relation to gender.

Gender

Another set of questions arises out of the debates about gender, the necessary realization of its historical and social construction as well as the need for its deconstruction and reconstruction. There exists a difficulty, however, in that the notion of 'gender', though applicable to both sexes, is currently mostly debated with regard to women. When looking at historical and cross-cultural data on religion, specific attention to gender issues is currently concentrated on women. It is important, though, to consider not only the construction of femininity but also that of masculinity, especially as far as it is grounded in specific religious teachings, and analyse it critically. I have seen few references to this so far. It also requires some explanation why the words 'feminist' and 'masculinist' do not function in a parallel manner in contemporary women's writing; the term 'feminist' is mostly given a positive connotation whereas 'masculinist' is seen as mainly negative.

Progress in the study of religion is slow, but there is no doubt that the perspective of gender is of increasing importance in theoretical and empirical studies, not only for the growing number of women scholars, but also for many men. Some of the most lively debates centre around this perspective, and some of the most creative insights occur here. Until very recently the study of religion has been undertaken in general terms, without specific attention to gender. Now many new questions arise, and new knowledge is discovered in relation to the gendered dimension of religious phenomena.

The idea of genderedness is an important new insight of feminism not derived from earlier philosophical positions. It represents a new breakthrough in the history of human consciousness (King, 1993a, p. 215f). As we have only just begun to study the implications of this insight, we do not yet fully understand how complex the relationship between religion and gender really is.

The analysis of gender is much discussed in contemporary sociology and anthropology where the construction of gender identity and gender relations are seen as central for the understanding of the social order of any society (Hess and Ferree, 1987; Sanday and Goodenough, 1990). Gender ideologies are frequently hierarchically organized and sexual inequality is embedded in thought, language and social institutions. Yet male and female roles and relations are affected by so many cultural variables that now, when the complexity and contradictions of local gender practices are better known, it is increasingly more difficult to state gender insights in terms of universals.

Alice Schlegel (1990, p. 23) has described gender as 'the way members of the two sexes are perceived, evaluated and expected to behave'. She simply states that it is generally agreed that gender is a cultural construct, but one can argue about this. Feminist theorists sharply divide sex from gender; sex referring to the biologically given differences between women and men whereas gender refers to the social and cultural meanings assigned to these differences. The historical and cultural construction of these interpretations is sometimes seen as too separate from the biologically given. Kari E. Børresen (1990) corrects this one-sidedness when she considers gender as a sociobiological category and not simply as the result of history and culture. She thus emphasizes the interaction between biologically determined sex and culturally expressed gender. Her attempt to achieve greater theoretical clarity and balance, grounded in her historical work on women in the Christian tradition (see chapter 11, this volume) is paralleled by several significant developments in contemporary gender studies.

Contemporary Gender Studies

Human genderedness is a primary source of individual and social identity. When used as an analytical category it is also an important perspective for organizing knowledge. But gender has two centres, not one. A holistic anthropology must pay attention to both female and male gender construction and overcome the polarization created by some representatives of women's studies and critical feminist thought. Earlier sociological studies of sex roles took sexual differences for granted by accepting and examining them from an overwhelmingly androcentric perspective whereby male experience and roles were valued as exemplary and normatively human. Women's studies critiqued such androcentric universalism by establishing the importance, specificity and inherent value of women's own experience. During the 1970s women's studies developed into a rich body of theory, ideas and facts. The impact of feminism on traditional academic disciplines was described by Dale Spender (1981) as *Men's Studies Modified*. However, during the 1980s the influence of this critique and of feminist theories on gender differentiation led to the emergence of a new field of quite different, critical and self-reflective 'men's studies' (Brod, 1987a, b; Kimmel, 1987; Robinson, 1992). These studies highlight the diversity of men's lives, the subjectivity of men's personal and private experience in contrast to male public roles, and critically analyse the construction of masculinity (Clatterbaugh, 1990; Doty, 1993) by examining its myths and heroes, and considering male–female relations from classical times to the present.

Many of the works in the newly developing field of men's studies not only deal with issues of masculinity and traditional male roles, but also reconsider male experience of and attitudes to work and war as well as wider issues of gender relations. Questions about the unequal distribution of power are central here and still have to be fully addressed. For some, men's studies are seen as a reaction, or even a backlash, a response to the current crisis of masculinity in the Western world. But at their most critical and best, men's studies are committed to a thorough examination of male genderedness, considered problematic in its traditional understanding and expression, and to a larger vision of profound social change. Harry Brod (1987b) has argued that men's studies is essential to fulfilling the feminist project, for it reconceptualizes the field by focusing on broader issues of gender rather than simply on women's studies. Yet Lillian S. Robinson (1992, p. 443) in her survey of contemporary men's studies has pointed out that 'even when it makes use of the insights and results of feminist scholarship, men's studies lack the urgency of women's studies'.

When studying the processes of engenderment we not only learn about gender differentiation, but often also accentuate gender dichotomies and gender polarization. In addition to women's studies and men's studies there now exists a growing number of critical gender studies which produce 'more fine-grained analyses of gender ideology' (Schlegel, 1990, p. 23), highlighting the variability and contradictory views on femaleness and maleness in different cultures. In her autobiographical work *Outercourse* Mary Daly (1992, p. 340) refers cursorily, though rather dismissively, to ' "gender studies" ... blender studies'. The post-Christian feminist theologian Daly is well known for her radically separatist approach which is so exclusively woman-centred that men have no place in it at all, except as oppressors. The passage just quoted continues with brief statements made by and about Daly herself: ' "No male-bashing!" they say. "That's very bad", they say "Bad girl" ' (Daly, 1992, p. 340).

Such radical separatism appeals to few women or men. The ever expanding literature on women, sexuality and gender produces a more nuanced understanding of sexual differentiation which appreciates the important contribution of new insights without denying their complexity, ambivalence and contradiction. The strength of a critical, but more inclusive gender studies approach lies in its greater comprehensiveness through seeing femaleness and maleness, and the attendant constructions of femininity and masculinity, as closely interrelated.

In the field of religion this tension between different approaches is reflected in the critical debates about the concept of God the Father where inherent difficulties are not overcome through recourse to a direct reversal by replacing God the Father with the figure of 'Goddess the Mother'. Some women writers have tried to get away from this polarization by developing a specifically androgynous model of the Godhead where both female and male aspects are combined together in the Divine. Others again find this an unsatisfactory solution and instead suggest a monistic concept of ultimate reality which transcends sexual distinctions.

A woman professor of psychology and women's studies at Cornell University, widely known for her studies on sex roles, androgyny and psychosexual identity, has recently moved away from her earlier emphasis on androgyny precisely because this concept reproduces the very gender polarization it seeks to undercut. In her study *The Lenses of Gender* Sandra Lipsitz Bem (1993) is concerned with transforming the debate on sexual inequality by looking at the lenses through which our culture views male and female gender. Bem calls the hidden assumptions about sex and gender 'the lenses of gender' through which we polarize human beings into females and males. She distinguishes three different beliefs or 'lenses' which affect the construction of femininity and masculinity. The first is gender polarization, which provides mutually exclusive scripts for being male and female, and defines any person or behaviour deviating from this script as problematic. The effect of these two processes 'is to construct and to naturalize a gender-polarizing link between the sex of one's body and the character of one's psyche and one's sexuality' (Bem, 1993, p. 81).

The two other lenses besides gender polarization are androcentrism, which considers men as inherently the dominant or superior sex, as providing the exemplary norm for being human, and biological essentialism which maintains that male–female difference and male dominance are natural. We must become aware of the pervasiveness of these three 'lenses of gender' which are deeply embedded in our cultural discourses, in social institutions and in the psyche of individuals. Yet we need no longer continue to accept these lenses as they are. Instead of looking *through* them, we can learn to look critically *at* them for what they are and what they do to our humanity. Sexual inequalities are an illegitimate form of discrimination which was first religiously defended as God-given and natural (Bem includes a brief examination of Judeo-Christian theology in her discussion of androcentrism) and then, with the rise of a secularized science, these inequalities have been argued for on scientific grounds in the biological and social sciences.

Bem argues for the abolition of androcentrism and of all gender polarization, including the new variety created by a 'woman-centred' approach in contemporary feminist thought. She wants to shift the debate about sexual inequality away from its focus on male–female differences on to how androcentric discourses and institutions – among which, I would add, may be counted much of religious life – transform male–female difference into female disadvantage. Her goal of eradicating gender polarization is described under the title 'Toward Utopia', a recognition perhaps of how difficult it is to create a society wherein the biology of sex might be considered as one of minimal presence in human social life, important only in the narrowly biological context of reproduction.

Bem's approach is grounded in a broad humanistic concern with the way gender polarization prevents women and men alike from developing their full potential as human beings. We have polarized human values and experiences into the masculine and the feminine, yet our culture has not yet developed a comparable concept of a 'real' human being. I would like to comment here that traditional religious teachings do contain high ideals of what it means to be fully human, but these ideals have mostly been propounded by men to the detriment and exclusion of women, and with no attention to gender specifities.

A new critical gender awareness requires that we seek a new, more differentiated and at the same time more inclusive definition of what it means to be human. This must also include the religious and spiritual dimension, but in a new way. To develop and embody such a comprehensive and humanly empowering vision demands a profound social transformation which cannot come about without the psychological revolution of which Sandra Lipsitz Bem speaks:

> ... a *psychological* revolution in our most personal sense of who and what we are as males and females, a profound alteration in our feelings about the meaning of our biological sex and its relation to our psyche and sexuality. Simply put, this psychological

revolution would have us all begin to view the biological fact of
being male and female in much the same way that we now view
the biological fact of being *human*. Rather than seeing our sex as
so authentically who we are that it needs to be elaborated, or so
tenuous that it needs to be bolstered, or so limiting that it needs
to be traded in for another model, we would instead view our sex
as so completely given by nature, so capable of exerting its influence to those domains where it really does matter biologically,
that it could be safely tucked away in the backs of our minds and
left to its own devices. In other words, biological sex would no
longer be at the core of individual identity and sexuality. (Bem, 1993,
p. 196)

I have devoted considerable space to *The Lenses of Gender*
because this work expresses so clearly a major direction in which
contemporary gender studies are moving through the critical examination of gender formation and gender relations, pointing to
their reconstruction from a different theoretical and practical
vantage point.

Gender and Religious Studies

In the area of religion more inclusive gender perspectives have been
explored by several studies, as for example in Patricia Altenbernd
Johnson's and Janet Kalven's (1988) edited volume *With Both
Eyes Open: Seeing Beyond Gender*. More recently a substantial
study of historical, cross-cultural and theological perspectives on
gender relations has been produced as a team project edited by
Mary Stewart Van Leeuwen et al. (1993) under the title *After
Eden. Facing the Challenge of Gender Reconciliation*. Concerned
with the 'decentring' of feminism, especially white, Western feminism, this project thoroughly explores the application of critical
theory to gender relations and challenges the concepts of masculinity and femininity by laying bare the sources of gender
brokenness in the Western world. Written from a Christian theological perspective the book examines ways of dealing with human
difference by proposing a model of gender reconciliation grounded
in a Christian feminist vision that embraces both women and men.

Caroline Walker Bynum, in her introduction to a volume on
Gender and Religion: The Complexity of Symbols (Bynum, Harrell
and Richman, 1986) also argues for a comprehensive rather than
an exclusively woman-centred approach in the study of gender by

investigating how religious symbols relate to 'genderedness' – to people's experiences as females and males – rather than studying women's religious roles and behaviour only. It is no longer possible to study religious thought, language, practice and experience as well as religious symbols without taking gender into account, but it is still not enough to investigate the construction of gender and of gender-related symbols, which may function very differently in different religious traditions, by examining female experience alone. A larger agenda for the study of gender in religion is indicated by Bynum's statement:

> Gender-related symbols, in their full complexity, may refer to gender in ways that affirm or reverse it, support or question it; or they may, in their basic meaning, have little at all to do with male and female roles. Thus our analysis admits that gender-related symbols are sometimes 'about' values other than gender. But our analysis also assumes that all people are 'gendered'. It therefore suggests, at another level, that not only gender-related symbols but all symbols arise out of the experience of 'gendered' users. It is not possible ever to ask How does a symbol – *any* symbol – mean? without asking For whom does it mean? (Bynum, Harrell and Richman, 1986, p. 2–3)

Put differently, many studies have demonstrated that while constructs of ultimate reality are conceived in a variety of ways and transcendence can be envisaged as male, female or androgynous, it is also seen as being beyond form and gender altogether. Yet at the empirical level world religions have 'maintained male social dominance in the prevailing social structure' (Young, 1987, p. 7). Another important insight concerns the fact that while 'the transcendent may or may not have a gender component, the prominent soteriology of a world religion is always gender inclusive, even when the transcendent is a supreme male being' (Young, 1987, p. 16). Most women scholars recognize the need to give priority to the female gender in their studies in order to invert the very asymmetrical treatment of women in the study of religion, but it must not be overlooked that the idea of genderedness has far wider ramifications than is often recognized at present.

The discussion so far has shown how the critical lens of gender can bring into view either a very specific or a more wide-ranging perspective. If the lens is one, it can yet centre on two different foci – the female or the male aspect of gender – or it can approach both together in their relational structure. As I have indicated above, theoretical developments have widened out from women's studies and feminist concerns to men's studies and more inclusive gender analyses. The significance of religion for gender formation and gender relations, and the impact of women's studies, feminism and gender studies on the study of religion, though relatively neglected in earlier discussions (Langland and Gove, 1981; Spender, 1981; Farnham, 1987), is now much more widely acknowledged in general surveys on the cross-cultural study of women (Sinclair, 1986) and in the social scientific analysis of gender (Briggs, 1987). Yet in men's studies the area of religion seems to remain unexplored apart from the field of classical mythology where certain ideals of masculinity have their origin. However, I have yet to find a critical examination of the influence of religion on masculine gender construction. For this reason most of what follows is concerned with women.

In religious studies the scholarship on gender has so far been closely connected with developments in women's studies and contemporary feminist theories. In 1987 Constance H. Buchanan described women's studies in religion in an exemplary article in *The Encyclopedia of Religion* edited by Mircea Eliade (vol. 15, pp. 433–40); Rosemary Radford Ruether provided a similarly helpful entry on the presence of androcentrism in religion in the same work (vol. 1, pp. 272–6). These were the only two articles to explicitly examine the impact of feminism on the study of religion in this large contemporary reference work of sixteen volumes (for a feminist critique of *The Encyclopedia of Religion* see King, 1990b, and chapter 10, in this volume).

Buchanan succinctly summarized the magnitude of the critical and constructive tasks undertaken by women scholars in religion. The critical task implies a critique of both the religious and anthropological assumptions found in the different religions of the world. The task of reconstruction involves detailed historical research in order to uncover the voices, experiences and contributions of women in the religious history and life of humankind. It also implies a reconstruction of religious beliefs – 'the task of reweaving the sacred symbolic fabric of culture based on distinctive female experience' (Buchanan, 1987, p. 437) – and the reconstruction of ethical thought as well as the creation of new religious worlds linked to women's spiritual quest and the celebration of the Goddess. Such critical reconstruction involves the deconstruction of false universalist claims relating to all women or all human beings. The development of feminist theory on gender, religion and culture is thoroughly cross-disciplinary: women scholars from different religious backgrounds are working on diverse religious traditions, drawing on methods and insights from several disciplines and gathering a new body of data which can form the starting point for further theoretical debates.

Also very helpful is the chapter on 'The scholarship of gender: women's studies and religious studies' in Anne E. Carr's (1990, pp. 63–94) book *Transforming Grace. Christian Tradition and Women's Experience*. This demonstrates how the insights of feminist history and philosophy are applied to the study of religion. While emphasizing the need for a feminist perspective in teaching women's studies, the author warns against a false ghettoization of women's studies within the university curriculum. This leads on to a discussion of the concept of gender in terms of 'an implied, assumed or explicit *meaning* of sexual differentiation whenever the study of women (and men) is undertaken' (Carr, 1990, p. 76).

Carr maintains that we have now reached a third stage of women's studies, which follows after a first stage of the deconstruction of error and a second stage of the reconstruction of reality from a feminist perspective. This third stage is devoted to the construction of general theories and seeks a unifying framework which may be developed around a more inclusive gender system. Carr also discusses some early examples of the critique of religious traditions and of the recovery of lost women's history in relation to Christianity. She argues for the development of an inclusive Western theology, not an exclusive feminist spirituality built on the new goddess movement.

The innovative research of women in religion means that:

> ... much of past scholarship is placed on a new map of religious reality. Less than half the story has been told. To begin to tell the other part is to acknowledge that women have always been involved (even when excluded or ignored) in everything human, in everything religious. As the distinct subject matter of women's studies is the experience of women, that of women's studies in religion is the religious experience, expression, and understanding of women. But the concept of gender reminds us that the experience of women has been and always is in relationship to men in the whole of human society. Thus women's studies affects the study of men (now seen as part of the whole), the study of the human in its wholeness, and religious studies generally. That wider whole will not be fully understood, given the androcentric history of the

disciplines, without women's studies as a subject matter in its own right and as a necessary transition to the transformation of scholarship and the university curriculum. (Carr, 1990, p. 93)

Carr stresses the pluralism of questions and methods together with the feminist perspective or angle of vision which distinguish contemporary women's studies from any traditional study of women. To discover the experience of women some of the major questions in any period or area of study are:

> What was/is happening to women, what were/are women doing and thinking, what was/is the relative status of women and men with regard to symbolization, valuation, creativity, participation, opportunity, power, institutional and informal support and constraint? What images of the female and the male are employed in any religious context, and how are these used? What are their practical effects? How is sexuality viewed? What issues of family and society, the public and the private, class and race, need to be taken into account? (Carr, 1990: 93–4)

This quotation points implicity to the dual nature of gender: on the one hand it is only a partial factor in explaining reality, relating to other factors such as race, class, ethnicity, generation differences, etc., but on the other hand it is also all encompassing as far as social relations are concerned. We have two sexes, no more, and the complex aspects of engenderment affect all areas of human life, not least the complex worlds of religion.

Women and Religious Traditions

The cross-cultural and interdisciplinary nature of women's studies in religion has already been mentioned and is perhaps more appropriately described as a transdisciplinary orientation. This is well brought out in the survey of feminist research in religion since 1980 undertaken by June O'Connor (1989) who has also contributed a chapter to this book (chapter 1). O'Connor has grouped the proliferating questions and studies about women and religion in terms of the three Rs of rereading, reconceiving and reconstructing religious traditions. By 'rereading' the traditions she means re-examining religious materials and traditions 'with an eye attuned to women's presence and absence, women's words and women's silence, recognition given and denied women'. 'Reconceiving' women in the different religious traditions requires 'the retrieval and the recovery of lost sources and suppressed visions'. Some speak of this task as 'reclaiming women's heritage'. In the study of the Christian tradition this has been linked with the development of a 'critical hermeneutics of liberation' which involves several 'moments': 'suspicion, proclamation, remembrance, historical reconstruction, ritualization and celebration'. Through this process we can uncover in Christian scripture and history 'woman as agent as well as object, woman as participant and leader as well as the one overlooked and rendered anonymous, woman as liberated by certain features of the Christian message as well as woman restricted by patriarchy'.

Such hermeneutical procedures can be applied to different religious traditions as is evident from the studies discussed by O'Connor under the section on 'Reconstruction'. Such reconstruction is described as involving two tasks: '(1) reconstructing the past on the basis of new information and the use of historical imagination; and (2) employing new paradigms for thinking, seeing, understanding and valuing.' (The quotations are taken from O'Connor, 1989, pp. 102, 103, 104.)

Theological reconstruction can apply to particular aspects of a religion or to the rethinking of a whole religious tradition from a feminist perspective. Examples of the latter are Rosemary Radford Ruether's (1983) *Sexism and God-Talk: Toward a Feminist Theology* which deals with Christianity, and Rita M. Gross's (1993) *Buddhism after Patriarchy. A Feminist History, Analysis and Reconstruction of Buddhism*. The work of theological reconstruction undertaken by scholars working on the goddess has been renamed 'thealogy' (for a discussion of the shift from theology to thealogy see Naomi Goldenberg, chapter 6, this volume). O'Connor's (1989) article on 'Rereading, reconceiving and reconstructing traditions: feminist research in religion' discusses many academic publications which are grouped under the headings: cross-cultural studies, goddess studies, Jewish studies, Christian studies, Afro-American studies, African traditional religions, native American religions, Islamic studies, Hindu studies, Buddhist studies, feminist religious ethics, journals and other resources for further study.

Such cross-cultural studies show that women's position in religion is often a reflection, however oblique, of women's status in society. Social scientists have frequently pointed out that religious systems both reflect and reinforce cultural values and patterns of social organization (Sinclair, 1986). Yet in spite of women's historical subordination and oppression many past examples can be found of women as active agents and religious subjects in their own right. Much attention is now given to women as religious actors, as shamans, witches, healers, nuns, mystics and ascetics. These figures are often seen and revered as women apart, as women who enjoy a high spiritual and moral authority rather than the institutional authority accorded to men. Such female religious specialists are often recruited from among women who eschew established female social roles. In fact, it is rare to find women who are at the same time religious officiants as well as wives and mothers.

Besides religious actors, women are also religious innovators. They develop strategies of resistance for coping with their own situation of oppression, but they also take part in wider religious and social protest movements. Numerous examples of women leaders and participants in dissident religious movements can be found throughout the history of religions. Of particular interest to contemporary researchers are the women founders and leaders outside mainstream religion in the new religious movements of our time (Knott, 1987; Puttick and Clarke, 1993; Wessinger, 1993; Puttick, 1994; see also chapter 12 of this book on 'Women and New Religious Movements in Africa' by Rosalind I. J. Hackett).

Another important area of research is concerned with women's experience of the sacred and female symbols associated with the sacred, or what some authors prefer to call the human constructs of ultimate reality. Many religions are rich in feminine imagery and symbolism, none perhaps more than Hinduism, but the symbolic ascendancy of the feminine often goes with a social denigration and low status of women in everyday life. Thus one must clearly distinguish between the place given to women in the world of religious imagination and that accorded to them in the actual world of religious life. These two often stand in an inverse relationship to each other and remain poles apart.

This tension is highlighted by some of the readings found in Serenity Young's (1993) anthology *Sacred Writings by and about Women*. Taken from the primary texts of the world's religions, such as sacred scriptures, law books, creation myths, hagiographies, tales of folklore and the stories of tribal groups, these readings about and by women present a rich store of male thinking about women while occasionally also voicing the religious experience of women themselves. Young analyses a number of different cross-cultural themes about women which are found persistently across religious traditions through time and space. A particularly striking contrast is that between the representation of women as both evil and wise. The complex issue of evil is tied up with other important themes, such as those of woman's body and sexuality, menstruation taboos, the figure of the witch and fear of death. The feminization of the spirit of wisdom appears in many religious traditions, whether as Sophia in the Judeo-Christian traditions or the goddess of wisdom in Mediterranean and Indian religions, or the female Bodhisattva of compassion in the Far East.

Another area of lively debate and creative development is that of feminist spirituality. This can be understood in the wider sense of women's contemporary spiritual quest or in the specific form of a new feminist consciousness and goddess spirituality (aspects of which are discussed in chapters 6, 7 and 8 of this volume). I have surveyed the explicit and implicit spiritual dimensions of contemporary feminism with reference to different religions and cultures in my book *Women and Spirituality: Voices of Protest and Promise* (King, 1993a). Other helpful bibliographical surveys are found in the articles by Joan Leonard (1990), 'Teaching introductory feminist spirituality: tracing the trajectory through women writers', Sally Noland MacNichol and Mary Elizabeth Walsh (1993), 'Feminist theology and spirituality: an annotated bibliography', Judith G. Martin (1993), 'Why women need a feminist spirituality', and Linda Woodhead (1993), 'Post-Christian spiritualities'. Indispensable for the understanding of feminist spirituality are the two by now classical collections of articles edited by Carol P. Christ and Judith Plaskow (1979, 1992), *Womanspirit Rising. A Feminist Reader in Religion* and Judith Plaskow and Carol P. Christ (1989), *Weaving the Visions. New Patterns in Feminist Spirituality*.

These rich scholarly resources raise many fundamental questions about women and religious traditions: How is women's spiritual quest experienced and explored? How do women experience their relationship with the sacred or divine spirit? How do they voice and describe it? What religious roles and rituals do women participate in and from which ones are they excluded? What religious rites, religious lives and religious communities have women created for themselves? What religious authority and power have women held, and how has the spiritually empowering authority of their experience been expressed and transmitted to others? What influence, if any, have women had in the creation and transmission of religious and theological knowledge?

These questions relate to women's actual participation in religious life. Further questions arise about the world of symbols created by the religious imagination: Which experiences of the sacred, by women or men, have found expression in female form and image? What are the female faces of the divine, or the feminine dimensions of ultimate reality present in different religions? How far are women themselves seen as sacred or, on the contrary, as demonic and taboo in some religious traditions?

Yet other questions relate to the importance of religion in women's history, questions to which feminist historians have not always paid the attention they deserve. Gail Malmgreen (1986; see Introduction, 1–10) has reminded us that women took to the public platform on behalf of religion long before they were stirred by politics. Examining the writings of the past where women's voices can be heard, she asks 'What was the nature of women's private devotions? Were women's religious beliefs consistently different from those of men? Does it make sense to speak of female-identified theologies in the eighteenth or nineteenth century, as it does in the twentieth? Can we discern a distinctively female ethical voice in the past, as Carol Gilligan has in the present?' (Malmgreen, 1986, p. 3). Looking at the women of the past from the angle of the present, one question above all others poses itself: 'To what extent did women's spiritual impulses and religious vocations, however expressed, persist in a more or less hostile environment as sources of strength, self-definition, and accomplishment?' (Malmgreen, 1986, p. 9). This question, raised in the historical context of Western Christianity, can be asked about women in all religions, past and present.

All these questions are not only questions of scholarly research and analysis. On the contrary, the perspective of women's studies, of feminism and of more inclusively conceived gender studies, includes as an integral part a strong commitment to contemporary personal and social transformation. It is this perhaps utopian goal, the strong wish to transcend all gender discrimination and polarization, to seek a holistic life-affirming spirituality and build a new society, which is the creative source of the often provocative and intellectually daring stance found among contemporary feminist scholars. Feminism is both a new academic method and also a new social vision. Both approaches have an impact on the methodologies of different disciplines. This is clearly reflected in the current methodological debates taking place among women scholars in religious studies.

Feminist Methodological Debates and the Paradigm Shift in Religious Studies

Methodological debates among contemporary women scholars in religion are much influenced by current feminist theory which fundamentally calls into question the basic assumptions of the prevailing organization of knowledge, its claims to universality, objectivity and value-neutral detachment.

In the study of religion and gender two fundamental problems arise for feminist scholars. One has to do with the subject matter of the research, the other with the attitude of the researcher. As to the subject matter, most religious phenomena, even when studied by women, still remain set in the context of an androcentric framework which defines our intellectual task in the very effort of deconstruction and reconstruction. The sources, concepts, models and theories of religious studies are male-derived and male-centred; they operate with a generic masculine which implies that men have almost always spoken for and about women. Even when studying the history, literature and religious experience of women themselves, we have to rely to a great extent on the materials and data described by men. The sacred writings of the world religions are all thoroughly androcentric. However, women are not only readers of androcentric texts, they are also writers and creators of such texts when they are schooled in and express themselves through the dominant modes of thinking of their age. Dissenting voices can be heard in the past, but they are few. A fully articulated critical consciousness of women has only developed in our own time and contemporary feminist 'gynocritics' (Showalter, 1986, p. 128), or what I prefer to call the gynocritical approach, is particularly interested in women as *writers*, that is women who as their own agents create their own structures of meaning. In religious studies such a gynocritical approach means that women scholars analyse and interpret religious phenomena specifically associated with, experienced, articulated and described by women.

As to the attitude of the researcher, there already exists a lively, wide-ranging methodological debate in contemporary religious studies in general. This is concerned with determining the most appropriate methods for studying religion. Many different approaches and positions are debated, such as that of insider and outsider, neutrality and commitment, for example. Many scholars criticize the over-intellectualist and heavily text-orientated approaches of traditional religious studies; many are beginning to recognize that the study of religion, especially of religious experience, involves one's own subjectivity and reflexivity. The religious position and commitment of the researcher can thus influence the subject matter that is being researched. However, the current general methodological debates in religious studies do not yet take into account the specific methodological insights and realignments found among feminist scholars.

Women's profoundly new experience of critical personal, social and religious transformation makes them ask challenging and uncomfortable questions. Critically aware of their own positioning in society, they question the existing structure of knowledge and their own place in it. The process of consciousness-raising has led women to the discovery of self autonomy and self agency, but also to that of solidarity and relationality. From the perspective of these experiences women criticize the suppression of personal, subjective human experience in general and of women's experience in particular in what traditionally counts as knowledge. Attention to gender is beginning to reshape both the perception of and the participation in knowledge. In the study of religion it is therefore no longer enough to ask *what* we know about religion, but equal attention must be paid to how we come to know what we know. Feminist research in religion has epistemological significance (as June O'Connor argues at length in chapter 1 of this book). Critical attention to gender variables not only affects the analysis of religious texts, but it also raises many questions about conceptual categories governing the gathering of data in fieldwork (as Kim Knott discusses in chapter 9).

Women scholars are searching for a more experientially grounded, more gender balanced and more dialogical methodology. In doing so, they still have to argue for a feminist perspective of gender analysis which cannot yet be taken for granted. Debates about the challenge of feminist methodological insights for the transformation of religious studies have been going on since the early 1970s. Yet so far mainstream methodological works have simply ignored them. Could this perhaps have something to do with the fact that detailed textual work and revision appear to be less threatening and more acceptable to male scholars than theoretical and interpretative work which reflects women's original and independent thinking?

Without claiming to be comprehensive I shall list some significant discussions on methodology. Rosemary Radford Ruether (1981) published an early article on 'The feminist critique in religious studies'. It focuses largely on the Judeo-Christian tradition and on theology rather than the more inclusive concerns of religious studies. But unlike other writings on the same subject, it raises the important question of how women's studies in religion can be translated into educational praxis in institutions of higher learning in terms of both curriculum development and staff appointments.

Other publications on methodology, criticizing the prevalent androcentrism in the history of religions, came from Rita M. Gross (1974, 1977, 1983) who must be recognized as a lonely pioneer in calling so early for a fundamental reorientation of the whole field of religious studies. I discussed her earlier work in my paper 'Female identity and the history of religions' (King, 1986), first delivered at the XIVth International Congress of the History of Religions in 1985. In it I emphasized that the feminist perspective is not yet part of the common horizon of religious studies and I argued 'that the development of a truly inclusive framework for the study of religion, of more differentiated conceptual tools as well as of different perspectives of analysis and synthesis requires that full space is given to the voices and perspectives of women' (King, 1986, p. 91). Women scholars in religion work in relative isolation. They can experience crises of identity due to the absence of role models and of a well-established community of discourse in their field. There exists also a continuing silence about the contribution of women scholars to the study of religion in the past (some historical examples are discussed in my chapter 10 in this volume).

The importance of methodological clarifications and of a basic shift in orientation is highlighted by numerous articles which the *Journal of Feminist Studies in Religion* has published since its foundation in 1985. Its second number included a roundtable discussion 'On feminist methodology' (1985, pp. 73–88) and a later volume presented another one on 'A vision of feminist religious scholarship' (1987, pp. 91–111). Other articles worth singling out are those by Carol P. Christ on 'Embodied thinking: reflections on feminist theological method' (1989) and on 'Mircea Eliade and the feminist paradigm shift' (1991).

Such methodological articles are evidence of how feminist scholarship makes use of alternative, non-traditional sources and methods which in turn produce alternative contents and structures in scholarly knowledge. The feminist paradigm in religious studies is one of transformation. Its critique of the traditional sources and content of an established field involves an alternative vision which transforms both the subject matter and the scholar at the same time.

The methodological process can be summed up as starting with a hermeneutics of suspicion *vis-à-vis* traditional sources and methods, followed by a critical deconstruction and reconstruction of the key elements of the discipline, eventually resulting in its transformation. The close alliance between feminism as an academic method and social vision born out of a new experience and consciousness has been challengingly expressed by Rita Gross, especially in the two methodological appendices of her book *Buddhism after Patriarchy* (1993). Her scholarly self-understanding and commitment is deeply rooted in a feminist perspective which leads to a large increase in the data to be studied and also to an increase in the critical reflection on the nature of religion and on the most appropriate methods for its study. Gross argues that religion is not reducible to its cultural matrix, but that the religious impulse for world-construction, for seeking meaning and orientation, constitutes an inalienable part of human life.

From her stance as an engaged, committed woman scholar she also argues against the division of the study of religion into separate, narrow theological and historical subdisciplines. The attitude of the scholar must in her view be one of empathy and commitment while maintaining honesty and objectivity in the sense of declaring one's interests and methodologies. As a feminist engaged in the cross-cultural study of religion Gross speaks of a 'double assignment' which on one hand requires to explain the world-view of patriarchy with empathy, yet on the other hand refuses to undertake scholarship 'that extends, perpetuates, legitimates, or justifies patriarchy' which she considers as a destructive traditional religious value that must be exposed (Gross, 1993, p. 315). Her feminist and scholarly experience and reflection converge in her conclusion that the 'engaged study of religion, with its combination of dispassionate de-absolutized understanding and passionate existential commitment to just and humane values, is the single most powerful lens through which one can view religion' (Gross, 1993, p. 317).

Much important work based on critical gender analysis exists in the contemporary study of religion. Yet one can still argue over the question of whether a paradigm shift in religious studies has already occurred or whether we are only at the threshold of a new paradigm. Feminist scholarly commitment expressed in both women's studies and wider gender studies requires nothing less than the transformation of the author's world-view and scholarship. The process of this transformation becomes visible at different levels: at that of one's personal existential and spiritual quest, at the level of scholarly discourse and knowledge construction, and also in the critique of whole religious systems. Numerous examples for these different forms of transformation can be found in contemporary scholarship on different religious traditions.

Some years ago Randi R. Warne (1989), when assessing the impact of women's studies on religious studies, spoke of moving 'toward a brave new paradigm'. She saw this move as occurring in three different areas: (1) in women asking new questions of traditional materials; (2) in the move from universality to particularity, from abstraction to engagement; (3) in the critique of objectivity and the revisioning of all knowledge as morally significant, thus raising basic questions about the nature of all knowledge. Critical feminist and gender perspectives are certainly much debated and attest to a profound transformative potential in their effect on traditional forms of knowledge. How far these debates have made a real impact on the dominant practitioners of the field and changed the way religion is studied in universities is another matter, however. Carol Christ, who has written on the feminist paradigm shift in religious studies more than once (Christ, 1987, 1991), still describes the field of religious studies as highly patriarchal and speaks of feminist scholars in religion as 'sojourners for a long time to come' (Christ, 1992, p. 87). Women's critical debates are set 'within an academic power structure which is not only male, but white, heterosexual, middle and upper class, for the most part Christian, and not particularly hospitable to feminism' (Christ, 1992, p. 86). Thus she concludes that a great deal remains to be done if feminist scholarship is to transform the teaching and research of religious studies in universities, although research and reflection on women and religion are flourishing both inside and outside the academic world.

Feminist scholarship offers exciting critical perspectives and, as mentioned earlier, these critical perspectives are also foundational for contemporary men's studies and the development of more inclusive gender studies. To maintain this critical momentum and challenge, to put into practice the transformative potential of such critical insights, necessitates that neither women's nor men's studies are ghettoized, and that gender studies are not simply reduced to 'blender studies', as Mary Daly maintains. A successful development of inclusive, balanced critical gender studies requires also a balanced gender representation and the full participation of both genders in all areas of religious studies – in religion as studied, taught, and practised. This requirement raises many practical questions, not least about institutional power and teaching authority. As Randi Warne has pointed out, to meet the challenge of women's studies, religious studies 'must ensure that its departments are materially constructed in such a way that the presumption of male privilege is not maintained' (Warne, 1989, p. 43). Will feminist scholars always remain sojourners in the field of religious studies or will they on the contrary soon become fully established citizens and inheritors of a whole field and its wide-ranging cluster of inquiries? This is a legitimate contemporary concern which invites further reflection.

Practical Considerations and Questions

As a discipline, religious studies remains thoroughly androcentric in its key concepts and paradigmatic perspectives of inquiry, but also in its institutionalized practice with its lack of recognition of feminist scholars and their work. The study of women is still marginalized in the study of religion, and the comprehensive study of gender as a category with even larger connotations has hardly begun.

The main question is this: Is the necessary paradigm shift in religious studies possible, and can it be practically brought about? A number of problems arise with regard to the teaching of new, gender-related perspectives in religious studies, but also with regard to larger issues pertaining to the training and employment of scholars teaching such courses and researching in this area.

Some feminists are emphatic in their exclusive stance and insist on addressing women alone, but they are in a minority. Many women scholars consider it important to develop a comprehensive, integral perspective on religion and gender and emphasize that both women and men students should participate in 'Religion and Gender' courses. While such courses may initially be of much greater interest to women, male students too can get deeply committed to the intellectual and experiential issues raised, and can experience a considerable transformation of their awareness and achieve excellent results.

The practical difficulties of introducing a religion and gender course will vary from institution to institution and from country to country. It is not only a question of getting such courses accepted by curriculum and programme committees, there is the additional difficulty of finding the funding and practical support for purchasing the necessary library materials. At one institution, I once submitted a long list of book titles to a librarian who was wholly unsympathetic to this field. It came as no surprise when I found out that only very few of my suggestions ever made it into the library. I can also think of the editor of a well-known Anglican theology journal raising the question of whether feminist books were ever of sufficient quality to warrant serious attention.

Even though high-quality literature on women and religion is steadily on the increase, it is not easy to build up a library collection for teaching, especially when one is dependent on the collaboration of librarians in sympathy with the subject. Most teaching institutions and their leadership are still thoroughly androcentric, and so is much that counts as accepted knowledge in most fields. To introduce change takes time, is hard work and demands a great deal of persistence and single-mindedness.

From what I have said, it is clear that I am strongly opposed to 'religion and gender' being treated as a 'ghetto subject' for women only, but even when the participant subjects of such a course are both female and male, the course itself can still be treated as marginal in the overall academic programme or as merely a temporary concession to current intellectual fashions. The ultimate aim of research and teaching on gender issues must be a more differentiated critical perspective in all courses and in the entire programme of religious studies. This can be achieved only if women scholars take a full part in the future shaping of the whole field of religious studies and eventually constitute 50 per cent of its practitioners.

At a professional level, in terms of academic posts, career structure, promotion and tenure there are still many obstacles to this. When being considered for promotion, I was once told that 'publications on feminism are academically not respectable' – this was the view of powerful, established figures in the field. Many younger colleagues, at the beginning of their career, may have even greater difficulties in getting their work accepted. It will take more than one generation to change the dominant academic power structure and to change some of the most influential methodologies which perpetuate the myth of 'objectivity' and 'detachment' derived from outmoded models of science. As is clear from the methodological debates referred to earlier, the feminist study of religion involves a 'participatory hermeneutic' on the part of both students and teachers which produces a new consciousness and new attitudes.

The study of religion and gender is a self-reflexive process which leads to a new, more differentiated consciousness on the part of those undertaking it. It also implies, of necessity, a self-critical examination of one's own beliefs, attitudes and experiences, and thus can lead to manifold transformations. Different teachers and students respond in a very personal and individual way to the study of religion and gender; they draw different conclusions from such a study for their own lives. In that sense no religion and gender course is a neutral, 'value-free' undertaking where cool analysis and traditional academic distancing in the name of objectivity and detachment can reign supreme. On the contrary such a course has existential implications, for it elicits personal decisions and commitment which may affect not only one's intellectual outlook, but one's entire life.

If critical attention to gender becomes a really integral part of religious studies, this will not only influence the study of religion, but also bring about deep changes in religious practice. Nowhere can this be seen more clearly than in the area of spirituality and religious ritual where women are experimenting with a fresh creativity and inventiveness unthinkable before. These experiments, and the new questions arising from them, may have consequences as yet difficult to foresee. At present, women are experimenting with old traditions and creating new ones. These prove spiritually empowering for women as individuals and groups, yet they often possess little cultural authority in a broader sense. Powerful religious institutions of the traditional kind continue to be led and shaped by men alone. Thus there is an urgent need to create a critical gender awareness and call for greater balance in the established religious institutions. Following the example of the World Council of Churches, there is also an urgent need to work for the greater visibility of women in traditional religious institutions by creating a 'Decade of Religions in Solidarity with Women', as I have argued elsewhere (King, 1993b). This would strengthen the work done at the academic level and make it easier for women to participate in equal numbers to men in the teaching and study of religion.

For historical and practical reasons the discussions on religion and gender occur at present primarily around a woman-centred focus. But this focus is itself but a part of the larger, bifocal angle of a critical gender lens. As Anne Carr has argued, feminist consciousness sharpens critical perspective, but it does not by itself guarantee the results, nor does it always necessarily produce important, insightful scholarship. Good scholarship in women's studies aims to meet the highest standards of scholarship anywhere, but it also calls into question what the most appropriate and best scholarly standards are, and what responsibilities such scholarship implies. But one thing is certain, women's critical work and reflection 'will inevitably alter perceptions of female and male, the masculine and feminine, and perceptions of gender in religious studies as a whole' (Carr, 1990, p. 94).

To sum up the developments, several dimensions can be discerned in the paradigm shift which the feminist critical awareness has introduced into religious studies. These dimensions are not sequential but coexist together and express the rich diversity which women scholars contribute to the contemporary study of religion:

1   There is a *descriptive* dimension: women's new awareness has made women ask new questions which have produced new materials and research results in the study of religions. Women's status, role, images and experiences, for so long neglected, have become new objects of investigation, even though these often remain androcentrically defined. Many publications and courses on women in world religions provide us with new data at the level of description, often with a minimum of critical analysis. We discern women's voices hidden in androcentric texts; we discover women's experiences and biographies, their contributions to the shaping of different religious traditions and spiritualities.

2   There is the *negative-critical* dimension of the analysis and deconstruction of the androcentric framework, perspectives and assumptions which mask much of the full meaning of these data. The feminist critical analysis of the history, literature and religious experience of women has to rely to a great extent on texts and data created or described by men. An additional, gynocritical analysis is concerned with women as independent, autonomous writers rather than simply as readers of androcentric texts. Women scholars now look critically at

works produced by other women rather than only those by men about women.

3   Following on from this there exists a *positive-critical* dimension where women undertake the reconstruction of experiences, insights and different elements of tradition to make them meaningful for us today. For some this may be a woman-centred reconstruction while others seek wider, more inclusive interpretations of religious materials. This may lead to an extended, new conversation between women and men scholars in the study of religion, a new phase of integration, a new stage of greater differentiation and complexity.

4   There is also the *methodological dimension*: women's critical approach undertaken from a new awareness as a gendered self in relation to others in community also requires different research methodologies which function differently from traditionally established methodological paradigms and elicit more empathetic involvement and personal concern in relation to one's studies. This does not mean abandoning scholarly objectivity and critical assessment, but they need to be modified and refined by taking into account current theoretical developments in critical gender studies.

Conclusion

As this essay has tried to show, critical attention to gender variables provides such a significant new orientation for the contemporary study of religion that one can justifiably speak of a paradigm shift in the entire field of religious studies. The important impact of gender on current theoretical and empirical work and on methodological debates provides us with critical tools for an alternative vision and different scholarly praxis which are beginning to transform and reconceptualize the study of religion.

Looking at religion through the sharp lenses of gender first developed by feminist theory produces a genuine advance in the intellectual processes, explanations and results of scholarship. Women's insights, academic inquiries and research efforts are currently at the cutting edge of contemporary scholarship. It is crucial that the knowledge gained is integrated into mainstream teaching and research without losing its critical edge and impact.

Considering the implications of the feminist paradigm for the contemporary study of religion, what are the possible directions for religious studies in the near future? It is impossible to prophesy, but it is clear that we need far more women scholars in the study of religion – ideally 50 per cent in all teaching and research positions – to effect not only a paradigm shift, but to get our new paradigm universally accepted and thereby transform our discipline more radically. In the view of some scholars, current studies on women and religion represent one of the liveliest, most creative and challenging developments in contemporary religious studies. Yet such studies are far from being given general academic recognition and acceptance. Some of the liveliest debates at present concern God-language, feminist ethics, feminist spirituality, religious attitudes to the body and sexuality, the relationship between feminism, religion and psychoanalysis. In feminist theology there is the additional significance of Third World theology which increasingly attracts attention (Russell et al., 1988; King, 1994). There is also fascinating new work being developed on feminism, religion and ecology (Primavesi, 1991; Ruether, 1992; Adams, 1993).

In looking for a future research agenda for religious studies we must also bear in mind that the feminist critical approach to the study of religion represents a paradigm shift *within* another paradigm shift which is larger still. This is the new discourse and consciousness about globality and globalization which has emerged over the last few years and which is of deep significance for religion as practised and studied, especially for spirituality. It is because of this global perspective that the theology of women from the Third World is of such great importance.

At present, the notion of difference and pluralistic diversity among women is widely discussed among feminists, but many of these discussions still remain too confined to local and regional boundaries. Women's studies are far from truly inclusive of all women, far from being comprehensive and global. This may be illustrated by just one example where others could be given. In a survey tracing the development of women's studies in religion Judith Plaskow (1993) strongly affirms that feminist work in religion belongs to a larger universe of feminist discourse, yet the universe surveyed by her is entirely restricted to North America (though it includes a few Asian women scholars teaching in the United States). North American studies on women and religion are leading in the field, but many of them suffer from their own parochialism by limiting their discussion only to other North American authors. Plaskow's (1993) article does not cite a single non-American publication and one may legitimately ask how representative her presentation of the development of women's studies in religion is. Such studies now have a truly global dimension and include publications from many countries, in many different languages, and on many different traditions.

It is impossible to develop thoughts on religion and gender in a global perspective further here, but globalization as a process whereby we become conscious of the whole world as a single place – a unity created by the bonds of one human family – has deep ramifications for feminism, gender and religion. In the future this may bring with it a further shift from woman-centred approaches to the study of religion – where religious thought, language, practice and structures are primarily examined with reference to women – to a wider focus on religion and gender where the field is enlarged to include critically reflected data about both sexes rather than about women alone.

Feminist critical analysis has called into question the false universalism of androcentric thinking. Women must not commit the mistake now of constructing a new, false unversalism of a different sort on the basis of female experience alone. We are faced with the difficulty that the notion of gender, though applicable to both sexes, is currently mostly investigated with regard to women. Women scholars, for fairly obvious reasons, concentrate their research on women; it is not their main task to critically investigate gender issues as they arise for men. Men have to do this for themselves. The next step in further reconstruction will be an additional phase of integration where female and male gender issues are brought into fruitful relationship with each other. Only then can we fully understand the complex interconnections between gender and power; and only then can we develop the strength and wisdom needed to shape the human community in a more just and balanced way and thereby radically transform the social order at both a local and global level.

Religious and spiritual values are vital for this. Women must be empowered and need to empower others to change the world as we know it. The critical voices of women in religion and in the contemporary study of religions must be heard and listened to – they are a promising sign of hope for the future of religious studies and for the future of our world.

The essays that follow exemplify as well as examine representative perspectives of contemporary women's critical studies on religion. Written by women scholars working in different countries around the world, they also demonstrate what Rosalind Shaw has called 'the gendering of religious studies' (see chapter 2, this volume). The following chapters acquaint readers with current perspectives and new research agendas in the field of religion and gender and will, hopefully, stimulate further critical debate and theoretical reflection. Each of the two parts of this volume is preceded by a brief introduction to the essays contained in it.

The bibliography at the end of this introductory essay does not only include references to the works cited but provides readers with the necessary bibliographical tools to enable them to examine the most significant debates on religion and gender for themselves. The bibliography, mainly based on publications of the last ten years, does not list the very large number of descriptive and comparative studies on women and religion (included in the extensive bibliography of my study *Women and Spirituality*, King, 1993a) but concentrates on titles primarily concerned with theoretical discussions of religion and gender.

Bibliography

Adams, Carol J. (ed.) 1993: *Ecofeminism and the Sacred*. New York: Continuum.

Ahmed, Leila 1992: *Women and Gender in Islam*. New Haven & London: Yale University Press.

Andolsen, Barbara H. 1985: Gender and sex roles in recent religious ethics literature. *Religious Studies Review*, 11, 3, 217–23.

Andolsen, Barbara H., Gudorf, Christine E. and Pellauer, Mary D. (eds) 1985: *Women's Consciousness, Women's Conscience: A Reader in Feminist Ethics*, New York: Seabury/Winston.

Atkinson, Clarissa W., Buchanan, Constance H. and Miles, Margaret R. (eds) 1985: *Immaculate and Powerful: The Female Sacred Image and Social Reality*. Boston: Beacon Press.

Atkinson, Clarissa W., Buchanan, Constance H., and Miles, Margaret R. (eds) 1987: *Shaping New Vision. Gender and Values in American Culture*. Ann Arbor/London: WMI Research Press, The Harvard Women Studies in Religion Series, vol. 5.

August, Eugene P. 1985: *Men's Studies: A Selected and Annotated Interdisciplinary Bibliography*. Littleton, CO: Libraries Unlimited.

Bell, Diane, Caplan, Pat and Karim, Wazir Jahan (eds) 1993: *Gendered Fields: Women, Men and Ethnography*. London and New York: Routledge.

Bem, Sandra Lipsitz 1993: *The Lenses of Gender. Transforming the Debate on Sexual Inequality*. New Haven and London: Yale University Press.

Børresen, Kari Elisabeth 1990: Women's studies of the Christian tradition. *Contemporary Philosophy. A New Survey*, 6, 2, 901–1,001.

Børresen, Kari Elisabeth (ed.) 1991: *Image of God and Gender Models in Judaeo-Christian Tradition*. Oslo: Solum Forlag.

Børresen, Kari Elisabeth and Vogt, Kari 1993: *Women's Studies of the Christian and Islamic Traditions*. Dordrecht, Boston, London: Kluwer Academic Publishers.

Briggs, Sheila 1987: Women and religion. In Beth B. Hess and Myra Marx Ferree (eds), *Analyzing Gender. A Handbook of Social Science Research*, Newbury Park, Beverly Hills, London, New Delhi: Sage Publications, 408–41.

Brod, Harry (ed.) 1987a: *The Making of Masculinities. The New Men's Studies*. Boston, London, Sydney, Wellington: Allen Unwin.

Brod, Harry 1987b: The new men's studies: from feminist theory to gender scholarship. *Hypatia*, 2, 1, 179–96.

Buchanan, Constance H. 1987: Women's studies. In M. Eliade (ed.), *The Encylopedia of Religion*, New York: Macmillan; London: Collier Macmillan, vol. 15, 433–40.

Bynum, Caroline Walker 1991: *Fragmentation and Redemption. Essays on Gender and the Human Body in Medieval Religion*. New York: Zone Books.

Bynum, Caroline Walker, Harrell, Stevan and Richman, Paula (eds) 1986: *Gender and Religion: On the Complexity of Symbols*. Boston: Beacon Press.

Cantwell Smith, Wilfred 1990: *The Meaning and End of Religion*. Minneapolis: Augsburg Fortress Press. (First edn, New York: New American Library, Mentor, 1964.)

Carmody, Denise Lardner 1982: Feminism and the world religions. *Horizons: The Journal of the College Theology Society*, 9, 2, 313–22.

Carr, Anne E. 1990: *Transforming Grace. Christian Tradition and Women's Experience*. San Francisco: Harper & Row.

Christ, Carol P. 1979: Why women need the goddess: phenomenological, psychological and political reflections. In Carol P. Christ and Judith Plaskow (eds), *Womenspirit Rising*, New York: Harper & Row, 273–87.

Christ, Carol P. 1983: Symbols of goddess and god. In Carl Olson (ed.), *The Book of Goddess Past and Present*, New York: Crossroad, 231–51.

Christ, Carol P. 1987: Toward a paradigm shift in the academy and in religious studies. In Christie Farnham (ed.), *The Impact of Feminist Research in the Academy*, Bloomington: Indiana University Press, 53–76.

Christ, Carol P. 1989: Embodied thinking: reflections on feminist theological method. *Journal of Feminist Studies in Religion*, 5, 1, 7–17.

Christ, Carol P. 1991: Mircea Eliade and the feminist paradigm shift. *Journal of Feminist Studies in Religion*, 7, 2, 75–94.

Christ, Carol P. 1992: Feminists – Sojourners in the field of religious studies. In Cheris Kramarae and Dale Spender (eds), *The Knowledge Explosion. Generations of Feminist Scholarship*, New York and London: Athene Press, 82–8.

Christ, Carol P. and Plaskow, Judith (eds) 1979: *Womanspirit Rising. A Feminist Reader in Religion*. New York: Harper & Row. (1992 edition: HarperSanFrancisco.)

Clatterbaugh, Kenneth 1990: *Contemporary Perspectives on Masculinity: Men, Women and Politics in Modern Society*. Boulder, CO: Westview Press.

Cooey, Paula M., Eakin, William R. and McDaniel, Jay B. (eds) 1991: *After Patriarchy. Feminist Transformations of the World Religions*. Maryknoll/NY: Orbis Books.

Culpepper, Emily Erwin 1987: Philosophia: feminist methodology for constructing a female train of thought. *Journal of Feminist Studies in Religion*, 3, 2, 7–16.

Culpepper, Emily Erwin 1988: New tools for theology: writings by women of color. *Journal of Feminist Studies in Religion*, 4, 2, 39–50.

Daly, Mary 1992: *Outercourse. The Be-Dazzling Voyage*. San Francisco: HarperSanFrancisco.

Doty, William G. 1993: *Myths of Masculinities*. New York: Cross Road.

Eliade, Mircea (ed.) 1987: *The Encyclopaedia of Religion*. New York and London: Collier Macmillan. (See for 'Androcentrism', Rosemary Ruether, vol. 1, 272–6; 'Goddess worship: theoretical perspectives', James Preston, vol. 6, 53–9; 'Women's Studies', Constance H. Buchanan, vol. 15, 433–40.)

Farnham, Christie (ed.) 1987: *The Impact of Feminist Research in the Academy*. Bloomington and Indianapolis: Indiana University Press.

Fiorenza, Elisabeth Schüssler and respondents 1985: Roundtable discussion: On feminist methodology. *Journal of Feminist Studies in Religion*, 1, 2, 73–89.

Goldenberg, Naomi R. 1993: *Resurrecting the Body: Feminism, Religion and Psycholanalysis*. New York: Crossroad.

Gross, Rita M. 1974: Methodological remarks on the study of women in religion: review, criticism and redefinition. In J. Plaskow and J. A. Romero (eds), *Women and Religion*, rev. edn, Missoula, MT: Scholars Press, 153–65.

Gross, Rita M. 1977: Androcentrism and androgyny in the methodology of history of religions. In R. M. Gross (ed.), *Beyond Androcentrism: New Essays on Women and Religion*, Missoula, MT: Scholars Press, 7–21.

Gross, Rita M. 1983: Women's studies in religion: the state of the art 1980. In P. Slater and D. Wiebe (eds), *Traditions in Contact and Change. Selected Proceedings of the XIVth Congress of the International Association for the History of Religions*, Waterloo, Ontario: Wilfred Laurier University Press, 579–91.

Gross, Rita M. 1993: *Buddhism after Patriarchy. A Feminist History, Analysis, and Reconstruction of Buddhism*. Albany NY: State University of New York Press. See in particular Appendix A 'Here I stand: feminism as academic method and social vision', 291–304; Appendix B 'Religious experience and the study of religion: the history of religions', 305–17.

Hagen, June Steffenson (ed.) 1990: *Gender Matters. Women Studies for the Christian Community*. Grand Rapids, Michigan: Academic Books, Zondervan Publishing House.

Henking, Susan E. 1991: Bibliographic resources on gender and religion. In Mark Juergensmeyer (ed.), *Teaching the Introductory Course in Religious Studies: A Sourcebook*, Atlanta, GA: Scholars Press, 275–9.

Hess, Beth B. and Ferree, Myra Marx (eds) 1987: *Analyzing Gender. A Handbook of Social Science Research*. Newbury Park, Beverly Hills, London, New Delhi: Sage Publications.

Heyward, Carter 1985: An unfinished symphony of liberation: the radicalisation of Christian feminism among white US women: a review essay. *Journal of Feminist Studies in Religion*, 1, 1, 99–118.

Hoch-Smith, Judith and Spring, Anita (eds) 1978: *Women in Ritual and Symbolic Roles*. New York and London: Plenum Press.

Hofman, Greta (ed.) 1987: *Women and Men – Interdisciplinary Readings on Gender*. Nemiroff, Montreal: Fitzhenry & Whiteside.

Jacobs, Janet L. 1991: Gender and power in new religious movements. A feminist discourse on the scientific study of religion. *Religion*, 21, 4, 345–56.

Johnson, Patricia Altenbernd & Kalven, Janet (eds) 1988: *With Both Eyes Open: Seeing Beyond Gender*. New York: Pilgrim Press.

Journal of Feminist Studies in Religion (1985–): Editors: Judith Plaskow, Manhattan College, and Elisabeth Schüssler Fiorenza, Harvard Divinity School.

Joy, Morny and Magee, Penelope (eds) 1994: *Claiming our Rites: Australian Feminist Essays in Religious Studies*. Adelaide: Australian Association for the Study of Religions.

Kaminski, Phyllis H. 1992: Teaching women and sexuality in the Christian tradition: mutual learning and pedagogical issues of voice, authority and power. *The Council of Societies for the Study of Religion Bulletin*, 21, 1, 1–5.

Kimmel, Michael S. (ed.) 1987: *Changing Men. New Directions in Research on Men and Masculinity*. Newbury Park, Beverly Hills, London, New Delhi: Sage Publications.

King, Ursula 1986: Female identity and the history of religions. In V. C. Hayes (ed.), *Identity Issues and World Religions*, Bedford Park: The Australian Association for the Study of Religions, 83–92.

King, Ursula M. (ed.) 1987: *Women in the World's Religions, Past and Present*. New York: Paragon House.

King, Ursula 1990a: Religion and gender. In U. King (ed.), *Turning Points in Religious Studies. Essays in Honour of Geoffrey Parrinder*, Edinburgh: T & T Clark, 275–86.

King, Ursula 1990b: Women scholars and the *Encyclopedia of Religion. Method and Theory in the Study of Religion*, 2, 1, 91–7.

King, Ursula 1993a: *Women and Spirituality – Voices of Protest and Promise*, second edn. London: Macmillan, and University Park, PA: Penn State Press.

King, Ursula 1993b: Rediscovering women's voices at the World's Parliament of Religions. In Eric J. Ziolkowski (ed.), *A Museum of Faiths. Histories and Legacies of the 1893 World's Parliament of Religions*, American Academy of Religion Classics in Religious Studies, Atlanta, GA: Scholars Press, 325–43.

King, Ursula (ed.) 1994: *Feminist Theology from the Third World. A Reader*. London: SPCK and Maryknoll, NY: Orbis Books.

Knott, Kim 1987: Men and women, or devotees? Krishna consciousness and the role of women. In U. King (ed.), *Women in the World's Religions, Past and Present*. New York: Paragon House, 111–28.

Kramarae, Cheris and Spender, Dale (eds) 1992: *The Knowledge Explosion. Generations of Feminist Scholarship*. New York and London: Athene Press, Teachers College Press, Teachers College, Columbia University.

Langland, Elizabeth and Gove, Walter (eds) 1981: *A Feminist Perspective in the Academy. The Difference it Makes*, Chicago and London: The University of Chicago Press.

Leonard, Joan 1990: Teaching introductory feminist spirituality: tracing the trajectory through women writers. *Journal of Feminist Studies in Religion*, 6, 2, 121–37.

Lloyd, Genevieve 1984: *The Man of Reason. 'Male' and 'Female' in Western Philosophy*. London: Methuen.

Lunn, Pam 1993: Why women need the goddess? Some phenomenological and sociological reflections. *Feminist Theology*, 4, 17–38.

MacNichol, Sally Noland and Walsh, Mary Elizabeth 1993: Feminist theology and spirituality: an annotated bibliography. *Women's Studies Quarterly*, XXI, 1 & 2, 177–96.

Malmgreen, Gail (ed.) 1986: *Religion in the Lives of English Women 1760–1930*. London and Sydney: Croom Helm.

Martin, Judith G. 1993: Why women need a feminist spirituality. *Women's Studies Quarterly*, XXI, 1 & 2, 106–20.

Meadow, Mary Jo and Rayburn, Carole A. (eds) 1985: *A Time to Weep, A Time to Sing: Faith Journeys of Women Scholars of Religion*. New York: Winston Press.

O'Connor, June 1985: How to mainstream feminist studies by raising questions: the case of the introductory course. In Walter E. Conn and Arlene Swidler (eds), *Mainstreaming: Feminist Research for Teaching Religious Studies*, Lanham, New York, London: University Press of America, 1–10.

O'Connor, June 1989: Rereading, reconceiving and reconstructing traditions: feminist research in religion. *Women's Studies*, 17, 1, 101–23.

Plaskow, Judith 1989: Religion and gender: the critical and constructive tasks. *The Iliff Review*, 45, 3–13.

Plaskow, Judith 1993: We are also your sisters: the development of women's studies in religion. *Women's Studies Quarterly*, XXI, 1 & 2, 9–21.

Plaskow, Judith and Christ, Carol P. (eds) 1989: *Weaving the Visions. New Patterns in Feminist Spirituality*. San Francisco: Harper & Row.

Prelinger, Catherine M. (ed.) 1992: *Episcopal Women: Gender; Spirituality, and Commitment in an American Mainline Denomination*. New York: Oxford University Press.

Preston, James J. 1987: Goddess worship: theoretical perspectives. In M. Eliade (ed.), *The Encyclopedia of Religion*, New York: Macmillan; London: Collier Macmillan, vol. 6, 53–9.

Primavesi, Anne 1991: *From Apocalypse to Genesis. Ecology, Feminism and Christianity*. Tunbridge Wells: Burns & Oates.

Puttick, Elizabeth 1994: Gender, Discipleship and Charismatic Authority in the Rajneesh Movement, PhD, King's College, University of London.

Puttick, Elizabeth and Clarke, Peter B. (eds) 1993: *Women as Teachers and Disciples in Traditional and New Religions*. Lewiston, Queenston, Lampeter: The Edwin Mellen Press.

Robinson, Lilian S. 1992: A good man is hard to find: reflections on men's studies. In Cheris Kramarae and Dale Spender (eds), *The Knowledge Explosion: Generations of Feminist Scholarship*. New York and London: Athene Press, 438–47.

Ruether, Rosemary Radford (ed.) 1974: *Religion and Sexism. Images of Woman in the Jewish and Christian Traditions*. New York: Simon & Schuster.

Ruether, Rosemary Radford 1981: The feminist critique in religious studies. In Elizabeth Langland and Walter Gove (eds), *A Feminist*

Perspective in the Academy. The Difference It Makes, Chicago and London: The University of Chicago Press, 52–66.

Ruether, Rosemary Radford 1983: *Sexism and God-Talk: Toward a Feminist Theology*. Boston: Beacon Press.

Ruether, Rosemary Radford 1985: The future of feminist theology in the academy. *Journal of the American Academy of Religion*, 53, 703–16.

Ruether, Rosemary Radford 1987: Androcentrism. In M. Eliade (ed), *The Encyclopedia of Religion*, New York: Macmillan and London: Collier Macmillan, vol. 1, 272–6.

Ruether, Rosemary Radford 1992: *Gaia and God. An Ecofeminist Theology of Earth Healing*. HarperSanFrancisco and London: SCM, 1993.

Russell, Letty M., Pui-lan Kwok, Isasi-Díaz, Ada Mariá and Cannon, Katie Geneva (eds) 1988: *Inheriting our Mothers' Gardens: Feminist Theology in Third World Perspective*. Philadelphia: Westminster Press.

Saint-Sens, Alan (ed.) 1991: *Religion, Body and Gender in Early Modern Spain*. San Francisco: Mellen Research University Press.

Sanday, Peggy Reeves and Goodenough, Ruth Gallagher (eds) 1990: *Beyond the Second Sex: New Directions in the Anthropology of Gender*. Philadelphia: University of Pennsylvania Press.

Schlegel, Alice 1990: Gender meanings: general and specific. In P. Reeves Sanday and R. Gallagher Goodenough (eds), *Beyond the Second Sex. New Directions in the Anthropology of Gender*, Philadelphia: University of Pennsylvania Press, 23–41.

Setel, T. Drorah 1985: Feminist insights and the question of method. In Adele Yarbro Collins (ed.), *Feminist Perspectives on Biblical Scholarship*, Society of Biblical Literature, Biblical Scholarship in North America Series, no. 10: Chico, CA: Scholars Press, 35–42.

Sharma, Arvind (ed.) 1987: *Women in World Religions*. Albany: State University of New York Press.

Shechter, Patricia and respondents 1987: Roundtable discussion: A vision of feminist religious scholarship. *Journal of Feminist Studies in Religion*, 3, 1, 91–111.

Shinn, Larry D. 1980: The goddess: theological sign or religious symbol? *Numen*, 30, 176–98.

Showalter, Elaine (ed.) 1986: *The New Feminist Criticism: Essays on Women, Literature and Theory*. London: Virago.

Sinclair, Karen 1986: Women and religion. In Margot I. Dudley and Mary I. Edwards (eds), *The Cross-Cultural Study of Women. A Comprehensive Guide*, City University of New York: The Feminist Press, chapter 5 under 'Theoretical perspectives', 107–24.

Skees, Sue R. 1990–91: Listening to women past and present: visiting scholars extend the boundaries of women's studies and religion. *Harvard Divinity Bulletin*, 20, 4, 14–17.

Spender, Dale (ed.) 1981: *Men's Studies Modified: The Impact of Feminism on the Academic Disciplines*. Oxford: Pergamon.

Swidler, Arlene and Conn, Walter E. (eds) 1985: *Mainstreaming: Feminist Research for Teaching Religious Studies*. College Theology Society, Resources in Religion 2, Lanham, New York, London: University Press of America.

Taves, Ann 1992: Women and gender in American religion(s). Review article. *Religious Studies Review*, 18, 4, 263–70.

Van Leeuwen, Mary Stewart et al. (eds) 1993: *After Eden. Facing the Challenge of Gender Reconciliation*. Grand Rapids, MI: William B. Eerdmans Publishing Company, and Carlisle: The Paternoster Press.

Warne, Randi R. 1989: Toward a brave new paradigm: the impact of women's studies on religious studies. *Religious Studies and Theology*, 9, 2 & 3, 35–46.

Weaver, Mary Jo 1989: Widening the sphere of discourse: reflections on the feminist perspective in religious studies. *Horizons: The Journal of the College Society*, 16, 302–15.

Wessinger, Catherine (ed.) 1993: *Women Outside the Mainstream: Female Leaders in Marginal Religions in America*. Illinois: University of Illinois Press.

Woodhead, Linda 1993: Post-Christian spiritualities. *Religion*, 23, 2, 167–81.

Young, Katherine K. 1987: Introduction. In A. Sharma (ed.), *Women in World Religions*. Albany: State University of New York Press, 1–36.

Young, Serenity (ed.) 1993: *Sacred Writings by and about Women: A Universal Anthology*. London: Pandora and New York: Crossroad.

Part I

Theoretical Reflections

Introduction

Ursula King

The following contributions discuss several theoretical points which arise out of the application of feminist insights to the study of religion, pursued at many different levels and from several disciplinary perspectives, whether those of philosophy, anthropology, psychology, theology or the history of religions. The wider, more inclusive approach of gender studies is well brought out in June O'Connor's chapter on 'The Epistemological Significance of Feminist Research in Religion', with which this section opens. What is our knowledge of religion, and how have we arrived at it? Feminist critical work is investigatory and transformative in character. O'Connor highlights this when she discusses how women's studies have not only made a difference to *what* we know but also in *how* we come to know. That is their special epistemological significance.

Such fundamental reorientation sharpens our sensitivities for investigating root metaphors, key concepts and foundational texts of religion as well as ethical and political issues. But epistemological shifts based on critical gender awareness, leading to gender-sensitive research in one's field of study, are not only significant for women, but for women and men alike. It is less a question of replacing a previously male-centred lens with a female-centred one than to draw attention 'to women's experience as an expansion or alternative or corrective to the historically prevalent male-based lenses'. Such a more balanced approach will yield more inclusive and less distorted, less partial knowledge.

But such an approach implies a profound transformation of one's own discipline. Depending on what this discipline is, such transformation may be fast or slow. Rosalind Shaw, who works in both anthropology and religious studies and conducts research on women in African religions, examines in chapter 2 the different impact which feminism has had on the transformation of her two disciplines. Religious studies has not questioned its own presuppositions as much as anthropology has done, and Shaw demonstrates how some of the dominant perspectives of religious studies – a primarily text-based view of religion, religion as reality *sui generis* and a positivistic paradigm of the 'science of religion' – all account for scholarship which sees religion as decontextualized and ungendered.

This makes it difficult to get a gender-orientated study of religion widely accepted, and it makes the study of women in African religions doubly difficult because of the quite different positioning of women and religion in African societies where the notion of power, 'the kinds of power which women exercise, and the kinds of power which others exercise over them', is central. In other words, religious roles, rituals and symbols cannot fully be understood without recognizing how the religious, social and political are closely interrelated and cannot be separated.

Chapter 3 articulates the possibility of a hermeneutics of gender, exemplified through a critical discussion of Paul Ricoeur's influential work and its bearing on the study of religious language, symbols and beliefs. Erin White shows how, on closer reading, Ricoeur's seemingly genderless theory proves to be quite androcentric, but she also mentions how he has become more aware of gender issues in more recent publications. White pleads for a critical attention to gender, defined as 'a construction of maleness and femaleness, in the study of all symbols and texts, and of their interpretations'. Yet, gender itself can be seen as a symbol. Operating at the semantic, mythic or rational level, this symbol is implicitly or explicitly present almost everywhere. A comprehensive hermeneutics of gender requires that neither an androcentric nor a gynocentric bias prevails. Only then can gender move to the centre as 'one of the key elements in the symbols of humanity'.

The next three chapters are less concerned with wider gender issues than with the impact of specific feminist perspectives on the study and practice of religion. Chapter 4 points to the tension between secular feminism, which seems to ignore religion, and religious studies which takes little notice of feminist theory and practice. Drawing on contemporary critical feminist and literary theory, Penelope Margaret Magee shows how the idea of the sacred, one of the central notions in the study of religion, is being disputed, challenged and destabilized by these theories. Is the sacred being erased in our culture? Are feminists helping to disrupt and deconstruct the sacred, or do their theories provide significant elements for its quite different reconstruction and for a profound rethinking of the problematic sacred/profane distinction?

Many feminist writers think so, as is evident from the reconceptualization of the Divine found in debates about God language and the Goddess. In chapter 5 Morny Joy examines the iconoclastic God-talk of several contemporary women theologians whereas Naomi Goldenberg assesses the significance of the modern Goddess movement from the perspective of psychoanalytic theory in chapter 6. From a somewhat different perspective the Goddess movement is also examined in chapter 7 where Donate Pahnke discusses the theoretical and practical consequences of studying feminist Goddess spirituality by showing how both 'religion' and 'magic' carry different meanings for its practitioners from that assumed in the traditional study of religion.

The last chapter of this section, chapter 8, returns to wider perspectives by relating gender awareness to a profound transformation of human consciousness, of great significance for the evolution of contemporary society. In a different context, such evolutionary transformation of person and society was already reflected upon by the Indian thinker Sri Aurobindo and the French writer Pierre Teilhard de Chardin, but neither of them took into account reflections on gender. Based on some of their ideas, and especially on Beatrice Bruteau's work, Felicity Edwards discusses the characteristics of 'neo-feminist consciousness', which recognizes gender polarity but transcends gender polarization and seeks to develop a new holistic spirituality based on participatory consciousness and on a new paradigm of social relationships which replaces domination and submission by communion.

The many different themes and theoretical points which these essays raise provide substantial evidence for the importance of critically examining the field of religion and gender. The insights gained here contribute not only to the transformation of our ways of knowing and of practising our scholarly discipline, but they are equally significant for transforming our understanding of spirituality and religious practice. Several of these points will be raised again, though from a different vantage point, in the second part of this book which is more concerned with empirical investigations.

1

The Epistemological Significance of Feminist Research in Religion

June O'Connor

Feminism is concerned with the shift in roles and the question of rights that have been unjustly denied women. But all of that, however important and even essential, is secondary. The main event is epistemological. Changes in *what* we know are normal; changes in *how* we know are revolutionary. Feminism is a challenge to the way we have gone about *knowing*. The epistemological *terra firma* of the recent past is rocking, and, as the event develops, it promises to change the face of the earth. (Maguire, 1986, p. 122)

Daniel Maguire's observation that the significance of feminism is primarily epistemological renders a judgement that invites attention. His interpretation offers a lens for approaching, understanding, assessing, and utilizing feminist research and analysis in religion.

The questions that characterize feminist inquiry are many and varied and can be clustered in a variety of intelligible ways. Elsewhere I have identified some of the questions being pursued in terms of the three 'Rs' of rereading, reconceiving, and reconstructing traditions (O'Connor, 1989).[1] The great variety of questions posed and pursued in feminist research arises out of curiosity about women's lives and ways of knowing, women's insights, aspirations and analyses. Feminist work also emerges from a sensitivity to and criticism of the androcentric manner in which many religions have been shaped and formulated and also the androcentric manner in which religions generally have been studied. Questioning the sources and strategies of study as well as the content of what has been forwarded and taught about women, men, and religion opens up new areas for study, new sorts of inquiry, new assumptions and standpoints. By asking previously unasked questions and by employing methods of social history, historical-critical textual hermeneutics, by drawing upon macro-historical perspectives of women's presence and work on the 'underside' of history, and employing the feminist movement's praxis for liberation from domination, feminist scholars have generated new questions and new findings (see, for example, Boulding, 1976; Fiorenza, 1983; Ruether, 1983; Plaskow, 1990). They have taken us behind the words of the world's religious literature and enabled us vicariously to move among disparate religious practices with eyes and ears open in order to see and hear anew. In doing so they alert us to a more nuanced, refined, and self-critical consciousness of women's presence and absence, participation and exclusion in religion and society. Because of this work, we now read inherited sources and conventional wisdom with a gender-sensitive hermeneutic that includes a variety of moments: (1) some measure of suspicion, given the androcentric context and content of inherited sources; (2) attention to recovery and remembrance of women's lives and history, together with efforts to reconstruct the lives of those who had little voice in their societies; (3) criticism, correction, and transformation of given concepts, such as inherited claims regarding what is universally human; (4) efforts to rethink and alter the ways scholarship itself is approached and carried out, given the findings of feminist perspectives; and (5) feminist self-critical examination, part of the process of following questions wherever they lead us and refusing to turn feminist inquiry into an ideology or orthodoxy.[2]

Paying attention to the findings of women's studies and feminist research has made visible the partial, selective picture we have inherited. In addition to the retrieval of lost or long-ignored sources, this work has opened up possibilities for recasting the concepts, theories, and methods that scholars think about in doing our work and reconstructing agendas for future work. But feminist contributions have done more than that. They have also opened up possibilities for recasting and reconstructing the concepts, theories and methods that *we think with*. Herein resides the most telling feature of the epistemological significance of feminist inquiry, I believe, because the ideas that have the most powerful hold upon us are not those *we think about* (and thus seek to get a 'handle' on, gain some 'control' over, or 'do' something with). The most powerful ideas are those *we think with*. They are the ideas that lie 'behind' our eyes, enabling us to see; what we do see is shaped by them. A Chinese proverb I regularly share with my students makes this point baldly: 'Two-thirds of what we see is behind our eyes' – a sobering and disillusioning insight for those of us working to see reality as is. And yet the proverb resonates a truth. Much of what we see, we see because we have been trained, educated and socialized to see in certain ways. This means there are also things we do not see, questions and insights to which we are blind, paths not taken, whole areas that are concealed to us as others are revealed. The alert are ever reminded that oversight, as well as insight, marks human knowing. These dynamics of expanding the boundaries of our thought by questioning the ideas we think with are not unique to feminist inquiry. Study in the liberal arts and humanities aims to alert students and scholars to become self-critically conscious about the very categories with which, by which, and through which we see and think and value. Feminist inquiry participates in this process by turning our attention to gender.

Feminist inquiry's most important feature is bringing to consciousness the ideas we think with regarding the sources of the traditions and their images for the sacred, regarding assumptions about spirit and body and ascetic materials that reflect and debate these assumptions, regarding understandings of sin and virtue and ignorance and enlightenment, and about ways of conceiving and implementing justice or love or compassion or harmony (see, for example, Atkinson, Buchanan and Miles, 1985: King, 1987; Sharma, 1987; Cooey, Eakin and McDaniel, 1991). Feminist inquiry questions, critiques, and reconstructs. It scrutinizes, relativizes and regularly rejects metaphors, concepts and approaches that have been cherished for years, indeed often for centuries. It also creates metaphors, searches for more adequate concepts, and proffers new approaches, bringing an air of detachment and an attitude of dispensability to inherited claims and categories. For these reasons, feminist inquiry and findings are not only interesting but, for many, deeply (and understandably) irritating.

The epistemological significance of feminist research in religion lies in its asking questions about how we know and what we know: How do we know what we know? What are our sources of knowledge and why do we trust them? It's not enough to tell me what you see. I want to know where you are standing as you see and speak, and also why you stand there.[3] How do we know what we claim to know (about women and men and religion and society)? What are the sources of our views (regarding gender identity and ability and power)? Who is making a given claim? How does the author/speaker know that and on what grounds, by what authority? Where is that voice coming from? Where does that speaker/author stand as she/he sees and speaks? Feminist theories and specific feminist analyses of texts, concepts and practices press us to reconsider how we know and what we think, how and why we see as we do. An array of sources awaits the attention and loyalty of serious inquirers. Why do we respect this source more than that one? Why do we rank our sources as we do (text over reader, reader more than text, religious community over either, personal experience and intuition or the voice of authority over all)? And what is at stake in the choices we make? What to gain? To lose? When feminist scholars ask us to examine the fact that the normative sources of Christianity, Judaism, Islam and other religions were authored by men, conveyed by men, and canonized by men, they ask us to notice a fact. When they ask on what grounds women were excluded from authoring, naming and establishing the canon, they ask questions that carry moral import as well as historical-critical connotations.

Feminist work is investigatory. It is also much more than investigatory. It is transformative in character. Investigative work informs us among other things that women have had diminished opportunity for study, diminished opportunity for participation in the institutions of learning and in the production of knowledge. Therefore, feminist scholars argue for and urge change such that women's voices join the public conversation that generates the production of knowledge. The investigative arm of feminist inquiry leads to the transformative function of feminist inquiry. For once the experience of women is taken as seriously as the experience of men, such experience must be utilized, that is, factored into our theories and methods.[4] How we hold and interpret our experience, what values we derive from it, and what hopes and aspirations we articulate are all moments in the process of constructing knowledge. Feminist theorists insist that women as well as men must have access to that process and a voice in the ensuing debates about the accuracy and adequacy of the knowledge produced.

Judith Plaskow's (1990) effort to examine Judaism from a feminist perspective and to transform it in light of the feminist value of gender justice exemplifies this work in process. Plaskow (1990, p. xviii) acknowledges the hard question many Jews rightly ask: 'At what point in the reinterpretation of Judaism does the Jewish tradition cease being Jewish and become something else?' Her response, in part, is to note that 'rabbinic Judaism itself was the product of enormous changes', effecting 'a shift from Temple sacrifice as the center of worship, to study and prayer as the dual foci of Judaism'. What she judges crucial is the fact that this 'profound change was perceived as a transition rather than a break only because the Jewish community willed it so, and undertook to reinterpret the past to meet the needs of a radically different present'. How the Jewish community will respond to the challenge of feminism is not yet decided, but Plaskow is confident that the mechanisms by which those decisions will be made are themselves 'old and tried'.

> Some feminist changes will endure because they are appropriate, because they speak to felt needs within the community and ring true to the Jewish imagination. Others will fall by the wayside as eccentric, mechanical, or false. To try to decide in advance which will be authentic is to confine our creativity and resources; it is to divert energy needed to shape the kind of Jewish community in which we want to live. (Plaskow, 1990, p. xix)

Plaskow vividly reminds us that radical transformation in and of a tradition is not an unprecedented phenomenon but is part of what tradition itself means and does. The rabbinic transformation occurred because the people willed continuity in the midst of radical question and change. Similarly, the feminist transformation will occur if the Jewish community wills continuity together with feminist appropriation.

Feminist research has sharpened my own epistemological sensitivities by stimulating my thinking about the root metaphors with which we think and the fundamental concepts we think about. It has freed me to appreciate and to propose alternatives that come from attentiveness to the concrete, lived experience of women and men alike. The Christian concept of sin provides one illustration.

Although *pride* has been one of the chief designations for defining and naming *sin*, feminist theological investigations have shifted the familiar categories, for when tested against the experience of women in many subcultures, women's sin is more aptly described not as pride but as self-denial, self-abnegation and debilitating dependence. While sin as pride makes sense for those who regularly experience power and authority in society and thus need self-critical reminders about how power is exercised and how authority is wielded, such a designation does not make sense to those who are relatively powerless, given their social and familial conditions. In her now classic 1960 essay, 'The human situation: a feminine view', Valerie Saiving (1978) initiated a radical rethinking of sin that characterizes feminist debate in Christian studies (for a recent discussion see Fulkerson, 1991; see also Plaskow, 1980; Yeager, 1988).

Since naming reality is a public function of the educated elites, and since the educated elites have in the main been men in the Western philosophical and religious traditions, sin has consistently been named on the basis of men's experience. The virtues of gratitude and humility, similarly, were proffered as important antidotes to sin (pride), given men's reflection on experience, and thus as virtues worthy of attention. Saiving finds pride notably inappropriate for women who, in the main, have not functioned in positions of power and who have had minimal exposure to the more commonly male experiences of independence and autonomy. Sin, for many women, she asserts, is not a matter of pride but 'is better suggested by such items as triviality, distractibility, and diffuseness; lack of an organizing center or focus; dependence on others for one's own self-definition ... in short, underdevelopment or negation of the self' (Saiving, 1978, p. 37). Humility and gratitude, she suggests, are not the virtues such women need to develop because these women do not relate to sin construed as pride. Women who are tempted by the sin of triviality, diffuseness and undue dependence, rather, are advised to develop and be publicly encouraged to develop the disciplines of initiative, responsibility and independence.

Saiving's critique can itself be critiqued on the grounds that the 'feminine experience' she alludes to is largely the domain of white, middle class, married women's experience. Since Saiving's analysis appeared, the fact of diversity among women has itself become part of the feminist agenda and is a good example of the way pursuit of new questions about gender has pushed the boundaries of feminist awareness to include discussion of differences among women with respect to race, class, sexual preference and the like.[5] This process of expanding the boundaries from within feminism itself enables feminism to resist becoming an ideology or orthodoxy. Thus, to explore the reality of sin from the standpoints of dominant and subordinate, race and class, margin and centre, men and women, engages a rethinking process that invites thought in multiple directions and exemplifies the open-ended nature of this inquiry. Mary McClintock Fulkerson (1991, p. 673) has observed that the genderization of sin has become a new universal that has entered 'the Christian vocabulary not only as a recognition of the documented forms of gender-specific sin', but also as 'a permanent area of investigation'.

Religious imagery for the Divine, similarly scrutinized, provides a second example of work that has sharpened my own epistemological sensitivities. Sallie McFague's (1987) focus on Christian metaphors and models critiques the ethical and political implications of prevalent images of God as father, king, and judge. Taking her own experience as a woman as one source for her reflections, she explores alternative metaphors of mother, lover and friend, judging these on ethical grounds to be more salutary, life-enhancing alternatives.[6] Examining the notions of relationship and relativity, process and openness, which she finds to be characteristic of reality as understood in nearly all branches of the sciences today, McFague wishes to expose and displace the inherited notion of hierarchical, authoritative order, with its connotations and denotations of dominance and subordination, superiority and inferiority as ways of arranging relationships. The relationships that concern her pertain to human beings with one another and with the entire natural world. Her line of thought has implications, then, not only for women's self-understanding, but also for the health and well-being of the entire planet and thus carries 'nuclear, ecological' import, as the subtitle of her book suggests. McFague's exploration of the way images mean and work and function in the life of a social body, feeding understandings, attitudes and actions, demonstrates the power that images carry and the ways attention to gender imagery both past and present opens us to new lines of inquiry and investigation.

A third example is evident in the work of biblical scholars with feminist interests who point our attention to the written sources of the tradition and urge us to note well what is not there as well as what is there. Kurt Marti articulates a probing question:

'What, for example, might a history of Israel look like if portrayed and written from the perspective of wives and mothers, who were allowed neither to bear weapons nor to join in worship?' (quoted in Moltmann-Wendel, 1982; unnumbered front page). Feminist biblical research alerts us to the silence as well as the words of women, to the lost and suppressed materials as well as the extant materials. Scholars urge us to notice the footprints and the shadows and the remnants that provide glimpses into stories that have not been showcased in the texts that have been preserved.[7] They alert us to the experience of early male and female Christians whose life circumstances varied significantly. What would have been attractive about Christianity to a first-century woman immersed in the Greco-Roman or Jewish world of the Mediterranean? What would have made Christianity attractive to a man from that social world? Since the normative sources of Christianity appear to have been authored by men, conveyed by men, and canonized by men, one wonders further, what were the early Christian women thinking, feeling, wanting, hoping for, wondering about, conjecturing? Given the scarcity of materials recording women's presence and participation, another series of questions emerges. Which women, what behaviours and what messages about women do find remembrance in the texts? Why these women? These voices? These messages? What was being communicated to and inculcated by aspiring Christian women of the founding Christian community, for example? Rereading canonical and non-canonical sources with these questions in mind has yielded multiple explorations and expositions (Wahlberg, 1975; Russell, 1976, 1985; Trible, 1978; Moltmann-Wendel, 1982; Fiorenza, 1984; Carmody, 1988).

A fourth example of epistemological shifts due to gender-sensitive inquiry is evident in the fields of ethics and politics. Influenced by Carol Gilligan's (1982) empirical studies of moral decision-making and the 'different voice' (see also Gilligan, 1987; Gilligan, Ward and Taylor, 1988) of women whom she heard address moral quandaries, many writers in the diverse fields of religious studies, philosophy, education and psychology (see Crysdale, 1994) are now exploring the varying ways in which people name and respond to ethical dilemmas. Given the emphasis on principles that has characterized philosophical ethics, philosopher Nel Noddings (1984, pp. 34–5) observes that ethics has been voiced largely in terms of the language of the father, which she equates with reason, rational principles and the judicial rule of justice. She wishes to develop an ethic based on the affective voice and language of the mother. The mother's response to the crying infant becomes Noddings' preferred model for ethics in so far as she would have us engage in ethical inquiry and reflection initially by sharing a feeling, not by formulating a problem, by feeling with before claiming to know about. Noddings places great weight on the affective element of moral knowing, convinced that feeling is constitutive of moral knowing. Shifting the focus of attention from moral reasoning, which has received sustained attention in theological and philosophical ethics, to *how we meet the other morally*, Noddings explores the underexplored dynamics of moral attitude, impulse and desire. At the heart of the ethic of caring which Noddings proposes and exposes, is the experience of reception rather than projection, based on a desire to see as and to feel with the other. By insisting on ethical attitude, orientation and inclination, Noddings addresses a new and less navigable terrain: namely, the affective ground out of which people receive moral perceptions and move to moral judgements.

Noddings' use of parental imagery is controversial among feminists. Critics lament her use of images that employ and perpetuate stereotypes (men as rational, women as emotional). Advocates acknowledge the criticism yet hold Noddings' images more loosely, benefiting from the points made without holding Noddings to an essentialist philosophy of male and female, father and mother. The very use of such images in methodological ethical debate illustrates the way gender-based images can amplify and broaden the discussion and simultaneously heighten awareness of the dangers of turning images into essences. Noddings does not use mother–father imagery to present a philosophy of male and female. She uses mother–father imagery, rather, as heuristic devices to raise issues about ethical inquiry and reflection and to encourage attention to be given to important dimensions of ethics that are too often neglected. Thus, by giving attention to differences in the ways women and men have been socialized to be parents in her own cultural context, Noddings invites us to look at the familial context and common social grounding in which their moral reasoning takes place, namely, the gender-influenced affections, feelings, desires, impulses and orientations out of which ethical reasoning occurs.

Mary Ann Glendon's (1991) critical look at what she deems to be exaggerated 'rights talk' characteristic of American political discourse, leads her to mine themes of empathy, care and community as currently underutilized resources for our body politic. Our society's preoccupation with individual rights would be moderated and enriched, she argues, by equal or greater attention to themes of responsibility and community. Glendon (1991, p. 174) attributes the women's movement and gender sensitivity as one stimulus to this badly needed line of critique, recovery and transformation of political and legal discourse (see also Addelson, 1986).

In exploring facets of experience which are gender-related, feminist analysts have also worked to include facets of experience that are affected by race and class. Gender, race, and class become primary categories for study, analogous to history-based inquiry and reason-based inquiry. Various liberation theologies and ethics share with feminist inquiry attention to the specifics of social location as relevant to how we know and what we know. Indeed, standpoint itself takes on new meaning as many women become conscious of standing in two places simultaneously – on the outside (with respect to the androcentrism of society) and on the inside (minority status *vis-à-vis* other minority voices or, as one example, as part of an oppressing majority *vis-à-vis* race or class). Contradictory social location is felt also by the Jewish feminist, Catholic feminist, academic feminist. Such feminists are working with, within, and yet against male-favoured institutions.[8] The thinker whose consciousness is bifurcated in so far as she identifies with women as a class, yet is an historically unique person (Bolivian or Chinese, rich or poor), is encouraged to use that tension as a resource for feeling and thinking and acting.[9]

As the standpoints to be studied proliferate, the universal-izability of knowledge claims appears ever more elusive. Does attention to gender relegate us to different worlds of knowing and meaning, valuing and preferring? Are these studies, these authors, and these lines of inquiry wittingly or unwittingly conspiring to polarize and oppose men from women, women from men, with respect to ways of knowing and valuing? Or do we, men and women, black and white, literate and illiterate, propertied and homeless enjoy a common basis for knowing and meaning, valu-ing and preferring? Is there a unitary basis in human consciousness – regardless of the human's gender, race, or class? Cynthia Crysdale (1990, p. 33) poses the question this way: 'What is the structure of knowing and does it have a unitary basis in human consciousness or are there two radically different foundations from which women and men know and create their worlds?'

The answer to this question is important because on it hangs our sense of confidence in knowledge itself, our sense of confidence in the possibilities of dialogue with persons of the other sex but also with persons of other cultures and ethnic heritages, other regions and religions, other races and classes. The answer to this question also tells us something about the possibilities for empathy with one another about matters of concern.

Citing Bernard Lonergan's description of human knowing as the activities of experiencing, understanding, deciding and judging, activities available to humans by virtue of their humanness, Crysdale (1990, p. 38) affirms a 'common basis of inquiry, a shared structure of human knowing', for the processes of knowing, questioning, analysing, and interpreting are not gender (race or class) specific, but have a basis in human consciousness as human. Curious and reflective men and women of diverse social location pay attention to experience and try to make sense of it by exploring and testing plausible and convincing explanations and by making judgements and decisions about what actions to take in the face of their understanding. Indeed, it is this unitary basis in human consciousness which makes the feminist critique possible and makes feminist inquiries intelligible to those who are indifferent or hostile to feminism as much as to those who share its curiosities and loyalties. In theory, it seems reasonable to assert, no one has a monopoly on the processes of attending to experience, exploring, accepting, criticizing, and adopting explanations, judging the adequacy of truth claims, making decisions and taking action.[10]

Much of what we know, however, is rooted not in our own personal experience, exploration, discovery and discernment, but in our trusting acceptance of what we have been told and taught. And most of what we have been told and taught in the Western religious and philosophical traditions has come to us from the voices of educated males. Women, in the main, did not have access to education and thus did not participate as fully in theological and philosophical debate and the dissemination of theological and philosophical knowledge. Taking a pointed look at what we have been told and taught about universal human existence has given rise to and continues to characterize feminist inquiries and analogous research that attends to ways that race and class, region and religion, affect knowing.

The source of gender differences remains a topic of debate as discussions about biology and history continue. The differing socializations, experiences, expectations and responsibilities afforded to men and women in many societies render a plausible and necessary rationale for the differences that are discovered when people tell their stories and interpret their lives. Whether the historical-cultural differences are sufficient to explain gender differences remains an unsettled question. What matters to me more than the nature/nurture debates and the search for a causal explanation, however, are the insights and resources for thinking that this research has generated. Feminist studies have focused our attention on the root metaphors and concepts with which we think by turning our attention to the datum out of which we do our thinking, namely, experience. When we attend to our own experience and when we attend to the experience of others whose lives and thoughts become the data for our studies, gender identity is very often a relevant factor. Gender is discovered as an item, as a feature of consciousness in the persons whose thought and writings scholars study. Awareness of gender as a lens relevant to understanding religion and other features of life is neither a modern invention nor a scholarly import.[11] The differing socializations of men and women, differing biological and life cycle participation in human life, differing interests and questions often (not always) give rise to different theological readings and ethical recommendations. By noticing these differences and taking them seriously, and by exploring the questions such noticing generates, feminist thinkers have shifted the epistemological grounds on which scholars think about issues and sources.

Feminist analysis contributes to the scholarly enterprise, the work of critique and corrective, *in order that our observations about human life, our theories about human knowing, and our claims and conclusions about what is good for human beings are informed by a broad data base that takes seriously the diverse ways in which human life is experienced, thought about and lived.* Whatever claims we come to make about our common humanness will be credible and trustworthy only if such claims are informed by attention to the concrete experience of lots of people. This means the experience of people who are men and women, black and white and brown and red, historical winners and losers, heterosexuals and homosexuals, colonizers and colonized, literate and illiterate, propertied and homeless.

Feminist research includes the retrieval and recovery of ignored or suppressed voices, but goes well beyond retrieval and recovery by proposing new ways of seeing, conceiving, hearing, listening, appropriating and valuing. Feminist study is, in part, a matter of including the lives and thoughts of women and other minority voices in the production and dissemination of knowledge. It is also more than this, in so far as this work then utilizes these lives as a starting point for asking further questions, developing concepts, designing research programmes, collecting data and interpreting findings (Harding, 1991, p. 268). Thus, feminist analysis contributes to the scholarly enterprise a transformative dynamic, for when gender-focused questions are seriously pursued, additional new questions, also new models, new metaphors, new presuppositions and new paradigms for thinking emerge. Sandra Harding (1991, p. 125) illustrates this point when observing that feminism teaches women and men to see male supremacy as a 'bizarre belief' rather than as an assumption.

Furthermore, it is important to note that this work is not for women only and that being a woman is not sufficient to generate feminist knowledge. Feminist inquiry is work that must be learned, a mode of inquiry that requires a critical consciousness. Without historical-critical consciousness, social relations are read as givens in nature rather than as constructs that can be reconfigured and practices that can be rearranged according to an alternative standard of value.[12] Men can utilize feminist perspectives to illuminate their own lives by critically examining the institutions and practices within which they think and believe and behave (Harding, 1991, pp. 286–7). A chastened understanding of one's social location (as privileged, as marginalized, as central or peripheral) carries the potential for thinking, conceiving, and proposing new ways of seeing and being. Men, too, can enjoy the benefits as well as the stresses of contradictory social location. This can be done, for example, by living consciously in a male-favoured society, yet choosing not to perpetuate or enable it and in this way participating in the feminist work of transformation.

Scholars interested in gender analysis are not working simply to replace male-centred lenses with female-focused lenses. They work, rather, to offer their attention to women's experience as an expansion or alternative or corrective to the historically prevalent male-based lenses. When this sort of inquiry rightly complicates our work by alerting us also to differences in experience due to race and class and region and religion, we note clearly the democratic bias to this line of research. Not only is there more to be known; there are more knowers to do the knowing and more lenses through which to see. This pursuit does complicate things terribly, irritatingly so for some. But it gets us closer to life which is itself irritatingly complicated. Our passion for the generalization comes from an understandable desire to simplify the complicated, to grasp in brief the many dimensions of life. Feminist and other, like-minded researchers work to slow down that process of generalization because it is too costly: it silences and ignores the voices of too many and in doing so precludes some very interesting and instructive ways of seeing and being and thinking and living. Limiting the sources also condones passive and active forms of injustice. With a gender-alert hermeneutic, feminist research offers the promise of a more complete, less distorted, less partial knowledge base because through it more is examined and less is assumed (Hawkesworth, 1989, p. 557). In this lies the epistemological import – and invitation – of feminist research in religion.

Notes

I thank the University of California, Riverside (USA) Senate Committee on Research for funds that supported the research, writing, and presentation of this paper. I thank also Leslie Hayes-Bolter for a critical reading of a draft of the paper and for offering helpful suggestions that served to inform my thought and to clarify my prose.

1   O'Connor (1989) is a bibliographical review essay, discussing a wide variety of works on feminism and religion published after 1980 and citing five review essays that examine materials published before 1980.
2   Mary Pellauer (1985, p. 34) rightly defines feminism as a 'method for creative inquiry' rather than 'a set of predetermined points'.
3   See O'Connor, 1985. Feminist authors voicing similar questions about how we know include: Lerner, 1979; Harding and Hintikka, 1983; Langland and Gove, 1983; Spender, 1985; Harding, 1991.
4   'Women's experience,' a fundamental normative source in feminist method, is itself a subject of scrutiny among feminist scholars who challenge one another's meaning and use of the term. See, for example, Davaney, 1987; Young, 1990. Mary McClintock Fulkerson (1991, p. 654) proposes turning to the postmodernist and post-structuralist language of 'discourse' as providing useful 'alternatives to the appeal to experience'.
    In this essay 'experience' refers to the process of encountering or undergoing life events in the course of time *vis-à-vis* the Divine,

oneself, communities, the world and the rest of nature, and the like. Experience is the datum on which all religious reflection rests and to which it returns. Feminist insistence on attention to women's experience is forwarded as a corrective to much of the past in which men's experience has served as the norm for reflection and insight. I refer to 'women's experience', then, as an alternative to and expansion of men's experience as norm, as an extension of the data base from which reflection emerges. 'Women's experience' means interpreted experience (not some sort of 'raw' or 'pure' or 'unmediated' experience). I refer to 'women's experience' in a generalized sense, not limiting it to biological experience, but including also historical, cultural and social expressions and understandings.

5 Some African-American feminists have replaced the word 'feminist' with 'womanist' as a way of drawing attention to the realities of black women and their differences from the stories, interests and concerns of white feminists (see Walker, 1983; Cannon, 1988; on issues of feminism, race, and class, see Davis, 1981; Hooks, 1981, 1984, 1989; Apthecker, 1982).

6 McFague identifies her standpoint in this way: '... though this essay is not a feminist theology in the sense that its guiding principle is the liberation of women, the fact that I am female is relevant to my perspective as author, for it is the form of oppression that has provided me with sufficient disorientation from middle-class, mainstream Christianity both to question it and to risk alternative formulations of Christian faith' (McFague, 1987, p. xiv).

7 Elisabeth Schüssler Fiorenza's (1983) *In Memory of Her: A Feminist Theological Reconstruction of Christian Origins* is particularly instructive in this regard.

8 Judith Plaskow (1990; p. xvi) illustrates the dilemma: 'Jewish feminists might agree that it is a matter of simple justice for Jewish women to have full access to the riches of Jewish life. But when a woman stands in the pulpit and reads from the Torah that daughters can be sold as slaves (Ex. 21: 7–11), she participates in a profound contradiction between the message of her presence and the content of what she learns and teaches. It is this contradiction feminists must address, not simply "adding" women to a tradition that remains basically unaltered, but transforming Judaism into a religion that women as well as men have a role in shaping.'

9 Sandra Harding (1991) makes this point in *Whose Science? Whose Knowledge? Thinking from Women's Lives* (pp. 284–5), as does Elise Boulding (1976) in *The Underside of History: A View of Women Through Time*. Domitila Barrios de Chungara (1978) illustrates the process in *Let Me Speak!: Testimony of Domitila, a Woman of the Bolivian Mines*.

10   Sidney Callahan (1991, p. 76) makes an analogous point with respect to moral judgement and decision. 'There can be no unique women's morality because the morally deciding, reflecting self is not gendered in intelligence, wisdom or charity. Thinking, feeling, deciding, acting on behalf of the good and the right is a complex holistic activity that does not depend upon one dimension of the self such as male or female gender.' Callahan continues: 'At the same time, the life experiences of many women in this culture give them different data to bring to the self's process of moral reflection.' Their experiences of 'oppression, subordination, and vulnerability', she asserts, can serve them by producing greater empathy, flexibility in outlook, and nurturing inclinations in their moral judgements and decisions.

11   Elizabeth Clark and Herbert Richardson (1977) provide a sampling of sources that illustrate this fact in Christian studies, in *Women and Religion: A Feminist Sourcebook of Christian Thought*. Exercepts display the awareness of gender-related issues in the scriptures and in the writings of spiritual leaders and intellectuals throughout the centuries (for example, Clement of Alexandria on gnosticism, women and sexuality: Jerome on Christian virginity; Augustine on sinfulness and sexuality; Julian of Norwich on revelations of divine love; Luther on marriage and the family; Schleiermacher on androgyny; Elizabeth Cady Stanton on women and the Bible; Karl Barth on women, men and the doctrine of creation).

12   Margaret Farley's (1991, p. 82) position that feminism is a work of justice leads her to assert that everyone should be a feminist: 'Feminism is a movement, but it is also a perspective, one that everyone should share. Everyone should be a feminist ... For me, concern for the well-being of women is within a larger framework of concern for the well-being of all.'

References

Addelson, Kathryn Pyne 1986: Moral revolution. In Marilyn Pearsall (ed.), *Women and Values: Readings in Recent Feminist Philosophy*, Belmont, CA: Wadsworth Publishing Company, 291–301.

Apthecker, Bettina 1982: *Woman's Legacy: Essays on Race, Sex, Class in American History*. Amherst, MA: University of Massachusetts Press.

Atkinson, Clarissa, Buchanan, Constance and Miles, Margaret (eds) 1985: *Immaculate and Powerful: The Female in Sacred Image and Social Reality*. Boston, MA: Beacon.

Barrios de Chungara, Domitila, with Viezzer, Moema 1978: *Let Me Speak!: Testimony of Domitila, a Woman of the Bolivian Mines*. Trs. Victoria Ortiz. New York: Monthly Review Press.

Boulding, Elise 1976: *The Underside of History: A View of Women Through Time.* Boulder, CO: Westview Press.

Callahan, Sidney 1991: Does gender make a difference in moral decision-making? *Second Opinion*, 17, 2, 76.

Cannon, Katie G. 1988: *Black Womanist Ethics.* Atlanta, GA: Scholars Press.

Carmody, Denise Lardner 1988: *Biblical Woman: Contemporary Reflections on Scriptural Texts.* New York: Crossroad.

Clark, Elizabeth and Richardson, Herbert (eds) 1977: *Women and Religion: A Feminist Sourcebook of Christian Thought.* New York: Harper & Row.

Cooey, Paula, Eakin, William and McDaniel, Jay (eds) 1991: *After Patriarchy: Feminist Transformations of the World Religions.* Maryknoll, NY: Orbis Books.

Crysdale, Cynthia 1990: Gilligan's epistemological challenge: implications for method in ethics. *The Irish Theological Quarterly*, 56, 31–48.

Crysdale, Cynthia 1994: Gilligan and the ethics of care: an update (bibliographical review essay). *Religious Studies Review*, 20, 1, 21–8.

Davaney, Sheila Greeve 1987: The limits of the appeal to women's experience. In Clarissa W. Atkinson, Constance H. Buchanan and Margart R. Miles (eds), *Shaping New Vision: Gender and Values in American Culture*, Ann Arbor, MI: UMI Research Press (The Harvard Women's Studies in Religion Series), 31–49.

Davis, Angela 1981: *Women, Race, and Class.* New York: Random House.

Farley, Margaret A. 1991: Love, justice, and discernment: an interview with Margaret A. Farley. *Second Opinion*, 17, 2, 80–91.

Fiorenza, Elisabeth Schüssler 1983: *In Memory of Her: A Feminist Theological Reconstruction of Christian Origins.* New York: Crossroad.

Fiorenza, Elisabeth Schüssler 1984: *Bread Not Stone: The Challenge of Feminist Biblical Interpretation.* Boston, MA: Beacon.

Fulkerson, Mary McClintock 1991: Sexism as original sin: developing a theacentric discourse. *Journal of the American Academy of Religion*, LIX, 4, 653–75.

Gilligan, Carol 1982: *In a Different Voice.* Cambridge, MA: Harvard University Press.

Gilligan, Carol 1987: Moral orientation and moral development. In Eva Feder Kittay and Diana T. Meyers (eds), *Women and Moral Theory*, Totowa, NJ: Rowman & Littlefield, 19–33.

Gilligan, Carol, Ward, Janie Victoria and Taylor, Jill McLean (eds) 1988: *Mapping the Moral Domain: A Contribution of Women's Thinking to Psychological Theory and Education.* Cambridge MA: Center for the Study of Gender, Education and Human Development.

Glendon, Mary Ann 1991: *Rights Talk: The Impoverishment of Political Discourse.* New York: The Free Press.

Harding, Sandra 1991: *Whose Science? Whose Knowledge? Thinking from Women's Lives*. Ithaca, NY: Cornell University Press.

Harding, Sandra and Hintikka, Merrill B. (eds) 1983: *Discovering Reality: Feminist Perspectives on Epistemology, Metaphysics, Methodology, and Philosophy of Science*. London: D. Reidel.

Hawkesworth, Mary E. 1989: Knowers, knowing, known: feminist theory and claims of truth. *Signs: Journal of Women in Culture and Society*, 14, 533–58.

Hooks, Bell 1981: *Ain't I a Woman: Black Women and Feminism*. Boston, MA: South End Press.

Hooks, Bell 1984: *Feminist Theory: From Margin to Center*. Boston, MA: South End Press.

Hooks, Bell 1989: *Talking Back: Thinking Feminist, Thinking Black*. Boston, MA: South End Press.

King, Ursula (ed.) 1987: *Women in the World's Religions: Past and Present*. New York: Paragon House.

Langland, Elizabeth and Gove, Walter (eds) 1983: *A Feminist Perspective in the Academy: The Difference it Makes*. Chicago: University of Chicago Press.

Lerner, Gerder 1979: *The Majority Finds Its Past: Placing Women in History*. New York: Oxford University Press.

McFague, Sallie 1987: *Models of God: Theology for an Ecological, Nuclear Age*. Philadelphia: Fortress Press.

Maguire, Daniel 1986: *The Moral Revolution*. San Francisco: Harper & Row.

Moltmann-Wendel, Elisabeth 1982: *The Women Around Jesus*. New York: Crossroad.

Noddings, Nel 1984: *Caring: A Feminine Approach to Ethics and Moral Education*. Los Angeles: University of California Press.

O'Connor, June 1985: On doing religious ethics. In Barbara Andolsen, Christine Gudorf and Mary Pellauer (eds), *Women's Consciousness, Women's Conscience: A Reader in Feminist Ethics*, New York, Seabury/Winston. (Originally published in *Journal of Religious Ethics*, 7 (1979), 1, 81–96.)

O'Connor, June 1989: Rereading, reconceiving, and reconstructing traditions: feminist research in religion. *Women's Studies: An Interdisciplinary Journal*, 17, 101–23.

Pellauer, Mary 1985: Moral callousness and moral sensitivity: violence against women. In Barbara Andolsen, Christine Gudorf and Mary Pellauer (eds), *Women's Consciousness, Women's Conscience: A Reader in Feminist Ethics*, New York, Seabury/Winston, 33–50.

Plaskow, Judith 1980: *Sex, Sin, and Grace: Women's Experience and the Theologies of Reinhold Niebuhr and Paul Tillich*. Washington: University Press of America.

Plaskow, Judith 1990: *Standing Again at Sinai: Judaism from a Feminist*

Perspective. San Francisco: Harper & Row.

Ruether, Rosemary Radford 1983: *Sexism and God-Talk: Toward a Feminist Theology*. Boston, MA: Beacon.

Russell, Letty M. 1976: *The Liberating Word: A Guide to Nonsexist Interpretation of the Bible*. Philadelphia: Westminster.

Russell, Letty M. (ed.) 1985: *Feminist Interpretation of the Bible*. Philadelphia: Westminster.

Saiving, Valerie 1978: The human situation: a feminine view. In Carol Christ and Judith Plaskow (eds), *Womanspirit Rising: A Feminist Reader in Religion*, San Francisco: Harper & Row, 25–42. (First published in *The Journal of Religion*, 40 (1960), 100–12.)

Sharma, Arvind (ed.) 1987: *Women in World Religions*. Albany, NY: State University of New York Press.

Spender, Dale 1985: *For the Record: The Making and Meaning of Feminist Knowledge*. London: The Women's Press.

Trible, Phylis 1978: *God and the Rhetoric of Sexuality*. Philadelphia: Fortress.

Wahlberg, Rachel Conrad 1975: *Jesus According to a Woman*. New York: Paulist Press.

Walker, Alice 1983: *In Search of Our Mothers' Gardens*. San Diego: Harcourt, Brace, Jovanovich.

Yeager, Diane 1988: The web of relationships: feminists and Christians. *Soundings*, LXXI, 485–514.

Young, Pamela Dickey 1990: Women's experience as source and norm of theology. In *Feminist Theology/Christian Theology: In Search of Method*. Minneapolis: Fortress Press, 49–69.

2

Feminist Anthropology and the Gendering of Religious Studies

Rosalind Shaw

Feminist projects of disciplinary transformation may be caught up in contradictions arising from the histories of the disciplines in which change is sought. In the history and phenomenology of religions, problems of disciplinary transformation appear to extend far beyond the difficulties of eradicating 'male bias' or of including women's standpoints. Such transformation may entail nothing less than the dissolution and reconstruction of the discipline itself. In anthropology, attempts to effect a feminist metamorphosis in the 1970s and early 1980s were subject to contradictions whose identification and critique by Strathern (1981, 1987) assisted scholars in rethinking the relationship between feminism and anthropology. Strathern's characterization of the 'awkward relationship' between anthropology and feminism finds important parallels in the history of religions, and her critiques may usefully be applied to certain forms of feminist religious studies today.

Strathern (1987) characterizes feminism and anthropology as close neighbours, enmeshed in a relationship of mutual mockery.

They do not so much contradict as 'mock' each other, she argues, because each so nearly attains the ideal which eludes the other. On the one hand, anthropologists have a comparative perspective which can give them a critical distance from dominant Euro-American understandings of gender and women's power – a distance which is highly valued in much of feminist thought. On the other hand, anthropologists are striving to reform anthropology from the conditions of its production, in which knowledge has been constituted within unequal power relationships between white Western anthropologists and colonized peoples of the Third World, among whom most anthropologists have worked. Anthropologists' struggles to effect a shift from a 'view from above' in order to reinvent anthropology contrast sharply with the apparent ease with which feminist scholars have assumed a 'view from below', in which relations of domination are analysed from a subordinate standpoint.

While anthropology 'mocks' feminism from its advantaged position for cultural critiques of Western social forms, then, feminism – from its own assumed standpoint of the subordinate's perspective – mocks anthropology. Anthropology can never really achieve its desired perspective of the 'view from below' until non-Western anthropologists have a stronger voice in its reinvention (see Moore, 1989). Because of this mutual mockery, 'feminist anthropology' is, for Strathern, not quite an oxymoron, but a hybrid beast. The awkwardness between feminism and anthropology thus involves disjunctions which extend beyond the problems of introducing women's perspectives into a discipline with a history of 'male bias'. This is because other forms of domination – in particular those of colonialism and racism – are just as central as that of gender inequality to the relationship between feminist thought and anthropology.

The same could be said of those forms of domination implicit in the relationship between feminism and the history of religions, but the mockery here is one-sided. Like anthropology, the history of religions has a long tradition of a perspective which is valued highly in feminist scholarship. A hermeneutic approach which makes empathy with lived religious experience central to interpretation and comparison was developed in the history and phenomenology of religions when other disciplines were working through their positivist phases (see, for example, Dudley, 1977; Allen, 1978). Since critiques of positivism have been prominent in many strands of feminist epistemology, the history of religions could be said to have had at its core an interpretive standpoint which many have seen as central to feminist scholarship.

But in practice, the history/phenomenology of religions is an apt illustration that a hermeneutic of empathy and experience is far from being automatically feminist. The question of *whose* subjective experience is being empathized with is crucial. All too typically, it is not that of real persons but of a 'collective subject' whose supposedly authoritative experience is either undifferentiated by gender, race, class or age, or defined explicitly as male. In particular, the writings of Eliade and his followers are premised upon this collective subject, usually known as '*homo religiosus*': 'Eliade understood that religious man will take a wife, build a house, make love, raise children, eat, sleep, go to war, make peace, and prepare for death out of [a] felt relationship to the gods, and what he believes they expect of him' (Idinopulos, 1994, p. 72).

What does 'lived religious experience' *mean* when it is located in a purportedly universal subject? And how universal can this impersonal subject be when represented through such unabashedly gender-specific depiction? In this totalizing but exclusionary empathy for a reified *homo religiosus*, the mockery of feminism by the history of religions – like the mockery of feminism by anthropology – falls flat.

This mockery, moreover, is not reciprocated. Those in mainstream history of religions have not typically striven for ideals represented by feminist scholarship. Allen, for example, draws attention to feminist critiques of Eliade (such as Saiving, 1976), and observes that 'one would never guess from Eliade's treatment that androcentrism and a theologically misogynist tradition, that patriarchal structures of exploitation and oppression, were key notions in the interpretation of witchcraft' (Allen, 1978, p. 117–18). Yet he does so merely to make a point about the perspectival nature of knowledge; he cites such critiques 'not ... so much ... to show that Eliade's scale is explicitly androcentric, but rather that his perspective emphasizes certain notions and overlooks or de-emphasizes other dimensions of the phenomena' (Allen, 1978, pp. 118–19). But to argue that the standpoint of mainstream history and phenomenology of religions and the standpoint of feminist critiques are merely two perspectives among many misses the point of such critiques: it is not just that all knowledge is partial, but that some perspectives represent a 'view from above'. In the history of religion, a 'view from above' is entrenched through, first, the overwhelming emphasis given to religious texts and, second, the concept of the *sui generis* nature of religion, in which religion is treated as a discrete and irreducible phenomenon which exists 'in and of itself'. Feminist scholarship can only collide with, rather than mock, mainstream history of religions: not only has the latter had a very poor record of overhauling itself in terms of critiques 'from below', but its central *sui generis* argument is incompatible with the very basis of such critiques.

The 'Distinctively Religious' and the Distinctly Apolitical

Both the textual and the *sui generis* definitions emphasized in religious studies scholarship are, in practice, 'bracketing' devices which support each other in representing religion as socially decontextualized and ungendered. Understandings of 'religion as scripture' tend, for example, to privilege (a) religions with texts, and (b) scholarly elites within scriptural religious traditions who claim the authority to interpret texts (and from whom women are usually debarred). The religious understandings of those excluded from authorizing discourses of textual interpretation are implicitly discounted and relegated to a 'lower' level. To 'saby book', as the Nigerian participants in Hackett's essay (chapter 11) in this volume put it, has indeed been used to define the centre of religious traditions – as well as of the discipline concerned with their study – and to relegate women to the periphery. That strand of women's scholarship which simply presents accounts of 'women who wrote texts too' thus does little to recast this dominant focus. This orthodoxy has recently been challenged, however, by feminist studies which explore innovative ways of reading and critically interrogating scriptures and other texts (e.g. Fiorenza, 1983; Atkinson et al., 1985).

Like the understanding of 'religion as text', the concept of the *sui generis* nature of religion also entails the decontextualization of religion. In mainstream history of religions, understandings of 'the uniquely religious' are usually constituted by excluding or peripheralizing social and political content in defining what really counts as 'religion'. Historians of religion who make the *sui generis* claim do not suggest that 'pure religious' phenomena can exist empirically, but that 'certain experiences or phenomena exhibit a fundamental religious character and that our method must be commensurate with the nature of our subject-matter. From the perspective of the History of Religions, the sociological, economic, or anthropological dimensions of the phenomena are "secondary"' (Allen, 1978, pp. 83–4).

Thus desocialized, 'the uniquely religious' is deemed interpretable only 'on its own terms': studies of religion which entail social or political analysis are typically dismissed as reductionist. Eliade, who more than anyone else has defined this dominant 'antireductionist' discourse in the history of religions, offers the following axiom: '[A] religious phenomenon will only be recognized as such if it is grasped at its own level, that is to say, if it is studied *as* something religious. To try to grasp the essence of such a phenomenon by means of physiology, psychology, sociology, economics, linguistics, art or any other is false (Eliade, 1963, p. xiii). As some of the contributors to a recent volume on reductionism and religion (Idinopulos and Yonan, 1994) point out, such essentializing assumptions close off the potentially awkward question of what 'the nature of religion' is:

> If I am right about the intellectual history of the notion of religion, it has shifted several times in the last hundred years already ... Eliade slams the door shut on possible competitors to his own 'spiritualist' position. Instead, he just insists on the identity of religious phenomena by appeal to 'what they are ...' But 'what they are' is or should be an open question; Eliade's anti-reductionist (by replacement) stance rejects alternatives out of hand. (Strenski, 1994, p. 101; see also Segal, 1989, 1994)

Since 'religion' as a category is not indigenous to most parts of the world, moreover, the *sui generis* concept often involves the imposition of 'the irreducibly religious' upon a landscape of human practices and understandings which do not divide up into the categories cherished by Western scholars.

As part of its discouragement of debates about 'the nature of religion', the discourse of irreducibility also deflects questions of power and inequality: the 'distinctively religious' is constituted as distinctly apolitical. Eliade writes, for example:

> Few religious phenomena are more directly and more obviously connected with socio-political circumstances than the modern messianic and millenarian movements among colonial people (cargo-cults,

etc.). Yet identifying and analyzing the conditions that prepared and made possible such messianic movements form only a part of the work of the historian of religions. For these movements are equally creations of the human spirit, in the sense that they have become what they are – religious movements, and not merely gestures of protest and revolt – through a creative act of the spirit. (Eliade, 1969, p. 6)

Eliade leaves us in no doubt that for him 'mere gestures of protest and revolt' are not part of the creative repertoire of 'the human spirit'. But for those within millenarian movements, politics and protest are *implicated in the very constitution* of their religious practice. Their experience of colonial power is 'interior' to – not somehow detachable from – their lived religious experience. Power, then, cannot simply be bracketed off as a 'dimension' or 'aspect' of religion (see Shaw and Stewart, 1994).

To take another example, attempting to understand a woman's experience of religion in terms of (not just 'in the context of') her position within a male-dominated religious tradition is reductionist only if we have severed 'religion' from 'power' in the first place. On the contrary, it *would* be a 'reduction' – in the rather different sense of a diminished and distorted representation of her experience – to bracket off 'male dominance' and 'gender asymmetry' as a mere biographical backdrop to, but not really part of, experiences which she calls 'religious'. With power and social organization detached from the analysis of gender and religion, we are left either with meaningless accounts of 'religious gender roles' ('the men do this; the women do that'), or with disconnected descriptions of female deities ('add goddesses and stir').

The *sui generis* concept thus stands in a contradictory relationship to the premises of feminist scholarship. By making power irrelevant to 'the nature of religion', it denies the scholar of religion a language with which to make a critique 'from below', relegating the very basis of a distinction between a 'view from above' and a 'view from below' to the realm of crass reductionism. By making it central to their discourse, scholars in the history of religions are effectively insulated from uncomfortable questions about standpoint and privilege – questions upon which feminist scholarship is based. The relationship between feminism and mainstream history of religions is not merely awkward; it is mutually toxic.

Institutional Embattlement and the Politics of Interpretation

The concept of the irreducibility of religion was not, of course, intentionally formulated as a bulwark against feminist critiques (even if this is, in fact, a consequence). Its hegemony has to be understood within the politics of disciplinary identity, in the embattled institutional position of the history of religions within the academy. Like feminist scholarship and women's studies, religious studies is ambiguously situated as both a distinct discipline and a multidisciplinary field analogous to American studies or science studies. As such, in many universities it has been in constant danger of being demoted from a department to a sub-department or an interdisciplinary programme. In other institutions it is perceived to be subsumed by – and hence institutionally indistinct from – theology: in British universities in particular, the era of cuts euphemistically described as 'rationalization' in the late 1970s and throughout the 1980s saw the closure of most departments of religious studies which were not sheltered within departments of theology. In public, secular American universities, on the other hand, religious studies is often attacked as an apparent anomaly. As Idinopulos writes:

> ... we who taught in the Department of Religion were faced with difficult questions from our colleagues about the appropriateness of such a department in a tax-supported, public university ... Why teach religion in a secular university? Does the study of religion really warrant a separate department? ... What are the special credentials which attach to a professor of religion that differ from the credentials of any social scientist who takes an interest in the study of religion and offers courses based on his research? (Idinopulos, 1994, p. 65)

In addition to this institutional embattlement, mainstream history of religions has for several decades been intellectually marginalized, consistently out of phase with broader debates and paradigm-shifts which cut across disciplines, such as feminism, structuralism, postmodernism, reflexivity and cultural critique. It has been so ignored by scholars in other disciplines who are concerned with religion that any attention from the latter tends to bring forth a spate of published reactions – witness Dudley's

(1977) response to an anthropologist's attack upon Eliade in a mere book review (Leach, 1966). Up to the 1960s, the strong phenomenological strand of the history of religions placed it, in many ways, ahead of its time. This also placed it beyond the pale, however, during the positivist and scientistic phase of anthropology and other social sciences during their structural-functionalist and structuralist eras. In the 1960s and 1970s, however, anthropological interests shifted towards a concern with meaning and interpretation which took the form of symbolic anthropology in the USA (e.g. Geertz, 1966) and semantic anthropology in the UK (e.g. Crick, 1976). These shifts entailed a reawakening of interest in religion and in phenomenology, but this took place for the most part as if the phenomenology of religion had never existed.

It has been in response to the double threat of institutional embattlement and intellectual marginalization that the boundary-defending argument of the *sui generis* nature of religion – and accompanying claims for the unique interpretive privilege of the history of religions – have been developed into a kind of disciplinary creed. 'Antireductionist' arguments, usually reiterated as a counter-critique of a structural-functionalist anthropology which has not existed for thirty years, are still part of the prevailing discourse of the history of religions today (when many anthropologists, ironically, can scarcely remember what structural-functionalism was).

The 'straw discipline' argument of antireductionism may sometimes be tactically useful in institutional battles over departmental autonomy and resources, but at the ultimately self-defeating cost of continued intellectual marginalization. 'By imagining a continuing struggle between religious studies and the social sciences', one scholar of religion observes sadly, 'we can be encouraged that someone is taking us seriously, even if that someone is mostly only we ourselves' (Elzey, 1994, p. 94). The high disciplinary walls which scholars of religion have created have cut them off from many new intellectual directions, debates and discourses, thereby transforming mainstream history of religions from an exciting approach ahead of its time in the 1950s and 1960s to a broken record endlessly rehearsing thirty-year-old debates in the 1990s. Some scholars in religious studies, aware of the missed opportunities entailed by Eliade's exaggerated claims of autonomy, argue for an end to 'all those interminable arguments about the transcendental reality of religion' (Strenski, 1994, p. 107): '...

despite the real risks of reconceptualization, we must resist looking on reduction like our cry-baby colleagues ... Reconceptualization also promises renewal and revival. ... We have to begin accepting conceptual change as a normal part of trading in the world of knowledge (Strenski, 1994, pp. 104–5).

The Gendering of Religious Studies

By reconceptualizing power as integral to – as opposed to a detachable 'dimension' of – religion, feminist religious studies has the potential to generate conceptual change and renewal. Yet its capacity for disciplinary transformation is currently cramped by hangovers from mainstream religious studies which some forms of feminist religious studies have carried with them. In this way, these (fairly dominant) strands of feminist religious studies are in a position analogous to that of feminist anthropology in the 1970s, which responded to the marginalizing of women in the discipline's mainstream by an essentializing discourse which placed it securely in a feminist 'ghetto'. Another article by Strathern (1981) consists of a critique of such writings, which eventually enabled feminist anthropology to reconceptualize itself, leave its ghetto and acquire a more audible voice in the discipline.

Particularly important here was Strathern's critique of the assumption of a unitary and essentialized category of 'woman' which unites the female researcher with the women in the (different) social and cultural context she is researching. Strathern's scepticism helped to sensitize white feminist anthropologists to criticisms of Western feminism by non-Western women and women of colour, who pointed out that their race and their history of colonization make a difference which makes it impossible to talk of a universal 'women's nature'. Currently, few feminist scholars in any discipline assume a universal 'female reality'. That many scholars in feminist religious studies are an exception to this derives, I believe, from the universalizing and essentializing tendencies of the discipline's mainstream.

In a recent critique of the 'transubstantiation' of women's experience into images of goddesses and cyborgs in some forms of feminist theory, Hewitt (1993) examines recent writings in feminist spirituality, best exemplified in the work of Carol Christ (e.g. Christ, 1985, 1987; Christ and Plaskow, 1979). As its alternative name of 'thealogy' suggests, feminist spirituality is directed against – yet implicitly shaped by – patriarchal traditions of Christian theology and practice. Thus God the Father is replaced by the Goddess as Mother, the embodiment of a cosmic femininity which 'refers back to a feminine ontology that is little more than the inverse of masculinist conceptualizations' (Hewitt, 1993, p. 138).

Although Christ is highly critical of Eliade (Christ, 1991), moreover, her methodology is closer to his than her criticism would suggest. Where Eliade proposed a universalized (but male) *homo religiosus* as the true subject of religious experience, Christ proposes a universalized female spiritual essence in which all women participate. Eliade felt free to construct his version of this collective subject, unhampered by the self-representations of real religious participants:

> 'It does not matter in the least,' says Eliade beginning his dismissal of any Dilthey-like advocacy of the native's point of view, 'whether or not the "primitives" of today realize that immersion in water is the equivalent both of the deluge and of the submerging of a continent in the sea ...' ... Instead, Eliade proposes nothing less than a total theory of religion, and thus one which *replaces* old meanings with (his) new ones. This 'totalizing' ambition explains why, in the end, Eliade does not care about what the 'natives' say or think ... (Strenski, 1994, pp. 102–3; see also Idinopulos, 1994, pp. 75–8)

Christ's approach – to use her own experiences of reconstructed goddess rituals as the basis for her interpretation of prehistoric goddess worship (e.g. Christ, 1985, p. 123) – is no less totalizing. With the aid of these experiences, she adapts Elisabeth Schüssler Fiorenza's method of 'imaginative reconstruction of reality'. Yet Fiorenza's method:

> ... is not easily adaptable to non-linguistic evidence from Neolithic times, which is where Christ ultimately wishes to apply it ... Without acknowledging the complexities involved, Christ uses Schüssler Fiorenza's method of 'imaginative reconstruction' as license for mythic and literary invention. By doing this, Christ hopes to avoid having to differentiate between the religious, symbolic meaning of the Goddess in her own spiritual life, and the public, historical claims that seek to establish the prevalence of Goddess worship, including the higher status of women, in prehistoric times. (Hewitt, 1993, p. 147)

Through such appropriation of the experience of women in other times and places, a feminized *homo religiosus* lives on. A feminist religious studies which does not incorporate differences between women – in particular between the researcher and the women she writes about – will merely invoke the concept of power without applying it to its own colonizing discourse. That sensitivity to these differences does not, of course, mean 'objectivity' is clear in examples of feminist studies of women's religion which demonstrate such sensitivity (e.g. Boddy, 1989; Brown, 1991). Quite the reverse: it requires more reflexivity rather than less; more attention to intersubjectivity; more attention to the voices of other women as personal actors that one cannot speak *for*; and more attention to the web of social relationships and cultural practices through which their power and experience are constituted.

References

Allen, Douglas 1978: *Structure and Creativity in Religion: Hermeneutics in Mircea Eliade's Phenomenology and New Directions*. The Hague: Mouton.

Atkinson, C. et al. (eds) 1985: *Immaculate and Powerful: The Female in Sacred Image and Social Reality*. Boston, MA: Beacon Press.

Boddy, Janice 1989: *Wombs and Alien Spirits: Women, Men and the Zar Cult in Northern Sudan*. Madison: University of Wisconsin Press.

Brown, Karen McCarthy 1991: *Mama Lola: A Vodou Priestess in Brooklyn*. Berkeley, CA: University of California Press.

Christ, Carol 1985: Discussion: What are the sources of my theology. *Journal for Feminist Studies in Religion*, 1, 120–3.

Christ, Carol 1987: *Laughter of Aphrodite: Reflections on a Journey to the Goddess*. San Francisco: Harper & Row.

Christ, Carol 1991: Mircea Eliade and the feminist paradigm shift. *Journal for Feminist Studies in Religion*, 7, 75–94.

Christ, Carol and Plaskow, Judith (eds) 1979: *Womanspirit Rising: A Feminist Reader in Religion*. San Francisco: Harper & Row.

Crick, Malcolm 1976: *Explorations in Language and Meaning: Towards a Semantic Anthropology*. London: Malaby Press.

Dudley, Guilford 1977: *Religion on Trial: Mircea Eliade and his Critics*. Philadelphia: Temple University Press.

Eliade, Mircea 1963: *Patterns in Comparative Religion*. New York: Meridian Books.

Eliade, Mircea 1969: *The Quest: History and Meaning in Religion.* Chicago: University of Chicago Press.

Elzey, Wayne 1994: Mircea Eliade and the battle against reductionism. In T. A. Idinopulos and E. A. Yonan (eds), *Religion and Reductionism*, Leiden: E. J. Brill.

Fiorenza, Elisabeth Schüssler 1983: *In Memory of Her: A Feminist Theological Reconstruction of Christian Origins.* New York: Crossroad.

Geertz, Clifford 1966: Religion as a cultural system. In M. Banton (ed.), *Anthropological Approaches to the Study of Religion*, New York: Praeger.

Hewitt, Marsha A. 1993: Cyborgs, drag queens, and goddesses: emancipatory-regressive paths in feminist theory. *Method and Theory in the Study of Religion*, 5, 135–54.

Idinopulos, Thomas A. 1994: Must professors of religion be religious? Comments on Eliade's method of inquiry and Segal's defense of reductionism. In T. A. Idinopulos and E. A. Yonan (eds), *Religion and Reductionism*, Leiden: E. J. Brill.

Idinopulos, Thomas A. and Yonan, Edward A. (eds) 1994: *Religion and Reductionism: Essays on Eliade, Segal, and the Challenge of the Social Sciences for the Study of Religion.* Leiden: E. J. Brill.

Leach, Edmund 1966: Sermons by a man on a ladder. *New York Review of Books*, 20 October, 28–31.

Moore, Henrietta 1989: *Feminism and Anthropology.* London: Polity Press.

Saiving, Valerie 1976: Androcentrism in religious studies. *Journal of Religion*, 56.

Segal, Robert A. 1989: *Religion and the Social Sciences: Essays on the Confrontation.* Atlanta: Scholars Press.

Segal, Robert A. 1994: Reductionism in the study of religion. In T. A. Idinopulos and E. A. Yonan (eds), *Religion and Reductionism*, Leiden: E. J. Brill.

Shaw, Rosalind and Stewart, Charles 1994: Introduction: Problematizing Syncretism. In C. Stewart and R. Shaw (eds), *Syncretism/Anti-Syncretism: The Politics of Religious Synthesis.* London/New York: Routledge.

Strathern, Marilyn 1981: Culture in a netbag: on the manufacture of a subdiscipline in anthropology. *Man*, 16.

Strathern, Marilyn 1987: An awkward relationship: the case of feminism and anthropology. *Signs*, 12, 276–92.

Strenski, Ivan 1994: Reduction without tears. In T. A. Idinopulos and E. A. Yonan (eds), *Religion and Reductionism*, Leiden: E. J. Brill.

3

Religion and the Hermeneutics of Gender: An Examination of the Work of Paul Ricoeur

Erin White

Several questions prompt the examination of the concept of gender in the hermeneutics of Paul Ricoeur. Is gender implicitly a factor in all hermeneutics? What construction of gender is operating surreptitiously in apparently non-gendered hermeneutics? If Ricoeur's hermeneutic is androcentric and patriarchal, can a more adequate concept of gender be constructed from hints within his own hermeneutic?

It is easy to show that Ricoeur's interpretation of specific symbols and texts is androcentric. This is unsurprising given the culture in which we of the West live and interpret. What is not so easy to show, however, is that Ricoeur's hermeneutical *theory* is also androcentric. The first section of this essay examines the connections between an apparently gender-neutral theory *and* the androcentric interpretations to which this theory gives rise. This examination hopes to detect the implicit and subtle gender references in an apparently innocent theory, and to explore their connections with the blatant androcentrism of specific interpretations. Entitled 'The gender of hermeneutics', this section subjects Ricoeur's own hermeneutic to a hermeneutic of suspicion.

The second section searches Ricoeur's subtle and comprehensive hermeneutic for resources with which to construct 'A feminist hermeneutics of gender'. Such a construction is a large task and I cannot undertake it here in full. I aim, however, to contribute to the task by naming aspects of Ricoeur's hermeneutic which are congenial to this construction: to show that Ricoeur's tensive understanding of language and symbol implicitly opposes patriarchy, and his exploration of text and interpreting community provides a resource for articulating the concept of gender. By making explicit the feminist possibilities within Ricoeur's own work, this section offers a restorative hermeneutics.

While the first section is a work of critique and the second a work of construction, both seek to throw light on how the subjugation of women and the dominance of men have occurred through language, and on the way patriarchy functions as the common ideology or prevailing hermeneutic in the West. My topic is the construction of *gender* in the context of *religion*, my method is to explore Ricoeur's hermeneutic from a feminist perspective, and my aim is to contribute to a more adequate construction of gender.

The Gender of Hermeneutics

Hermeneutics is, ostensibly at least, a non-gendered discipline. For Ricoeur, hermeneutics has to do with interpreting the texts and symbols by which humanity has expressed its 'effort to exist' and its 'desire to be' (Ricoeur, 1974, p. 18). It is a theory for deciphering the documents of life so that some understanding of human subjectivity can finally be reached. Hermeneutics is a theory of understanding.

From his earliest work Ricoeur has maintained that human self-understanding can come only via texts and symbols, or, put negatively, that the self cannot immediately and intuitively know itself. Self-understanding is always mediated. This is stated in embryonic form in the first volume of Ricoeur's philosophy of the will, *Freedom and Nature* (published 1950):

> The act of the *Cogito* is not a pure act of self-positing; it lives
> on what it receives and on a dialogue with the conditions in which
> it is itself rooted. (Ricoeur, 1966, p. 18)

With Ricoeur's famous hermeneutical turn in *The Symbolism of
Evil* (published 1960), statements expressing his belief in the
mediated *Cogito* become clearer:

> ... the task of the philosopher guided by symbols would be to
> break out of the enchanted enclosure of consciousness of oneself,
> to end the prerogative of self-reflection. The symbol gives reason
> to believe that the *Cogito* is in being, and not vice versa. (Ricoeur,
> 1969, p. 356)

In a later essay, 'Existence and hermeneutics' (written in 1965), he
says:

> Reflection is the appropriation of our effort to exist and of our
> desire to be by means of the works which testify to this effort
> and this desire. (Ricoeur, 1974, p. 18)

And again in a 1985 interview he says[1]:

> There is no self-knowledge without some kind of detour through
> signs, symbols and cultural works etc. ... (Our own existence)
> cannot be separated from the account we can give of ourselves.
> It is in telling our own stories that we give ourselves an identity.
> We recognize ourselves in the stories we tell about ourselves. It
> makes little difference whether these stories are true or false, fiction
> as well as verifiable history provides us with an identity. (Quoted
> in Madison, 1988)

Such quotations abound in Ricoeur's work, from 1950 and before
right up to the present. If his work is about self-understanding,
about what it means to be human,[2] and it is, then it is also
about making a detour through cultural symbols, the only means
by which we come to self-understanding. For Ricoeur, consciousness is not a given but a task, the task of becoming more
conscious[3], of reappropriating the self and recovering the *Cogito*,
via the interpretation of texts.

The hermeneutical theory represented in the above quotations
is non-gendered. We can presume that the work of becoming

conscious is a human work proper to men and women. What happens though when this thinker applies his own hermeneutical theory to a specific cultural work, say to the Genesis myth of Adam and Eve as he does in *The Symbolism of Evil* (Ricoeur, 1969)? In this work, Ricoeur sets out both a comprehensive hermeneutic, largely innocent of any gender bias, *and* a most androcentric interpretation of a particular myth. Strangely, when Ricoeur speaks in general theoretical terms his hermeneutic is or appears to be unbiased, but when he applies this theory to one of the foundational myths in the West a strong androcentric bias appears. Are there, then, seeds of this bias within the theory itself? Or is it rather that the theory arises out of androcentric myths? I will return to these questions after considering Ricoeur's interpretations of Adam and Eve – figures, as he sees it, with quite different roles (see Ricoeur, 1966: part II, chapter III, 'The "Adamic" myth and the "Eschatological" vision', esp. pp. 235–60).

Ricoeur's Adam is identified as *sinner* in relation to God and as *victim* in relation to Eve. Being sinner means representing humanity's freedom to do evil (and by implication not to do evil) and being victim means representing humanity's lack of full responsibility for evil. So the one figure, Adam, represents the freedom and responsibility of the sinner *and* the lack of responsibility of the victim. This is a most flattering view of Adam. With meaning oscillating between the poles of freedom and innocence, Adam represents the saving aspects of being sinner and victim.

This is not the case with Eve. Ricoeur identifies Eve as *victim* in relation to the serpent which means she represents the human experience of being seduced. He also identifies her, along with the serpent, as '*evil emissary*' in relation to Adam, which means she represents evil itself. This identification of Eve with the serpent is one of the most damaging aspects of all traditional interpretations, for it makes no allowances for the figure of Eve.

So while Ricoeur sees Adam as partly innocent or at least less guilty because he is Eve's victim, he does not see Eve as less guilty because she is the serpent's victim. Adam as victim is allowed a degree of innocence which Eve as victim is never allowed. Even more tellingly, Ricoeur interprets Adam's sinfulness as an expression of freedom, but he completely ignores the aspects of freedom and responsibility implied in Eve's sinfulness. In the case of Eve, meaning oscillates as she is seen first as almost powerless victim in relation to the serpent and then as evil personified in relation to Adam. Neither is a flattering picture.

Significantly, Ricoeur never considers Eve as representative human in relation to God.

The lack of mutuality in interpeting these mythic figures is not surprising. After all, Ricoeur is doing nothing more than following the patriarchal interpretations of the New Testament, Paul and of the entire Christian tradition. Commonly, and lopsidedly, Adam represents the freedom of the human race, and Eve represents its inclination to evil. For Ricoeur, as for Paul, the myth is mainly about Adam, the archetypal human person. As Ricoeur (1969, p. 235) says: '... the central intention of the myth is to order all *other* figures in relation to the figure of Adam, and to understand them in conjunction with him and as peripheral figures in the story which has Adam as its principal protagonist.'

And even more pointedly, he says: '... the Biblical myth in spite of Eve and the serpent, remains "Adamic" – that is to say anthropological' (Ricoeur, 1966, p. 260). Androcentrism could hardly be expressed more clearly. In this reading all the figures – not only Eve but God and the serpent as well – are ranged around Adam. He is the sole figure by virtue of which the myth qualifies as anthropological. Eve and the serpent are the excluded others.

This reading is clearly inaccurate and unjustified. Undoubtedly the myth is androcentric and patriarchal but not to the degree that later interpretations would have us believe. My purpose here, however, is not to examine the degree of androcentrism in the myth or the particular inaccuracies of Ricoeur's interpretation. My purpose is to examine the androcentrism of the Ricoeurian reading itself. This appears in Ricoeur's failure to critique adequately the actual bias in the myth, and also in his implicit approval of the myth's perceived intense androcentrism. So the Ricoeurian reading is androcentric in that it increases the androcentric bias in the actual myth *and* implicitly approves of that bias.[4]

Does this androcentric reading of an ancient myth have any bearing on today's men and women? Does it matter that the mythic Eve is consistently subordinated to the mythic Adam? It does. By constantly identifying with Eve or Adam and with the patriarchal institutions engendered by these mythic figures, women and men maintain unjust gender arrangements. The self-understanding of women and men is shaped by modern interpretations of mythic figures and by the political structures and philosophical concepts to which they give rise. Unconsciously, we are assimilated to their meanings.[5] In the next section I will return to these claims, all of which are in keeping with aspects of Ricoeur's own hermeneutical theory.

Ricoeur himself is aware of the dangers of identifying only women with Eve. In one place, having stated that 'the woman represents the point of least resistance of finite freedom to the appeal of the ... evil infinite', he immediately goes on to say: 'Eve ... does not stand for woman in the sense of "second sex". Every woman and every man are Adam; every man and every woman are Eve; every woman sins "in" Adam, every man is seduced "in" Eve' (Ricoeur, 1969, p. 255). This is an even-handed statement, but is it true to common experience? In one sense it is. All humans, men and women, do have the experience of being 'sinners', that is of being free to do (and not to do) evil, and all have the experience of being seduced, of being tempted, almost compelled by some source of evil outside the self. Humans are at the same time free and not free, or, to use religious terms, are both sinners and victims. In another sense, however, the statement is not true, for Eve does indeed stand for woman and Adam for man.

Consider the myth itself. The punishments meted out to Adam and Eve are quite different. While Adam has to earn his bread by the sweat of his brow, Eve has to endure a peculiarly female punishment. To her, God says: 'I will greatly multiply your pain in childbearing; in pain you shall bring forth children, yet your desire shall be for your husband, and he shall rule over you'. (Genesis 3: 16 (RSV)). It is clear that here all women are addressed in Eve. It is also clear that all men are excluded, for they cannot possibly identify with Eve in this punishment, even if they can identify with her in the experience of succumbing to temptation. Some feminist scholars have pointed out that these punishments do not dictate the way things are meant to be; they are, rather, descriptions of the unredeemed patriarchal society which resulted from disobeying (see, for example, Trible, 1978, pp. 126–8). The subtlety of this feminist reading is largely lost, however, as Jewish and Christian and even post-Christian traditions continually identify women with the condemned Eve. So these mythical punishments growing out of a sex-roled society subordinating women and superordinating men have maintained this unjust arrangement for thousands of years.

Ricoeur himself fleetingly acknowledges this when he says:

... why is the woman chosen for the confrontation of interdict and desire? In the Biblical account she represents the point of weakness and giving way in the presence of the seducer; the serpent tempts the man through the woman.

No doubt it must be granted that the story gives evidence of a very masculine resentment, which serves to justify the state of dependence in which all, or almost all, societies have kept women. (Ricoeur, 1969, p. 254)[6]

Ricoeur is aware, then, of the bias in the myth and its role in maintaining patriarchal societies. Yet even in this passing acknowledgement the androcentrism of his own reading is apparent. Does the woman really represent 'the point of weakness' in the biblical account or has this reading been imposed by a patriarchal tradition? A gynocentric interpretation would suggest that Eve was chosen for the confrontation because she was the stronger: that it was only after much discussion with the serpent, the figure representing evil itself, that she finally succumbed, and that Adam by contrast succumbed immediately on the mere suggestion of his human companion (for a similar interpretation, see Trible, 1978, p. 113). And is it not androcentric of Ricoeur to say, 'the serpent tempts the man through the woman' whereby the woman becomes no more than a vehicle for the interaction between the serpent and the man? A gynocentric reading would say, 'the serpent tempts the woman and the woman tempts the man', a statement that acknowledges the woman for herself. But little is to be gained by scoring feminist points in this way. It is more productive to examine some connections between this (no worse than usual) androcentric interpretation and what appears to be a finely balanced hermeneutical *theory*.

It is clear from the above discussion that *tension* plays a vital role in Ricoeur's hermeneutic. The tensions between the voluntary and the involuntary, for example, are fully articulated as Ricoeur conceptualizes evil within humanity and outside of it, evil as read in the psyche and on the cosmos. Tirelessly, his hermeneutic builds a relation between a schema of interiority and one of exteriority, between an ethical vision by virtue of which humans are guilty and responsible *and* a tragic vision by which we are innocent and blighted. At the one time, humanity is *and* is not responsible for evil. Exploring the advantages and disadvantages of each vision and the need to keep them in tension, Ricoeur constructs a most complex and even-handed hermeneutic couched in non-gendered philosophical terms.

Yet this admirable hermeneutic translates into a biased reading. It is worth exploring the complex nature of this translation. It is not that the voluntary aspect is always associated with Adam and the involuntary with Eve. If the transition from myth to hermeneutical theory and back were so neat, it would be relatively easy to identify it as simply another example of a harmful dualism. But Ricoeur's reading does not consistently align Adam with one pole of the tension and Eve with the other. Instead, it consistently associates Adam with the *desirable* aspects of both the voluntary and the involuntary, and Eve with the *undesirable*. Not that the desirable and undesirable are ever alluded to. They remain deeply presupposed factors dictating whether the male or female figure will represent specific meanings. So when the *voluntary* aspect of evil signifies freedom and responsibility then the representative figure is Adam, and when this *same voluntary* aspect signifies guilt then the representative figure is Eve. Similarly, when the *involuntary* aspect of evil signifies innocence or a lessening of guilt then the representative figure is Adam, and when the *same involuntary* aspect signifies powerlessness then the representative figure is Eve. Favourable and unfavourable meanings are applied, unconsciously, to male and female figures respectively.[7]

While this gender bias is present in the myth itself, it is intensified in Ricoeur's reading, influenced as it is by the New Testament myth of the second Adam as well as by two thousand years of patriarchal tradition. The above example is not an isolated one. Androcentric myths and symbols have constantly given rise to androcentric philosophical concepts. The difficulty is that these concepts appear, not as androcentric, but as neutral. The abstracted concepts of the voluntary and the involuntary appear to have nothing to do with gender but this is a false appearance. The voluntary and the involuntary have everything to do with gender because they are experienced only by men and women, by gendered humanity. Once the concepts are translated back into myths, stories, historical accounts, as they demand to be, then their implicit gender bias becomes visible. Ricoeur's articulation of the tensions *within* the concepts actually makes it easier to detect the nature of gender bias. With great skill Ricoeur shows that the concepts of the voluntary and the involuntary support tensive meanings not only between themselves but also within each one, and it becomes apparent that these meanings are always related to desirability and undesirability. It is complex, though, because what is considered desirable and undesirable continually shifts according to context.

Feminist scholars have already uncovered a long list of harmful dualisms by which women are consistently aligned with what is judged as less desirable and men with the more desirable.[8] These scholars show that this alignment can shift as the poles of the dualism change. So, for example, in the soul–body split men are traditionally associated with soul and women with body, but when the body is considered in itself as in the head–heart dualism, men belong with head and women with heart. This scholarly exploration of dualisms has undoubtedly contributed to uncovering the roots of patriarchy. The thesis is, however, oversimplified, for it suggests that tensions occur solely or principally between the poles of the dualism. Here I am suggesting that: (1) significant tensions occur *within* each pole of any dualism (a suggestion derived from Ricoeur's work), and (2) that androcentric meaning arises when these tensions are continually interpreted in favour of male figures and to the detriment of female figures. This means that androcentrism is extremely difficult to pin down as single concepts constantly give rise to tensive meanings which can be applied selectively to male and female figures.

To return to the example of the voluntary and the involuntary: there is an obvious tension between these abstract philosophical concepts, and feminist analysis can easily show that the male is more frequently aligned with the voluntary and the female with the involuntary. But the tension is not only between the concepts, it is also *within* each of them. Each concept gives rise to desirable and undesirable meanings which Ricoeur consistently attaches to Adam and Eve respectively. This patriarchal practice is by now largely unconscious and Ricoeur's androcentric hermeneutic is not an isolated example. An examination of most myths and philosophies will reveal the same sleight of mind. If Ricoeur is right and if meaning arises out of tensions, then the possibilities are endless for aligning female figures to the less desirable and male figures to the more desirable poles of any tension, and also for exploiting the conflicting meanings to which the single concept or practice gives rise. The discipline of hermeneutics, taking advantage of these possibilities, functions in an androcentric and patriarchal manner.

A Feminist Hermeneutics of Gender

The above critique of Ricoeur's hermeneutic already begins the constructive work of articulating a more adequate hermeneutics of gender. This critique highlights the key concept in Ricoeur's hermeneutic, the role of tension. Now I turn to the most comprehensive of all Ricoeurian tensions, that between symbol and self, or between the objectivity of the text and the subjectivity of the interpreting community. While Ricoeur deals at length with the interactions within texts (*intra*textuality) and between texts (*inter*textuality), his principal concern is the elusive connection between these textual interactions and the interpreting subject.[9]

The relation between text and self is circular: the text gives self-understanding, and self-understanding opens the reader to the text. Ricoeur chooses to enter this hermeneutical circle at the point of the text, not at the point of the self. He gives priority to the text because he believes that the text gives the mediated self and not the other way round. The reflexive self is the gift of the text; the text is never the gift of the reflexive self. This much is clear from the quotations at the beginning of the above section on 'The Gender of Hermeneutics'.

The priority of the text remains a theme of Ricoeur's work. In his first hermeneutical work, *The Symbolism of Evil* (Ricoeur, 1969), meditating on the Kantian adage 'the symbol gives rise to thought', Ricoeur emphasizes the active, giving power of the symbol (Ricoeur, 1969, pp. 347–57). For him, the symbol or text evokes thought and if this priority is changed so that the symbol or text is subordinated to the interpreting self, then narcissism, scepticism and rationalism result. Only by attending to the text and letting go the ego is the mediated self received. The immediate self must be emptied, decentred, so the matter of the text can be received. As Ricoeur (1979, p. 219), somewhat tersely, says, '*listening* excludes founding the self'. And at greater length:

> To understand is not to project oneself into the text but to expose oneself to it; it is to receive a self enlarged by the appropriation of the proposed worlds which interpretation unfolds. In sum, it is the matter of the text which gives the reader his dimension of subjectivity; understanding is thus no longer a constitution of which

the subject possesses the key ... if fiction is a fundamental dimension of the reference of the text, it is equally a fundamental dimension of the subjectivity of the reader: in reading I 'unrealize myself'. Reading introduces me to imaginative variations of the *ego*. The metamorphosis of the world in play is also the playful metamorphosis of the *ego*. (Ricoeur, 1981b, p. 94)

There is much to be learned from this statement, and much to be wary of. Basically Ricoeur is right. Self-understanding does come through appropriating proposed worlds which interpretation unfolds. 'The symbol (does) give rise to thought' and the text gives subjectivity. But what if symbol and text are patriarchal? What if nearly all symbols and texts propose worlds in which males are dominant and females subordinant? What if most 'imaginative variations of the *ego*', most 'playful metamorphos(e)s' are androcentric? What if the female 'I' receives a self, not 'enlarged by the appropriation of proposed worlds', but diminished by them? Ricoeur may speak truer than he knows when he says 'it is the matter of the text which gives the reader *his* dimension of subjectivity'. And again when he says, 'in reading I "unrealize myself"'. A feminist hermeneutics suggests that women, appropriating a patriarchal tradition, do indeed constantly and pathologically 'unrealize' themselves.

With the question of gender introduced, the above Ricoeurian statements expressing complete trust in symbols and texts, neatly summarize the problem. If most symbols and texts are patriarchal and if they provide the only key to self-understanding and self-constitution, then the possibilities for male and female self-realization are severely limited. Patriarchal symbols and texts must give rise to patriarchal thought, to patriarchal subjectivity. Since we are all born into a world of patriarchal texts and symbols, we all become assimilated to their warped meaning intentions.

The way out of this dilemma requires undertaking certain tasks. One is to attend to that minority of non-patriarchal texts which, eschewing dominance and subordinance, fully affirm womankind as well as mankind. Appropriating the meaning intentions of these texts, men and women receive a mediated self that is not inappropriately gender-biased. Another task is to attend to the *critical* moment in the process of interpretation itself. Provided we pay proper attention to this moment, even patriarchal myths can be a means to an adequately mediated self. So these two therapeutic moments, the first involving a hermeneutics of consent and the second a hermeneutics of suspicion, can contribute to a more adequate concept of gender. I begin with the vital moment of suspicion.

Ricoeur's hermeneutic has always included a critical moment, even if this moment has remained subordinate in a philosophy that is more concerned with avowal than critique. Appearing in different guises in successive phases of his work, this critical moment constantly modifies the absoluteness of Ricoeur's faith in symbols and texts. In some places, he warns as strongly against absolutizing the text as he does against absolutizing the self, for such unquestioning faith in texts leads variously to fundamentalism, naivete, romanticism, credulity, fideism and idolatry.[10] Critical hermeneutics, engaging in a process of demythologization, ensures against these outcomes.

The critical moment appears in Ricoeur's early work in the guise of qualified approval for the work of Freud, that 'master of suspicion'. While Ricoeur disapproves of Freud's reductive understanding of religious symbols, he does not reject it outright, for he wishes to incorporate Freudian suspicion into his own hermeneutic: 'One should not be in a hurry to correct this reductive hermeneutics but should rather stay with it, for it will not be suppressed, but retained, in a more comprehensive hermeneutics' (Ricoeur, 1970, p. 447). Ricoeur transforms the reductive hermeneutic of Freud into the critical moment of his own more comprehensive hermeneutic. This moment is required because 'The symbol is a phantasm disavowed and overcome but not at all abolished. It is always on some trace of archaic myth that the symbolic meanings appropriate to reflective interpretation are grafted'.[11]

For Ricoeur, then, the critical moment of hermeneutics is demanded by symbols themselves. All symbols must be subjected to a hermeneutics of suspicion because all incorporate 'phantasms', that is traces of archaic myths expressing degrees of false consciousness. Implicit in every symbol is an *arche* as well as a *telos*, a disguise as well as a disclosure. On account of this overdetermination, all symbols demand regressive as well as progressive interpretations.[12]

But despite this critical theory, so congenial to a feminist hermeneutics, Ricoeur never identifies misogyny as a phantasm operating within most symbols. Although he wrote this critical theory in conjunction with a detailed interpretation of the cultural and religious symbol of fatherhood,[13] he failed to detect the obvious misogynous intentions of this key symbol. Along with Freud and most male thinkers, Ricoeur has never identified patriarchy as the great archaic myth underlying Western culture. The vast substratum of this myth is continually being uncovered by a body of feminist scholarship which shows that male desire posing as normative human desire is encoded in most texts. 'I the Lord am your God and you will have no strange gods before me.' I the Father, Husband, King, President, Judge ..., I the Powerful Male am your God and you will have no other. Enscribed on the minds and bodies of women and men, on animals and nature, this myth appears in countless forms. Consider the major myths of Judaism and Christianity, and the dominant myths of a secular post-Christian society. Consider Western classics in whatever art form and Western institutions. The phantasm of patriarchy, that pyramid of male power,[14] permeates the entire culture imparting a warped subjectivity. To participate uncritically in such a culture is to remain alienated from the self in a state of false consciousness.

This regressive interpretation, a disavowal of the phantasm at the heart of Western culture, begins a more constructive work. Ricoeur's hermeneutic is valuable precisely because it articulates connections between the two moments of suspicion and consent. Indeed the very moment of suspicion is itself a form of consent, since suspicion of one text grows out of consent to another. Creative suspicion of patriarchy arises, not from the unmediated and non-reflexive self, but from the self that has appropriated myths and concepts that give rise to non-patriarchal meanings. Suspicion arises from the clash of myths and concepts. Basically, Ricoeur is right: the symbol *gives*. If the patriarchal symbol gives patriarchal subjectivity, so the feminist symbol gives feminist subjectivity. Symbols are best able to give when they are in collision with other symbols, for the reflexive self is given in the very act of mediating conflicting interpretations.[15] So the reflexive self is received in the process of determining what will be avowed and what disavowed, in the process of saying yes and no. But unless gender is a factor in this interpretive process, the self will remain patriarchal and, as a consequence, less reflexive.

Ricoeur's critical hermeneutic also warns against the iconoclastic nature of symbols: each symbol seeks to oust competition, claiming for itself alone absolute authority.[16] Undoubtedly God the Father has been the most iconoclastic of all symbols in a patriarchal culture. Since the Enlightenment, however, the power of this symbol has altered, for science and technology as well as the human sciences have exposed many of the phantasms lurking in the *God* symbol. The symbol of *Fatherhood*, on the other hand, has scarcely been critiqued at all save by feminist scholars. Instead, it has been uncritically appropriated so that fatherhood or authoritative maleness has become God. What is an appropriate response to this form of idolatry? It is not to deny and ignore the symbols of God and Father, for this simply drives them underground where they function even more powerfully as phantasms. The appropriate response is to attend to those symbols whose meanings compete with the symbols of God and Father, not to destroy the latter but to jostle them and relativize their meanings. Mediating between competing symbols and allowing the moment of suspicion to incorporate a moment of consent and vice versa, one receives self-understanding and self-constitution, the gift of the mediated self.

Different *levels* of symbols are also iconoclastic. Ricoeur distinguishes three levels.[17] Primary symbols such as dreams are the places where experience first wells up in language. Being closest to experience, these semantic symbols are the least articulated. Secondary symbols appearing in the form of myths are more clearly articulated and more removed from experience. And tertiary symbols taking the form of logical and dogmatic concepts are most removed from experience. In a rationalistic age, this third type of symbol is the most iconoclastic seeking to deprive other types of discourse, like myth, fiction and poetry of all truth value. So third-level symbols such as those of science and philosophy need to be deconstructed constantly so they do not congeal into the pretence of absolute truth. One of the never-completed tasks of a critical hermeneutics is to deconstruct symbols as concepts and reconstruct them as myths and stories. The traffic must be two-way, though, as myths need to be articulated again and again as philosophical concepts.

This articulation of experience in semantic, mythic and rational symbols is demanded by experience itself. In Ricoeur's (1981b, p. 115) words: 'Experience can be said, it demands to be said. To bring it to language is not to change it into something else, but, in articulating it and developing it, to make it become itself.' While this statement is unbiased, it prompts several questions. Has *female* experience been adequately said, or has it remained largely unsaid or wrongly said? To what degree has female experience, through articulation, 'become itself'? To answer these questions one has to examine specific symbols and texts, particularly those considered classics. These questions become especially difficult, however, when applied to third level symbols because, being generally couched in ungendered terms, these symbols easily hide their gender bias. As already noted, it is impossible to detect any gender bias in Ricoeur's discussion of the voluntary and the involuntary, and the bias appears only when this discussion is associated with an androcentric reading of the Adam and Eve myth. Only in the deconstruction, then, from philosophical concept to myth – that is, from third to second level symbol – does the bias clearly appear. In other words, when the imagination mediates between different levels of symbols, phantasms can more easily be detected.

Essential to Ricoeur's hermeneutic, then, are the tasks of deconstructing and reconstructing symbols, and of mediating between them. These tasks are the work of the 'productive imagination',[18] the key term on the subject side of Ricoeur's hermeneutic just as symbol or text is the chief concern on the object side. Ricoeur trusts symbols and texts to the degree that the imagination mediates both the conflicts within and between them, and those between texts *and* the interpreting subject. An adequate mediation of conflicts leads to the appropriation of meaning which provides self-understanding and self-constitution.

This constructive work remains the key element in Ricoeur's theory which resists being reduced to a hermeneutics of suspicion. Critique, for Ricoeur, is but one moment in a more comprehensive hermeneutics demanding consent to the meaning intentions of symbols. This broader hermeneutic seeks the restoration of meaning on the far side of criticism: 'a metaphor faith beyond demythologization', 'a second naivete beyond iconoclasm' (Ricoeur, 1978), a reorientation after disorientation.[19] 'Beyond the wastelands of critical thought we seek to be challenged anew' (Ricoeur, 1974, p. 288). This desire for the affirmation of meaning so necessary for the constitution of the mediated self finds frequent expression in Ricoeur's work.

Does this hermeneutics of consent also provide resources for a more adequate construction of gender? I believe it does. Just as I have begun to show that a Ricoeurian hermeneutics of suspicion is helpful in exploring gender, it can also be shown that his restorative hermeneutics has a part to play. As an example, I briefly explore Ricoeur's extensive theory of metaphor in conjunction with the symbol of gender.[20]

Ricoeur's theory of metaphor proposes that new meanings and new referents arise from the tension between 'is' and 'is not' at the heart of metaphorical discourse. Briefly, Ricoeur explores the tensions within metaphor by referring to the notion of 'stereoscopic vision', or the ability to entertain two points of view at the same time. Any metaphor demands that principal and subsidiary subjects maintain their normal meanings as well as take on new meanings, for the metaphor exists in the tension between meanings. To take an example, one considered by Ricoeur: in the metaphorical statement, 'nature is a temple where living columns ...', nature both *is like* a temple and *is not* a temple (Ricoeur, 1978, p. 247). This tension between 'is like' and 'is not', that is between sameness and difference in the verb 'to be', creates new meaning and new reference. This new creation constitutes a 'world' projected *'in front of'* the text, a 'world' in which readers can dwell.

Such a theory, making both epistemological and ontological claims, never reduces metaphor to embellishment. Through metaphor, a new cognitive element exists, and a new way of being is possible. This theory stresses that this new creation, this 'world', is 'in front of' the text and not behind it, for Ricoeur is opposed to any psychologizing interpretation which tries to get back to the mind of the author or to the minds of the original audience. By a process of 'distanciation' or 'decontextualization', any text is removed from its original author, audience and meaning (see, for example, Ricoeur, 1973). The metaphorical meaning and reference await appropriation through the recontextualizing activity of the current reader or listener. In other words, a tension exists not only within the text, but also between text and reader, a tension which is resolved only through appropriation including critique.

This Ricoeurian theory never averts to gender, but what happens if it is introduced? I begin with the example: 'nature is a temple where living columns ...'. Here the tension within the metaphorical 'is' creates an interaction between 'nature' and 'temple', and the denotation of both these ungendered terms is straightforward enough. But what is the denotation of 'living columns'? To what does this term refer? The obvious reference is to trees and pillars of stone, and the less obvious, to the human spinal column.[21] Clearly or dimly, the poetic imagination is aware that the human body is one of the connotations of this fragment. The three stated terms – nature, temple and living columns –

all evoke the human body: the temple of the body belongs to nature and the spinal column renders it like (and unlike) both the trees of nature and the pillars of a temple. The metaphorical statement holds sameness and difference in tension: 'living columns', being grounded and stretching upwards, share a vertical dimension, and, being movable and immovable and made variously of stone, wood and bone, are quite different. Nature both is and is not a temple. The human body is and is not like the temple of nature.

With the reference of the human body introduced, this reading has gone far enough. Given that the body is one of the connotations of the above text, does the reader imagine a male body or a female body? Does either the text itself or the tradition from which it comes give preference to the image of male or female? Does the choice depend on individual readers, or on the interpreting community to which they belong? Does a choice have to be made, or can the imagination image a neuter or androgynous body? With only a fragment of text available, these questions cannot be answered definitively, and they might well remain unanswerable even with the whole text at hand. It is likely, however, that on account of the connotations of sacredness, strength, height, and power, this fragment suggests a male body. In a patriarchal culture where the male body is paradigmatic, the imagination automatically turns to it unless a female body is specified. This depressing conclusion is not the main point of my reading, however. The main point is to demonstrate how the symbol of gender lurks in a text which at first reading appears non-gendered. And this text is not unusual. A careful examination of most texts and symbols shows that gender is nearly always present, at least implicitly.

Texts that are not specifically gendered allow 'imaginative variations' within themselves, and can give rise to androcentric and/or gynocentric meanings and referents. In Ricoeur's (1981b, p. 94) terms, the 'imaginative variations' within the text can introduce the reader to 'imaginative variations of the *ego*', fiction being a fundamental dimension of both text and reader. Consequently, readers can play with gender possibilities within texts, allowing meanings to range freely between maleness and femaleness, and refusing to restrict meaning or referent to one or other unless the text itself demands such restriction. Playing is part of the 'dynamic activity of the reader', part of the process of decontextualization and recontextualization. This scope for play both within the text and between text and reader, is one of the elements of Ricoeur's restorative hermeneutic most congenial to a feminist hermeneutics, for it allows gynocentric meanings and referents to emerge.

So Ricoeur's metaphor theory actually throws light on how the current patriarchal construction of gender has arisen. The tensions within the metaphorical verb 'to be', the play of possibilities within texts as well as between texts and readers, the polyvalence of language itself, all allow for multiple interpretations. Taking advantage of this multiplicity, a patriarchal tradition has consistently interpreted texts in favour of men and to the detriment of women. The result is that the Western tradition has constructed maleness as normative and in some sense invisible, with the specific symbol of maleness rarely mentioned. That is why gender needs to be brought to consciousness. Gender is an ubiquitous symbol, in Ricoeur's terms 'a phantasm', currently working underground. Until it surfaces to general consciousness, a patriarchal tradition can continue to align maleness and femaleness arbitrarily with the metaphorical 'is' and 'is not' according to whichever aspect is more desirable in a given context. In short, it can continue to allot favourable and unfavourable meanings to maleness and femaleness respectively.

Ricoeur's restorative hermeneutic implicitly shows that this destructive split along gender lines need not occur. If a patriarchal tradition has taken advantage of the essential fluidity of meaning and reference in language in order to serve its own interests, a feminist tradition can take advantage of the same fluidity in the interests of women and men. Because of this fluidity, the entire Western tradition can be reread so as to include the female as well as the male in non-gendered texts, and to critique those texts in which the female is inappropriately excluded. Such a reading is necessary for any adequate construction of gender.

In conclusion, my examination of gender in conjunction with Ricoeur's theory is a beginning. It would be most profitable to explore the symbol of gender in the context of Ricoeur's entire hermeneutic, with special reference to his earlier work on freedom and his latest work on time and narrative. The following concluding statements bring together some key elements in this brief Ricoeurian examination.

Gender, being a construction of maleness and femaleness, is itself a symbol operating on the semantic, mythic and rational levels.[22] Implicitly or explicitly, gender is an element in nearly all other symbols and texts and in all interpretations. While a feminist tradition explicitly acknowledges gender, it frequently remains implicit in a patriarchal tradition. Suppressed by this tradition, gender functions as a 'phantasm' or an idol expressing unacknowledged fear, guilt and desire. This suppression of gender-consciousness means that a patriarchal tradition fails to notice the inappropriate androcentric bias in specific texts and symbols, and imposes a further bias through androcentric interpretations. A feminist tradition, on the other hand, critiques and appropriates all texts in a gender-conscious way. Sometimes this latter tradition also imposes an inappropriate bias, this time a gynocentric one, in which case gender functions as a phantasm in a feminist tradition. Currently, attention to gender remains an activity on the fringes of some institutions such as the academy and the church, and is completely ignored by others. Yet, as one of the key elements in all symbols of humanity, gender needs to move to the centre.

To adapt a Ricoeurian adage: only when the idol of universal androcentrism dies can the symbol of gender begin to speak.[23] Such is the task for a hermeneutics of gender.

Notes

1 'History as narrative and practice', interview with Paul Ricoeur by Peter Kemp in *Philosophy Today* (1985, pp. 193–4), quoted by Madison (1988, p. 95).

2 Various commentators have noted that the principal question motivating Ricoeur's work is: What does it mean to be human? See, for example, Rasmussen (1971, p. 3) and Ihde (1971, p. 20).

3 'The hermeneutics of symbols: II', in Ricoeur (1974, p. 324); 'Consciousness and Unconscious' in Ricoeur (1974, p. 108).

4 In his paper, 'The Bible and the imagination' Ricoeur (1981a, p. 72) comments on the transition from 'the work of imagination *in* the text' to 'the work of imagination *about* the text'. In these terms, not only does Ricoeur fail to critique the patriarchal imagination at work *in* the Adam and Eve myth, he also engages in a work of patriarchal imagination *about* the myth.

5 Ricoeur terms this process of being incorporated into the meaning intention of myths, 'symmorphosis'. Speaking of the symbol of 'pardon', he says: 'It is not that the individual undergoes a certain experience and then projects it onto a world of images; on the

contrary it is because he is incorporated into that which those "images" signify that the individual attains the experience of pardon' (Ricoeur, 1969, p. 275).

6   Ricoeur's work shows evidence of an increasing awareness of gender. For example, a more recent paper, 'The human being as the subject matter of philosophy', presented at the World Congress of Philosophy, Brighton, 1988, uses inclusive language. Ricoeur says in the first footnote of this paper, 'I shall use the inclusive language "humans" instead of "men" which is suspect to many of us' (Ricoeur, 1989: 101).

7   Feminist interpretations can easily turn this process inside out, applying all desirable meanings to the female and leaving undesirable meanings for the male. The polyvalence of language easily allows gender-biased meanings. Some recent articles critical of feminism have accused feminist theorists of doing precisely this. See, for example, Arnold (1989).

8   Rosemary Radford Ruether was one of the first scholars in religion to draw attention to the dualisms. See, for example, her two articles, 'Women's liberation in historical and theological perspective' (Ruether, 1970), and 'Misogynism and virginal feminism in the fathers of the Church' (Ruether, 1974). The listing of dualisms or 'dichotomous oppositions' has become commonplace in feminist texts. As one example, see Cixous (1986), 'Sorties: out and out: attacks/ways out/forays'.

9   The relation between text and interpreting subject is a constant theme of Ricoeur's work. For succinct early statements, see the following essays in (Ricoeur, 1974): 'The hermeneutics of symbols and philosophical reflection: II' written in 1961, especially parts III and IV, and 'Existence and hermeneutics' written in 1965, especially parts IV and V. Ricoeur is critical of structuralism precisely because, to his mind, it reduces the text to an object to be analysed and ignores the role of the interpreting self. See 'Structure, word, event' written in 1967, and 'Structure and hermeneutics' written in 1963.

10 Ricoeur articulates a finely nuanced relation between text and self. In his essay, 'Towards a hermeneutic of the idea of revelation' (Ricoeur, 1980), for example, Ricoeur warns specifically against absolutizing either object or subject. Rhetorically he asks, 'If to understand oneself is to understand oneself in front of the text, must we not say that the reader's understanding is suspended, derealized, made potential just as the world itself is metamorphosized by the poem?' (Ricoeur, 1980, p. 137).

11 'Fatherhood: from phantasm to symbol' (Ricoeur, 1974, p. 350).

12 This thesis is presented in detail in Ricoeur (1970), where Ricoeur brings into a tensive relation the regressive hermeneutic of Freud and the progressive hermeneutic of Hegel.

13 The thesis of the massive work, *Freud and Philosophy* (Ricoeur, 1970), is presented succinctly in Ricoeur's interpretation of father-hood: 'Fatherhood: from phantasm to symbol' in Ricoeur (1974).

14 The image of patriarchy as a 'male pyramid' is Elisabeth Schüssler Fiorenza's. In Fiorenza (1984) she defines patriarchy thus: 'I do not use the concept (patriarchy) of "all men dominating all women equally", but in the classic Aristotelian sense. *Patriarchy* as a male pyramid of graded subordinations and exploitations specifies women's oppression in terms of the class, race, country or religion of the men to whom we "belong"' (p. xiv).

15 See, for example, Ricoeur's mediation of the conflicting approaches to symbols of psychoanalysis and phenomenology in 'The herme-neutics of symbols: II' (Ricoeur, 1974, pp. 318–26).

16 Ricoeur, 1969, p. 354; and 'The hermeneutics of symbols I' (Ri-coeur, 1974, p. 293).

17 In *The Symbolism of Evil*, Ricoeur (1969) 're-enacts' the struggle within and between semantic and mythic levels of symbols, but omits any 're-enactment' of rational symbols. This latter 're-enactment' is confined to two essays, 'The hermeneutics of symbols: I' and 'Original sin: a study in meaning' (both in Ricoeur, 1974). Nowhere does Ricoeur 're-enact' the dynamics of third-level sym-bols of evil, although he does state that the semantic, mythic and rational levels of symbols must not be separated. See 'The herme-neutics of symbols: II' (Ricoeur, 1974, p. 316).

18 The productive imagination has remained a theme of Ricoeur's work. In a succinct article, 'Metaphoric imagination', Mary Schaldenbrand (1979) traces Ricoeur's philosophy of the imagination through his works, *Freedom and Nature* (1966 [1950]), *Fallible Man* [1960], *The Symbolism of Evil* (1969 [1960]), *Freud and Philosophy* (1970 [1965]), and *The Rule of Metaphor* (1978 [1975]). Imagination remains a central concern of his latest three-volume work, *Time and Narrative* (1983, 1984, 1985).

19 Ricoeur says, for example, that the parables provide 'a re-orienta-tion after a disorientation' (Ricoeur, 1979–80, p. 76). While Ri-coeur makes much of the disorienting function of the parables, he always allows for re-orientation, though never in any definitive way. The process of orienting, disorienting and re-orienting is never completed.

20 My brief treatment of Ricoeur's metaphor theory draws on Study 7, 'Metaphor and reference', of *The Rule of Metaphor* (Ricoeur, 1978). Catherine Keller in her article, 'Goddess, ear, and metaphor: on the journey of Nelle Morton' (Keller, 1988, pp. 56–9), also draws on Ricoeur's theory of metaphor in the interests of a feminist analysis. She too is critical of Ricoeur's theory, but her critique is, I believe, misplaced. First, she states that Ricoeur cuts short 'the

iconoclastic moment', a conclusion based on one Ricoeurian essay, 'Metaphor and symbol' (Ricoeur, 1976). But an examination of Ricoeur's major work on metaphor, *The Rule of Metaphor* (Ricoeur, 1978), does not support this assertion. Neither can it be supported in terms of his overall work, for his 1960s work on Freud and his 1970s work on the parables can all be read as explorations of the 'iconolclastic moment' or interpretation. Far from cutting this moment short, Ricoeur who coined the term 'hermeneutics of suspicion' shows evidence of being devoted to iconoclasm and dissonance. Second, Keller states that metaphor in Ricoeur's theory, 'becomes a disembodied word' (p. 58). Again, this claim cannot be supported in the light of Ricoeur's work. Over fifty years, Ricoeur's work has articulated the relation between text and experience. See, for example, note 9.

21   The term, 'living columns', may instantly recall the phallus. This is, I believe, the effect of a patriarchal tradition on the imagination. I do not mention the image of the phallus in my own text as I want to suggest that the spinal column is a more appropriate and more comprehensive interpretation. While all texts need to include as many meanings and referents as possible and while the phallus is undoubtedly a possible referent of 'living columns', it is, in this text, a subsidiary one. What I am drawing attention to here is the constant and damaging priority given to the phallus within patriarchy.

22   This essay has not entered the lively debate on the sex–gender distinction as discussed, for example, in *Australian Feminist Studies* (No. 10, Summer 1989). My understanding of gender in this paper cuts across this distinction. I use the terms 'maleness and femaleness' in preference to 'masculinity and femininity', for the former terms better reflect the link, even unity, between sexed body and socially constructed gender. A succinct exploration of the construction of 'male' and 'female' in the Western philosophical tradition can be found in Lloyd (1984).

23   'Religion, atheism and faith'.(Ricoeur, 1974, p. 467): 'An idol must die so a symbol of being may begin to speak.'

References

Arnold, Patrick M. 1989: In search of the hero: masculine spirituality and liberal Christianity *America*, 161, 9 (7 October), 206–10.

Cixous, Hélène 1986: Sorties: out and out: attacks/ways out/forays. In Hélène Cixous and Catherine Clément, *The Newly Born Woman*, trs. Betsy Wing, Manchester: Manchester University Press, 63–100.

Fiorenza, Elisabeth Schüssler 1984: *Bread Not Stone: The Challenge of Feminist Biblical Interpretation.* Boston, MA: Beacon.

Ihde, Don 1971: *Hermeneutic Phenomenology: The Philosophy of Paul Ricoeur.* Evanston, IL: Northwestern University Press.

Keller, Catherine 1988: Goddess, ear, and metaphor: on the journey of Nelle Morton. *Journal of Feminist Studies in Religion*, 4, 2, 56–9.

Lloyd, Genevieve 1984: *Man of Reason.* London: Methuen.

Madison, G. B. 1988: *The Hermeneutics of Postmodernity.* Bloomington and Indianapolis: Indiana University Press.

Rasmussen, David 1971: *Mythic-Symbolic Language and Philosophical Anthropology: A Constructive Interpretation of the Thought of Paul Ricoeur.* The Hague: Martinus Nijoff.

Ricoeur, Paul 1966 (1950): *Freedom and Nature: The Voluntary and the Involuntary.* Trs. Erazim V. Kohak. Evanston, IL: Northwestern University Press.

Ricoeur, Paul 1969 (1960): *The Symbolism of Evil.* Trs. Emerson Buchanan. Boston, MA: Beacon Press.

Ricoeur, Paul 1970 (1965): *Freud and Philosophy: An Essay on Interpretation.* Trs. Denis Savage. New Haven and London: Yale University Press.

Ricoeur, Paul 1973: The hermeneutic function of distanciation. *Philosophy Today*, 17, 2 & 3.

Ricoeur, Paul 1974 (1969): *The Conflict of Interpretation: Essays in Hermeneutics*, (ed.) Don Ihde. Evanston, IL: Northwestern University Press.

Ricoeur, Paul 1976: *Interpretation Theory: Discourse and the Surplus of Meaning.* Forth Worth, TX: Texas Christian University Press.

Ricoeur, Paul 1978 (1975): *The Rule of Metaphor: Multi-Disciplinary Studies of the Creation of Meaning in Language.* Trs. Robert Czerny with Kathleen McLaughlin and John Costello. London and Henley: Routledge & Kegan Paul.

Ricoeur, Paul 1979: Naming God. *Union Seminary Quarterly Review*, xxxiv, 4, 215–27.

Ricoeur, Paul 1979–80: A response. *Journal of the Chicago Society for Biblical Research*, XXIV–XXV, 70–80.

Ricoeur, Paul 1980: Towards a hermeneutic of the idea of revelation. In Lewis Mudge (ed.), *Essays on Biblical Interpretation*, Philadelphia: Fortress Press, 73–118.

Ricoeur, Paul 1981a: *The Bible as a Document of the University.* Chico, CA: Scholars Press.

Ricoeur, Paul 1981b: Hermeneutics and critique of ideology. In John B. Thompson (ed. and trs.), *Hermeneutics and the Human Sciences*, Cambridge, UK: Cambridge University Press, 63–100.

Ricoeur, Paul 1983–5: *Time and Narrative*, 3 vols. Chicago: University of Chicago Press.

Ricoeur, Paul 1989: The human being as the subject matter of philosophy. Paper presented at the World Congress of Philosophy, Brighton. In Peter Kemp and David Rasmussen (eds), *The Narrative Path: The Later Works of Paul Ricoeur*, Cambridge, MA: MIT Press, 89–101.

Ruether, Rosemary Radford 1970: Women's liberation in historical and theological perspective. In Sarah Bentley Doely (ed.), *Women's Liberation and the Church*, New York: Association Press.

Ruether, Rosemary Radford 1974: Misogynism and virginal feminism in the fathers of the Church. In Rosemary Radford Ruether (ed.), *Religion and Sexism: Images of Women in the Jewish and Christian Tradition*, New York: Simon & Schuster, 150–83.

Schaldenbrand, Mary 1979: Metaphoric imagination. In Charles E. Reagan (ed.), *Studies in the Philosophy of Paul Ricoeur*, Athens, OH: Ohio University Press.

Trible, Phyllis 1978: *God and the Rhetoric of Sexuality*. Philadelphia: Fortress Press.

4

Disputing the Sacred: Some Theoretical Approaches to Gender and Religion

Penelope Margaret Magee

I take as my starting point the observation that religious ideas are seen as anomalous or difficult to approach from the viewpoint of much feminist theory and practice. Speaking of feminists working in the area of religious ideas, Rosemary Ruether (1979, p. 307) notes that for some, the revolutionary change intended in feminist thought and practice is 'so fundamental that it must bury all patriarchal faiths forever in the scrap heap of history as outworn and, indeed, demonic world-views'. 'Secular', political, or 'academic' feminist theory and practice (which I will argue is very problematic terminology) is even more likely to condemn patriarchy in its religious dress; even feminist religious dress is suspect.[1]

The various invented postmodern 'methodologies' which claim descent from Derrida have made much of the deconstruction of binary oppositions. Yet an exploration of some of the problems raised by feminist distancing from the sacred highlights the real difficulty experienced with leaving a fundamental binary opposition ('sacred/profane') unquestioned in general feminist discourse. In this essay, I first examine an example of what I see as problems experienced by feminist writers in relation to religious ideas, then experiment with the matching of some different, but connected theoretical insights (Derrida, Wilden, Jay, Spivak) about binaries and the problem of absolutes: two concepts which circumscribe the exposition of the 'sacred' in Western discourse.

Theism, Atheism and Discursive Strategies

When Elaine Marks and Isabelle de Courtivron (1981, p. xi) decide that the French feminist tradition 'is resolutely atheistic', whereas American feminists are often women with a 'strong religious background', we are alerted to some kind of anomaly. The signal in this case for there being something amiss is the sheer absurdity of contrasting the French against a group who come from a strong religious background and also the very solid oppositional signification. The reference seems to be about 'belief' in a particular traditional Western understanding of 'God'. No acknowledgement is made of the scholarly practice of referring to, disputing and exploring the naming and function of the sacred in conversation with one's cultural tradition – for instance, the work of Caroline Walker Bynum and others. All is seen in the oppositional sense of believers versus unbelievers. The clue to this problem is given in Stephen Moore's (1989) lively discussion of the 'modern' in the 'postmodern', in biblical scholarship, philosophy and *l'écriture féminine*. He locates the 'uncompromising iconoclasm' of Irigaray, Kristeva and others in the 'modernist content/postmodern politics' category and contrasts this with 'the more complicitous approach' of American feminists. 'American feminist readers of the Bible', he says, 'for better or for worse, and unlike Spivak ... and a number of other secular feminists, ... are postmodernist critics who have never known a modernist revolution' (Moore, 1989, p. 556).

It is in the English-speaking tradition's relation to French feminism that some aspects of the problem of the unapproachability of religious ideas are found. In her outstanding interpretative work *Sexual Subversions*, Elizabeth Grosz (1989) unweaves the most delicate and obscure writing about the sacred by Luce Irigaray with great sensitivity and careful consideration of her texts. However, in relation to Irigaray's recent work, she remarks that her themes ('divinity', 'alterity' in Levinas' sense of the other's necessity for the self, and ethics) are a 'surprising cluster of terms ... not usually associated with academic feminism, but, if anything, with a more "spiritually" minded feminism' (Grosz, 1989, p. 140).

She describes this 'mystical feminism' as tending to be 'strongly anti-theoretical, more interested in matriarchal religions, astrology, separatist lifestyles and naturalist conceptions of the two sexes than in interrogating philosophical paradigms' (Grosz, 1989, p. 140). Grosz does not say whose work she has in mind. It certainly cannot be that of Mary Daly, Rosemary Ruether, Elisabeth Schüssler Fiorenza, Mieke Bal, Judith Plaskow or any other of the major European or American scholars and theologians whose work examines some of the fundamental myths and conceptual distinctions which interweave with Western philosophy. What is defined as 'academic' feminism virtually never includes scholars such as these; the Academy is essentially secular, *tout court*. The two most influential summaries of contemporary feminist thought used in Australian tertiary institutions (Eisenstein, 1984; Tong, 1989) do not mention feminist research in relation to the Hebrew and Christian scriptures or scholarly feminist analyses and critiques of theological ideas in Judaism and Christianity. These are, of course, concerns about divinity, alterity and ethics. Feminist theologians and scripture scholars have been marginalized or made invisible as humanist-liberal 'reformers' within religions which, it is assumed, should either be condemned or ignored. Grosz (1988, p. 92) has observed that 'only in the late 1980s have feminists acquired a perspective from which to assess traditional knowledges from the point of view of their capacity to accommodate women's particularity'. Yet scholars in theology and the history of religions had ventured into 'thoroughgoing critiques and displacements [of prevailing knowledges]' (Grosz, 1988, p. 103) long before the late 1980s. An obvious example is Mary Daly.

Although Grosz' exegesis of Irigaray is delicate, empathetic and emotionally powerful, her fear of interpretative lapses into religious essentialism causes her to reassure her readers that Irigaray is not 'a "born-again" Christo-feminist' (Grosz, 1988, p. 155), an unnecessary warning which carries with it an implied horror of 'Christo'-feminism, rather than any helpful information about Irigaray. Irigaray is presented as a political and scholarly strategist who uses unusual sources, rather than as a scholar who is able to draw on the history of religious ideas and practice in the context of Western philosophy. Within Grosz' 'spiritual'/'academic' dichotomy, Irigaray is placed within the 'academic', almost in spite of possible contamination by theological concerns. The context of this interpretation is Grosz' struggle to combat misreadings of Irigaray's understanding of 'woman' and the 'feminine', misreadings which 'substantialize or ontologize what, for Irigaray, is a discursive or deconstructive strategy' (Grosz, 1988, p. 241, endnote 7). Grosz could be interpreted as implying that what she calls (*pace* Derrida) the '*end* of metaphysics and the *demise* of onto-theology' (p. 155, my emphases) is the end of spiritual and religious 'meaning' altogether. The banishing of the sacred as metaphysical-essential substance results in the triumph of the essentially secular as solid strategy.

The distinction between secular and religious became absolutized in the post-Enlightenment separation between theology and philosophy, yet philosophy did not cease consideration of the foundations of theology. Grosz' hierarchy of sources is made clear in her defence of Irigaray, which includes pointing out that Irigaray deals with 'philosophical (not simply theological) texts' (Grosz, 1989, p. 155). Grosz' own exegesis of Levinas and Feuerbach shows the difficulty of clearly separating philosophy from theology (see Grosz, 1988, pp. 141ff; 1987). In the context of a discussion about Heidegger's critique of metaphysics, Levinas (Levinas and Kearney, 1986, p. 21) himself states that 'philosophy can be ethical as well as ontological, can be at once Greek and non-Greek in its inspiration. These two sources of inspiration coexist as two different tendencies in modern philosophy ...'

Acknowledgement of the sources in this way would seem to be a first requirement for feminist philosophy; otherwise, crucial master-knowledges remain unchallenged or, as has occurred, the challenges become marginalized and boxed in a mystical/spiritual/theological no-woman's land. It is Irigaray's great contribution that she has had 'a *fling with the philosophers*' (Irigaray in Grosz, 1989, p. 137), knows the masters she interrogates with such force, and has no 'fear of the God question' (Levinas on Sartre, Levinas and Kearney, 1986, p. 17).

There is, of course, on the other side of the great divide, fear of the questions of philosophy: Seyyed Hossein Nasr (1981, p. 84) speaks of the struggle between 'profane philosophy' and 'sacred knowledge' and argues that those who seek sacred knowledge must 'express their categorical opposition to modernism' which he calls a 'revolt against Heaven'. The revolt takes many forms of course. Mary Daly's fierce and denunciatory retreat to a Hag-ridden mystical-metaphysical world is also a revolt against the Heaven of God the Father. The label of 'metaphysical feminism' has been attached to the Daly enterprise with a certain amount of distaste and put aside from the concerns of 'academic feminism'. Her work has been interpreted as elitist, oppositional and essentialist,[2] and I would argue that her seeming 'capture' of the sacred is anomalous and threatening in itself; while it may be fanciful to connect the feminist flight from interrogating the sacred with Mary Daly's theft of it, none the less there is a residual vacuum in much feminist discourse. The retreat into the 'profane' is no more satisfactory. The declaration of total war on one polarity of an opposition is always repressively anti-intellectual and exclusivist.

For Emmanuel Levinas the displacement of metaphysical essences does not mean the reduction of ethics, alterity and the divine to mere political strategy. He says: 'Where he [Derrida] tends to see the deconstruction of the Western metaphysics of presence as an irredeemable crisis, I see it as a golden opportunity for Western philosophy to open itself to the dimension of otherness and transcendence beyond being' (Levinas and Kearney, 1986, p. 28).

Although Irigaray is notoriously difficult to interpret in particular definite 'meanings', I think it is very clear, both from her own writing and also from Grosz' presentation of her work, that in denying transcendence as metaphysical certainty, she opts for something more than strategy. She speaks of a 'sensible transcendental' (Grosz, 1989, p. 181), a 'divine' which Grosz describes as 'the field in which creativity, fertility and production must be positioned ... the space for what is new, what remains unthought, the space for the projection of possible futures ... a becoming without *telos*, a movement linked, above all, with love, self-love, love of the other and of the Other' (Grosz, 1989, p. 162). Levinas' Jewish understanding of the divine ('founded on lack, on infinite interpretation and uncertainty, not truth' – Levinas in Grosz, 1989, p. 156) is carefully explained by Grosz in the context of his priorities of 'the good' and of alterity: the 'demand made by the very face of the Other' (Grosz, 1989, p. 156) Levinas' divine is accurately differentiated from the ontotheological metaphysics-of-Presence of Hellenized Christianity. Irigaray's divine, on the other hand, while neither Jewish nor

Christian but elsewhere acknowledged by Grosz as equally complex and passionately understood, is finally reduced to the academic/political: a 'principle, or ideal, a projection of the (sexed) subject – a kind of ego-ideal specific to the concrete subject' (p. 159), part of a 'strategy of deconstructive textual reading' (p. 155). The religious/the sacred in any and every sense, is banished.

Maybe this is because 'the religious/mystical/spiritual' is understood as being absolutely Hellenic-Christian, or absolutely patriarchal, or if feminist, absolutely soft-minded and 'anti-theoretical', or in Kristeva's terms, a neutralizing and homogenizing force which represses the semiotic (Grosz, 1989, p. 53). Whatever the explanation, the impression given is that the sacred/religious/mystical/spiritual is an altogether unredeemable group of concepts. Grosz acknowledges Irigaray's concern that 'For men to be conceived as the other and for women to conceive of themselves as subjects requires a major shift in our conceptions of theory, of psychical relations and the sacred' (Grosz, 1989, p. 181), but it is as if a new and subversive reading of religious texts cannot have 'religious' impact or any hint of 'spiritual-mindedness'. In contrast, Irigaray's theory-embedded-in-materiality, the 'rare coming together of political and academic concerns' (Grosz, 1989, p. 140) is taken very seriously. Here is strategy signifying social *reality*. As Meaghan Morris (1988a, p. 46) notes: 'For Luce Irigaray, the importance of discourse is imbrication in the social.' I would want to assert that it is equally imbrication in the 'religious', which does not mean (following Levinas) that it involves either belief or unbelief. Who other than Irigaray (1986, p. 9) would insist that women 'need a religion, a language, and either a currency of their own or a non-market economy [and that] these three conditions go hand in hand'? Irigaray's acting/writing/intervention *is* playful, poetic, transgressive strategy, but her signification of the sacred, however self-conscious, even reluctant, open and uncertain, is not an absolute Absence, any more than it is absolute Presence.

The Sacred as Master-Knowledge

The very awkward and doubtful essentialist oppositions between theism and a-theism, between political strategy and religious belief, between 'academic' and 'mystical' are symptomatic of the difficulties major strands of Anglo/American/Australian feminism have in beginning to rethink the sacred/profane opposition. In the manner of Durkheim this opposition is treated as sacred in itself, the very basis of Western thought in the grand tradition of the metaphysical essences of Aristotle: 'In all the history of human thought, there exists no other example of two categories of things [sacred/profane] so profoundly differentiated or so radically opposed to one another' (Durkheim, cited in Jay, 1981, p. 40). It is a familiar post-Enlightenment stance that each category sees the enemy as the other, of course, but the language has changed. Sacred knowledge is master-knowledge in many guises and this is a clue to feminist 'fear of the God question'.

In a brief discussion of Arthur Danto's *The Philosophical Disenfranchisement of Art* and Fukuyama's *The End of History* Ron Gilbert (1990) speaks of the seductive presentation of master-knowledges as theoretical imaginaries from which profane elements of the social, historical and artistic are expelled. Theory emerges as impersonal, ' "pure" and "sacred" ' (Gilbert, 1990, p. 45). 'Modernity' is seen as a process which:

> ... denotes a space in which the sacred, as the dominant marker of certainty, has been destroyed. But there seems to be a deep denial of this ... the disintegration of the old markers of certainty has given rise to an intellectual dream, namely that the theorist can escape from the general economy by producing a discourse that is removed from the everyday – the profane. In so doing theory becomes sublime and empty. And seductive, because it is difficult to resist the intellectual fantasy that there is a space to be had free from the mundane affairs of the general economy. (Gilbert, 1990, p. 48)

As Meaghan Morris (1988b, p. 55) remarks, for theorists in the academy and other workplaces, 'there is always the pressure to feel that "Practice" always lies elsewhere (on the streets, on the beaches ...)'. She identifies the 'ever discreditable and ridiculous political question: the (shaky and shifting) place within the women's movement, and beside it, of academics, intellectuals: or "theorists" ...', and points out that 'an ivory tower of dreams called Theory' is very rare – academics and other theory-builders have workplaces where the practicalities of being a woman are inescapable (p. 57). Gilbert and Morris differ about the potential of theory to exclude the 'profane', but both use 'dream' as a metaphor for Theory as (sacred) master-knowledges. It cannot be just chance that there is an echo of Derrida: 'The "knowledge" of the philosopher places him among the dreamers, for knowledge is a dream. But the philosopher "knowingly" agrees to dream, to dream of knowledge, agrees to "forget" the lesson of philosophy, only so as to "prove" that lesson. ... It is a vertiginous movement' (cited in Spivak, 1976, p. lxxviii). It would seem that the intellectual dreamers do not hear the alarm clock ringing; others find it difficult to dream at all: the alarm clock is too insistent. The experience of the 'vertigo' of both forgetting and remembering the lessons of philosophy, of both dreaming and being awake, can be paralysing.

Destabilizing Absolutes: Jacques Derrida and Anthony Wilden

Neither Jacques Derrida nor Anthony Wilden discusses the sacred/profane distinction as such, although Derrida never lets Being and Presence out of his sight and Wilden analyses aspects of these, including a brief comparison of Jewish and Christian expressions of the sacred. I wish to argue a case for an interpretation of their work which undercuts those (mis)understandings of the deconstruction of 'oppositions' which reinforce particular dogmatics about 'secular/academic/political' and 'religious/spiritual' feminisms. Derrida has made it quite clear that there is no escaping metaphysics and no need, if one sees the shifting ground which both enables metaphysics *and* removes metaphysical certainties: 'One could reconsider all the pairs of opposites on which philosophy is constructed and on which our discourse lives, *not in order to see opposition erase itself* but to see what indicates that each of the terms must appear as the différance of the other ...' (cited in Hart, 1989, p. 53). We cannot opt for absolute groundlessness as a solution to the problems of ground: 'It is not enough "simply to *neutralize* the binary oppositions of metaphysics"' (Derrida in Spivak, 1976, p. lxxvi). The total removal of one term in a hierarchy, or the mere reversal of that hierarchy leaves the full presence of both terms intact. Thus the sacred and the profane always exceed themselves in supplements which reflect the necessity of the other term. Although Irigaray agrees with Derrida that 'The Divine has been ruined by God' (Derrida in Hart, 1989, p. 47 n.) she wryly remarks: 'the exclusion or suppression of the religious dimension seems to be impossible' (Irigaray, 1986, p. 6).

In tracing Derrida's philosophical sources in the introduction to her translation of *De la Grammatologie*, Gayatri Spivak (1976, p. xxviii) cites Nietzsche: 'only from the oppositions of logic do we derive the concept of opposites – and falsely transfer it to things.' Nancy Jay has detailed some of problems with A/Not-A traditional logical categories in relation to gender. The Law of the Excluded Middle makes the boundary between A and Not-A impermeable. Everything in a particular range of experience or perception *must* fall on either side of the divide. Further, the A category takes on a powerful superiority because it is the indicator by which everything-which-is-not-A is excluded from A and put over the wall as Not-A. Thus, in relation to 'sacred/not sacred', purity, transcendence and order must exclude pollution, materiality and disorder. Such is the weight of the threat of chaos and general corruption, the boundary must be shored up at great cost to prevent total dissolution of all categories, and life itself as we know it (or think we do). The association of gender with the profane in these terms is notorious (see Jay, 1981; Lloyd, 1984).

Given the traditional strength of the sacred/profane opposition, it is understandable that for some women, avoidance of a sacred that validates masculine dominance and master knowledges in which women are oppressively enclosed or invisible, can lead to avoidance of the sacred altogether. It is thought that Derrida also celebrates the de(con)struction of the sacred. What Kevin Hart calls the 'common theory of deconstruction' has opted easily for an interpretation of Derrida as a-theistic, and his deconstruction as determinedly 'secular'. In the words of Carl Raschke, 'Deconstruction is the dance of death upon the tomb of God' (in Hart, 1989, p. 144). By his own words, Derrida cannot and has not opted for the kind of dogmatism which interprets Presence as Absence. It is precisely this essentialist either/or of Presence/Absence, Theism/A-theism that he radically transforms. Derrida finds that not only is the boundary between 'oppositional' terms not impermeable, but that in most matters of importance, the relation is a great deal more complex than simply A/Not-A.

Anthony Wilden and the Analogue/Digital in Communication

We need to find a way around the invented constraints of either/or in this matter of the sacred. I now want to consider either/or distinctions in the context of Anthony Wilden's theoretical world.[3] I use Wilden because cybernetics and information theory use visual/mathematical imagery which gives the concepts of difference, distinction and opposition a concreteness which complements the more abstract analysis of philosophy. My summary of part of Wilden's work does not do him justice. It is notable that feminist writers universally ignore Wilden in spite of the honest and intelligent analysis of gender in all his works (for example, ch. X, 'Critique of Phallocentrism' in *System and Structure*, 1980).

Wilden is the original translator of Jacques Lacan's work. Lacan has sharply criticized Wilden's own theory-base – communication theory is seen by some as too transparent in its assumptions about signification. However, Wilden is not the average communication theorist; he combines a number of disciplines very creatively, including linguistics, cybernetics and general systems theory, psychoanalysis, philosophy and literary criticism. In particular he tackles the problems in essentializing 'either/or' relations.

Wilden remarks that the two most fundamental kinds of experience in human life and thought are 'continuity and discontinuity' (see Wilden, 1980, ch. VII; 1987a, ch. 7; see also Jay, 1981, p. 42). Cybernetics describes either/or terms as discontinuously coded information such as on–off, plus–minus and so on, known in systems theory as digitally coded information. This is information about things, 'facts' and events for which one needs an either–or descriptive content, and where there are no degrees of choice (Wilden, 1980, p. 164). Each piece of digitally coded information has boundaries. Nameable information and most of the functions of analytic logic are digitally coded.

'Both/and' relations describe continuously coded information in analogue form in which there are no intrinsic boundaries. The hands of a clock give analogue-coded information. In an analogue model, there can be no zero, things are either more or less but never nothing at all, and there can be no negation. Analogue-coded information can describe only relationships, not things. Difference and similarity are its markers. It cannot express most of the truth functions of analytic logic; a digital syntax is required for this.

In the matter of difference, there is a vital distinction between analogue and digital: 'Analog differences are differences of magnitude, frequency, distribution, pattern organization and so on ... Digital differences are those such as can be coded into distinctions and oppositions, and for this, there must be discrete elements with well-defined boundaries' (Wilden, 1980, p. 169). Confusion about difference in the two modes of communication is commonplace.

For a description of human communication systems, as well as the modelling of organisms, it is necessary for *both* 'either/or' *and* 'both/and' information to be included *in relation to one another*. Digital framing in an analogue context operates much like the visual effect of figure and ground. Wilden uses the word 'icon' for representation. An icon is a 'combination of analog and digital information ... patterns, or patterns of patterns, fixed or moving, made up of infinities of information in one or more dimensions, framed and punctuated by one or more digital boundaries in one or more dimensions' (Wilden, 1987b, p. 2). An icon could be a word, an image, an idea or a text in Derrida's sense of 'writing', but these are not 'things'; they are 'relationships' (Wilden, 1987b, p. 1).

In relation to language and communication Wilden (1980, p. 123) says that 'the problem of the punctuation of the analog by the digital is irresolvable for humankind'. Most knowledge is in analogue form, but we are forced to digitalize it in the syntax and grammar of language. Derrida describes this problem in terms of 'translation'. Further problems arise in that an analogue message may contradict a digital message. In this case, neither 'yes' nor 'no' is an adequate answer – the classic double bind in which we oscillate between the positive and negative. We also experience serious problems of movement between the two modes – in our effort to process complex information we muddle them up and manufacture fallacies, become reductionist and destroy diversity and complexity to opt for the simple equation – 'the reduction of the other to the categories of the same' (Levinas in Levinas and Kearney, 1986, p. 17). Wilden maintains that most knowledge is analogue, but that this is not recognized; 'the (analog) context of (digital) knowledge' especially, is 'denied, rejected, or ignored' (Wilden, 1980, p. 167). Somewhat like dreaming with the alarm clock ringing, consciousness of context, complexity and ambiguity can threaten us into simple solutions. Wilden (1980, p. 98) points out that the judgements we make in dealing with complexity and the way in which we 'punctuate' it digitally to organize it, are ethical judgements.

In cybernetics terms, differences and similarities (unboundaried) are analogue, and of a higher logical type than distinctions and oppositions (boundaried) which are digital. By confusing analogue and digital and the two modes of differentiation, we become entrapped into an 'epistemology of opposition and identity' and what Wilden (1980, p. 108) calls the 'counter-adaptive antinomies of class, caste, race and sex'. 'Irreducible difference becomes the "fact" of irreducible opposition ...' (1980, p. 458). Boundaries which should be able to be crossed are thus made into solid barriers. Self and not-self are reified; self and other similarly. In using binary oppositions as foundational signifiers or root metaphors, we collapse both–and relations with their infinite variety and diversity and potential for creative change in an open system.

In fact, what we see as pairs of 'apparently equal imaginary opposites at a single level [are actually] real relations between levels in (illegimate) hierarchies of power' (Wilden, 1987a, p. 80). Wilden lists various pairs, such as culture/nature, reason/emotion, white/non-white, and says that 'not one of these pairs is a real opposition. They are the symmetrization – the reduction to a single level – of a dependent hierarchy ... the second term in each pair is in fact the environment that the first term depends on for subsistence and survival' (Wilden, 1987a, p. 82). The application to gender of this explanation of dependent hierarchy is particularly apt. As Wilden (1980, p. 424) notes: 'Because ... binarism is described as a fundamental process of human thought, we find our deepest social prejudices confirmed in it.' Nancy Jay (1981, p. 48) points out that the A/Not-A dichotomy (the either/or of cybernetics) 'is necessarily distorting when it is applied directly to the empirical world, for there are no negatives there. Everything that exists (including women) exists positively' (the analogue of cybernetics). It is when we are led to believe that our realities are naturally arranged in flat oppositions in negative and positive terms, that strategies of resistance themselves become absolutist. The struggle becomes centred on power, rather than the quality of the ethics applied to social and political structures.

Différance as the key to analogue/digital relationships

The relation between two 'opposed' terms is the heart of 'deconstruction'. Derrida states that 'one of the terms [of a binary opposition] appears as the différance of the other, the other as "differed" within the systematic ordering of the same' (in Spivak, 1976, p. xxix). When Gayatri Spivak talks of the 'horizon of indefinite meaning with the provisional anchor of the text never given up' (1976, p. lxxvi), she is describing the non-absolute nature of all digital coding in its analogue context of both/and. There is, she says, *both* the desire/necessity for seeking knowledge *and* also showing a text [or an icon] 'what it "does not know"' (Spivak, 1976, p. lxxvii), which is another kind of certainty. These certainties dissolve and there is no end to this process, no final fixed truth-statement – as you grasp one element, it is already erased – meanings are plural and never complete. 'Différance' is *not* a strategy or method. In Derrida's words:

> *Différance* is neither a *word* or a *concept* ... is not theological, not even in the most negative order of negative theology. The latter ... always hastens to remind us that, if we deny the predicate of existence to God, it is in order to recognize him as a superior, inconceivable, and ineffable mode of being ... For us, différance remains a metaphysical name ... *'Older' than Being itself* [my emphasis], our language has no name for such a différance. ... Not even the name 'différance' which continually breaks up in a chain of différant (*différantes*) substitutions. (Spivak, 1976, p. lxxi)

Theos, différance and absolute origin

Wilden comments that Derrida's 'trace' is an analogue inscription, 'trace' (cf. footprint/track) being for Derrida that which 'presents itself as the mark of an anterior presence, origin, master' (Spivak, 1976, p. xv) – it is another term for différance. For Derrida, 'The trace is in fact the absolute origin of meaning in general. This amounts to saying ... that there is no absolute origin of meaning in general. The trace is the différance which opens up the world of appearance and signification' (Derrida in Wilden, 1980, p. 399).

As for 'theology', both Derrida and Spivak use the word in its traditional ontological context: as having to do with the Being/Not-Being (A/Not-A) of an Origin/Logos/Theos. Spivak (1976, p. lxxviii) shows something of the same anxiety about falling into some kind of theological trap as does Elizabeth Grosz: 'this terrifying and exhilarating vertigo is not "mystical" or "theological"'. In this she is echoing Derrida who, together with Spivak and Grosz, interprets theology *as* totalizing metaphysics, with no other possibilities. While rejecting theology in this way, Derrida does not totally erase it – the footprint cannot be absolutely obliterated. Spivak and Grosz worry that the writing of their subjects of analysis (Derrida, Irigaray) may somehow be seen wrongly in ontotheological terms. The problem is that in re-assuring their readers and in avoiding the 'theological' in other contexts, they are both betraying a desire to totalize 'theology' in Absence.

Kevin Hart is made especially irate by what he calls this 'gap' in Spivak (more than a gap I would say; a gap full of Presence). He notes her 'avoidance of any links between deconstruction and religion' (Hart, 1989, pp. 44–5) and energetically reverses the environment in which Spivak places Derrida (Nietzsche, Freud and Heidegger), by linking him with three Jewish intellectuals, including Levinas. Perhaps Hart totalizes religion where Spivak totalizes philosophy. (He also manages to totalize 'feminists' in the very few acknowledgements he makes and in so doing, he has neglected the poetry, wit, deconstructive art and intellectual generosity of Luce Irigaray on the one hand and her 'imbrication' in the social and religious analogue context on the other: the latter in particular would alert him to some of the problems of 'negative' theology.)

Seeking the Sacred, but not locating it

The icon or text, while enclosing propositions and looking solid, is actually a palimpsest. Behind and in front of it are an infinite number of icons, texts, words, images. To communicate, we must 'decide', act, speak and write – 'fix' a text with some kind of confidence. Spivak (1976, p. lxxvii) asks: 'Why should we undo and redo a text at all?' We simultaneously pursue a goal, look for a solid foundation, *and* undo what we have done; following Derrida, she explains the desire we have for that which is other than ourselves: 'our desire ... forever differs from and defers the text of ourselves' (Spivak, 1976, p. lxxviii). In 'the open-ended indefiniteness of textuality', our desire leads us into the double-bind of the 'search for a foundation and the need to "undo and redo" ("the pleasure of the bottomless")' (p. lxxvii). Our desire is never satisfied; yet we cling to the possibility of mastery and forget that the will to knowledge is also the will to ignorance (p. lxxviii).

In his discussion of Derrida, Wilden (1980, p. 399) also con-cludes that 'it is the *seeking* and not the goal which is at the origin of human affairs'. In understanding this, the only thing we stand to lose perhaps is some of our own arrogance, but this is a difficult lesson to learn. We cling to the absolutization of difference and distinction in the habit of taking refuge in a closed system. Spivak (1976) reminds us that Nietzsche spoke of our 'will to power', and (in Spivak's phrases), the 'desire for unity and order' (p. xlix), 'the drive to appropriate and conquer' (p. xxiii), 'to have plenitude and exercise authority' (p. xix). Spivak diagnoses: 'It is this longing for a center, an authorizing pressure, that spawns hierarchized oppositions. The superior term belongs to presence and the logos; the inferior serves to define its status and mark a fall' (p. lxix). Wilden calls this our 'enslavement to an Imaginary Other' which 'depends on a value-system based on the maintenance of exploitative oppositions and identities'. If our species is to survive, he insists, 'humankind must find a way of reintroducing the mediating function of difference and similarity into the social ecosystem' (Wilden, 1980, p. 109). Recalling Marx, Wilden believes that 'the resolution of the *theoretical* contradictions is possible *only* through practical means, only through the *practical* energy of man' (Marx in Wilden, 1980, p. 109, Wilden's emphases).

Feminism and Authorizing Pressures

And what of the *practical energy of woman*? The process by which certain flat oppositional readings of the sacred are adversarily possessed and codified in artefacts of social, political and economic power is the real locus of destructive dispute in relation to women and men; but we cannot magically and permanently erase any concept in an oppositional pair that has alarmed us, if only for the reason that we do not know what it is we imagine we have destroyed.

Feminist theory/practice is now turning towards difference and similarity as the key to avoidance of reifying 'woman', 'man' and 'Other women', especially in post-colonial criticism (Gayatri Spivak, Chandra Mohanty and others). There is, however, in mainstream English-speaking feminism, no sign of deconstructive and practical energy in relation to the secular/religious and the sacred/profane, which are fundamental categories of the Imaginary Other. In her conclusion to *Sexual Subversions*, Elizabeth Grosz (1989), separating theory and practice, says that the three French intellectuals seem 'more concerned with femininity as metaphor and concept than the empirical reality of women's lives in patriarchy'

(p. 234). She goes on to defend them, explaining that without the analysis of feminist knowledges 'women will remain tied to a series of concepts and values which oppress them' (p. 234).

In 1978, when she completed the essay 'The Pirate Fiancée' (1988b, p. 69), Meaghan Morris had doubts about the possibility of theorizing difference in a politically powerful manner. She pointed to the emphasis on establishing identity and equivalence, acknowledging difference only 'in vague and general terms' and complained that 'for attacking the analysis of confrontations, it [theory] simply has no teeth' (Morris, 1988b, p. 62). Here she was referring to the obsession with the *problem* of subjectivity: the dogmatic denunciation of the 'errors' of humanism, anti-humanism, essentialism, totalization. She complained that such were the constraints of this discourse that 'analysis is largely deprived of any operative means of distinguishing between strategies of power and tactics of resistance, between statements in common ... and antagonistic discourses ...' (p. 61). Philosophy she saw as 'that wheezing science', able to demonstrate only 'its own limitations' (p. 63). Quite a few years later, I have a much more optimistic view of the potential of philosophy and the teeth of theory (of which Morris herself is an exemplar), but the problem of dogmatics to which she was referring is still with us.

In a related discussion of *écriture féminine*, she notes that 'The language of the feminine body, woman's desire, is a deliciously cultural ploy; entirely organized by the binary logic which Luce Irigaray alone attempts (and wittingly refuses) to dismantle' (Morris, 1988b, p. 65). In the remainder (and there is an element of suspicion lingering about Irigaray), she saw only 'the next same old two-step' (p. 65). Her suspicion of the English-speaking feminist obsession with 'the subject' (for which she blames Derrida et al., rather than misreadings/non-readings of them) was justified and her warnings in relation to the 'common theory of deconstruction' are still relevant.

In the context of *écriture féminine* and the anxiety about what Morris (1988b, p. 65) calls 'the cult of the signifier', it is understandable that Elizabeth Grosz found it necessary to argue strongly (and correctly) that in the case of Kristeva, Irigaray and Le Doeuff, the 'next same old two-step' has been disrupted/ruptured/subverted. In the face of a large feminist misunderstanding of Derrida and deconstruction, Grosz's task (in relation to Irigaray especially) was a very difficult one, achieved with elegance and precision. The spectre of the determining defensiveness of 'academic' feminism and its uncertain relationship to 'the empirical reality of women's lives' remains, however, in a way similar to the 'cult of the signifier'. If it were not for the constraints of the doctrine of what constitutes 'academic' feminism, underpinned as it is by the acceptance of the sacred/profane distinction as totalizing opposition, it might be possible to link and cross-reference feminist theory and practice in deconstructing 'religion' and its themes. Divinity, alterity and ethics could be seen as fundamental academic/theoretical *and* practical *loci* of intervention and subversion for feminism. The 'real' business of living does not take place 'elsewhere'.

Emmanuel Levinas says that philosophy in the sense of 'critical speculation and interrogation ... is by no means near its end' (Levinas in Levinas and Kearney, 1986, p. 33). Furthermore, his concern with ethics is very much embedded in the social. The 'self' has meaning only in *relation* to the 'other' (which puts the cult of the subject nicely in its place). It is precisely in Levinas' sense of critical speculation and interrogation that women should have their 'fling' with philosophy. We must avoid setting up adversarial positions which invoke, by means of Absence, traditional metaphysical certainties. 'Fear of the God question', fear of 'divine women' and fear of their irrelevance to 'empirical reality' can only maintain constraints that reinforce the ideology of the sacred-profane 'opposition'.

Traditional philosophers, theologians and clergy have already achieved much success keeping the sacred and the profane (as defined by them) at war with one another, and we know who are the colonized. Feminism should not sell arms to the combatants. This is, in Derrida's (1976, p. lxxvi–lxxvii) terminology, 'a violent hierarchy', and both terms must be put under erasure. If René Girard (1977), Luce Irigaray (1986) and Nancy Jay (1985) are right about the violence of sacrifice as the foundation of the sacred, the politics of subversion will be a dangerous undertaking – the pleasure and the terror of keeping our shoes on and striding towards the burning bush. If 'Being in their place is what makes [things] sacred' ... 'but so, equally, does their being *out* of place' (Brubaker, 1982, p. 204, commenting on Lévi-Strauss), who knows what disorder might result?

Notes

This essay has survived many different readings over a long period. I am grateful to those who responded with helpful criticism and support in seminars given at the University of Adelaide (1987), at the Australian Association for the Study of Religions Conference in Perth (1989), at Deakin University (1990) and during a four-month Fellowship in the Religious Studies Department of La Trobe University in 1990. The support and enthusiasm of feminist scholars during the 1990 International Association for the History of Religions Congress in Rome (1990) (especially that of Morny Joy and Ursula King), and individual critiques by Jackie Cook (University of South Australia) and Greg Bailey (La Trobe) assisted me enormously in opting for authorship rather than in a continuing series of deconstructed texts imprisoned in my files.

1 See Susan McKernan's (1991) diagnosis of the causes of Australian feminist concerns about 'too much' of a women's conference programme being 'devoted to spirituality, psychoanalysis and religion'; '... for English speakers the traditions of empiricism die hard. French theory's elevation of motherhood, mysticism and poetry worries many Australian and English feminists who have been nurtured on Marxism, liberal radicalism or Protestant individualism.'
2 By far the most empathetic and critically aware analysis of aspects of Mary Daly's work is Meaghan Morris' (1988a), 'A-mazing Grace: Notes on Mary Daly's poetics'. This essay also includes a stimulating comparison of Irigaray and Daly.
3 Anthony Wilden's most stimulating and controversial theoretical work (which I first read on the advice of the anthropologist Deborah Bird Rose) is *System and Structure: Essays in Communication and Exchange* (1980). Two further works, based on *System and Structure* are: *The Rules are no Game: The Strategy of Communication* (1987a) and *Man and Woman, War and Peace: The Strategist's Companion* (1987b).

References

Brubaker, Richard 1982: The Goddess and the polarity of the sacred. In John S. Hawley and Donna W. Wulff (eds), *The Divine Consort: Radha and the Goddesses of India*, Berkeley, CA: Berkeley Religious Studies Series, 204–9.
Daly, Mary 1978: *Gyn/ecology: The Metaethics of Radical Feminism*. Boston, MA: Beacon.
Daly, Mary 1986: *Beyond God the Father: Towards a Philosophy of Women's Liberation*. London: Women's Press. (1st edition 1973.)

Derrida, Jacques 1976: *Of Grammatology*. Trs. Gayatri Spivak. Baltimore: Johns Hopkins University Press.

Derrida, Jacques 1978: *Writing and Difference*. Trsl. Alan Bass. London: Routledge & Kegan Paul.

Eisenstein, Hester 1984: *Contemporary Feminist Thought*. Sydney: Allen & Unwin.

Gilbert, Ron 1990: Endings. *Meanjin*, 49, 1, 43–8.

Girard, René 1977: *Violence and the Sacred*. Trs. Patrick Gregory. Baltimore and London: The Johns Hopkins University Press.

Grosz, Elizabeth 1987: 'The people of the Book': representation and alterity in Emmanuel Levinas. *Art and Text*, 26, 32–40.

Grosz, Elizabeth 1988: The in(ter)vention of feminist knowledges. In Barbara Caine, E.A. Grosz and Marie de Lepervanche (eds), *Crossing the Boundaries: Feminists and the Critique of Knowledges*, Sydney: Allen & Unwin, 92–104.

Grosz, Elizabeth 1989: *Sexual Subversions*. Sydney: Allen & Unwin.

Hart, Kevin 1989: *Trespass of the Sign: Deconstruction, Theology and Philosophy*. Cambridge: Cambridge University Press.

Irigaray, Luce 1986: Women, the sacred and money. *Paragraph*, 8, 6–18.

Jay, Nancy 1981: Gender and dichotomy. *Feminist Studies*, 7, 1, 38–56.

Jay, Nancy 1985: Sacrifice as remedy for having been born of woman. In Clarissa W. Atkinson, Constance H. Buchanan and Margaret R. Miles (eds), *Immaculate and Powerful: The Female in Sacred Image and Social Reality*, Boston, MA: Beacon, 283–309.

Levinas, Emmanuel and Kearney, Richard 1986: Dialogue with Emmanuel Levinas. In Richard A. Cohen (ed.), *Face to Face with Levinas*, New York: State University of New York Press, 13–33.

Lloyd, Genevieve 1984: *The Man of Reason: Male and Female in Western Philosophy*. London: Methuen.

McKernan, Susan 1991: Feminist literary criticism. *24 Hours*, April, 40–1.

Marks, Elaine and de Courtivron, Isabelle 1981: *New French Feminisms: An Anthology*. New York: Schocken Books.

Moore, Stephen 1989: The 'post-'age stamp: does it stick?: Biblical studies and the postmodern debate. *Journal of the American Academy of Religion*, LVII, 3, 543–59.

Morris, Meaghan 1988a: A-mazing Grace: Notes on Mary Daly's poetics. In Meaghan Morris, *The Pirate's Fiancée: Feminism. Reading, Postmodernism*, London and New York: Verso, 27–50.

Morris, Meaghan 1988b: *The pirate's fiancée*. In Meaghan Morris, *The Pirate's Fiancée: Feminism. Reading, Postmodernism*, London and New York: Verso, 51–69.

Nasr, Seyyed Hossein 1981: *Knowledge and the Sacred: The Gifford Lectures 1981*. New York: Crossroad.

Ruether, Rosemary Radford 1979; A religion for women: sources and strategies. *Christianity and Crisis*, 39, 19, 307–11.

Spivak, Gayatri 1976: Translator's preface. In *Of Grammatology*, Baltimore: Johns Hopkins University Press. (French edition, 1967.)

Tong, Rosemarie 1989: *Feminist Thought: A Comprehensive Introduction*. London: Unwin-Hyman.

Wilden, Anthony 1980: *System and Structure: Essays in Communication and Exchange*, 2nd edn. New York and London: Tavistock. (Trs. into French (1983) by Georges Khal, Montreal: Boreal Express.)

Wilden, Anthony 1987a: *The Rules are No Game: The Strategy of Communication*. New York: Routledge & Kegan Paul.

Wilden, Anthony 1987b: *Man and Woman, War and Peace: The Strategist's Companion*. New York: Routledge & Kegan Paul.

5

God and Gender: Some Reflections on Women's Invocations of the Divine

Morny Joy

Theology has traditionally been alien territory for women. This is not just because, as with many other disciplines, it was a male preserve. God-talk itself has remained a captive of the human predilection to conceive of the absolute in masculine imagery and terminology. As a result, many women today no longer feel constrained by its demands and have taken their allegiance elsewhere. On the other hand, there are women who are not inclined to abandon a belief in some form of Ultimate Reality, and their responses are various. There are those who have elected to remain within their traditions, i.e. Christianity and Judaism, while others have declared that these traditions are bankrupt and sought alternate divine consolations. What all these women have expressed is a desire for the experience of women to be acknowledged as the basis of any explorations in theology. God-imagery and God-talk is, as a result, invigorating and iconoclastic. What may happen eventually to the discipline of theology, as a form of second-order reflection, is not easy to ascertain. I do feel it is safe to say that theology, despite some rearguard reactions, will never be the same again.

Women are indeed emphasizing that part of their feminist agenda which is the recognition of their ability to name and claim their own experiences. This impetus shatters ingrained stereotypes and caricatures not only of what is regarded as 'feminine' behaviour, but also of what are the 'masculine' attributes of God. But this focus on the centrality of experience, of specific ways of being and knowing, introduces a basic dilemma into women's discussions of God. Controversy has ensued as to whether this experience is primordial or contextual. Depending on one's preference in this debate, it would appear the only options are those of essentialism (where certain attributes are seen as integral to women) or relativism (where a definition of woman becomes context dependent).

But these choices seem to me to limit the parameters of the needed exchange on this topic. Women sorely need to move beyond any dualistic impasse. The God that has been rejected was one made in the image of ideals alien to most women's experience. Yet even appeals to experience itself can be suspect, for the subject of Cartesian modernity (where the thinking subject controls the process of knowledge) still posits itself over against an external object. The empirical self of these exchanges validates experience according to criteria of logical or scientific verification. So the vital question would seem to be: how can women move beyond this conundrum posed by empirical objectivity, while at the same time avoiding the shoals of relativism and essentialism? A tall order.

First I would like to survey the numerous options available today for the reconception of God. Not all of these are novel, as they have been integral (if neglected) elements of the symbolic matrix available to both Judaism and Christianity. Some are significantly of a political nature and emphasize not only women's plight, but that of all disadvantaged humanity. All, however, seek to reverse the autocratic and austere atmosphere that has pervaded male-oriented God models. The counter-claim need not be made that women are inherently non-hierarchical and relational. The fact is that their interests and concerns have predominantly been organized in this fashion, and it is with these values they resonate and that they wish to promote. Within this framework I would like then to discuss some of the problems that beset women's divine experimentation. I do not intend to concern myself here with the ratification of these speculations *vis-à-vis* scriptural requirements, which is a debate concerning the grounds of theology and introduces the problem of establishing the dynamics of a canon.[1] What interests me more is the status of these speculations in relation to current philosophical mediations. My own perspective is that of a white, middle-class North American female, subject to all the vicissitudes of such a stance.[2]

God-language today proliferates in books by women. This God has many guises. Not all these models are mutually exclusive, nor should they be. A brief survey of divergent positions advocated by different feminist thinkers reveals the spectrum of opinion as women challenge the theological edifice.

Mary Daly, perhaps the most iconoclastic of all, envisages an end to all anthropomorphisms and suggests a form of God that is in touch with our dynamic and creative core.

> Why indeed must 'God' be a noun? Why not a verb – the most active and dynamic of all? ... The anthropomorphic symbols for God may be intended to convey personality, but they fail to convey that God is Be-ing. Women now who are experiencing the shock of nonbeing and the surge of self-affirmation against this are inclined to perceive transcendence as the Verb in which we participate – live, move, and have our being. (Daly, 1973, pp. 33–4)

Elizabeth Dodson Gray visualizes this verb as a swirling, radiant, rhythmic presence that informs all the interconnections of our cosmic environment.

> Here are a few possibilities. God is the 'power of relationship', as in an ecological web. We live in a totally interconnected system, and the truth is that we would disintegrate in the life system without such things as gravity, electromagnetic fields, without all that holds both planets and electrons, the very large and very small, in their orbits ... What I invite you now to do is take off your hierarchical-ranking eyeglasses and put aside your patriarchal vision so that we may all join with other species and come inside the circle of creation, and join the great dance. (Gray, 1988, pp. 54–5)

Rosemary Ruether depicts a pivotal element, a primal and neutral source of energy pervading all life, infusing it with peace and harmony that is the right of all.

To return Home; to learn the harmony, the peace, the justice of body, bodies in right relation to each other. The whence we have come and whither we go, not from alien skies but here, in the community of earth. Holy One, Thy Kingdom come, Thy will done on earth. All shall sit under their own vines and fig trees and none shall be afraid. The lion will lay down with the lamb and the little child will lead them. A new thing is revealed; the woman will encompass the warrior. Thou shalt not hurt, thou shalt not kill in all my holy mountain.

The Shalom of the Holy; the disclosure of the gracious *Shekinah*; Divine Wisdom; the empowering Matrix; She, in whom we live and move and have our being – She comes; She is here. (Ruether, 1983, p. 266)

Carol Christ commends the Goddess as a form which endows women with pride and self-affirmation in their quest for recuperating those qualities that have been diminished by patriarchal platitudes.

The symbol of Goddess has much to offer women who are struggling to be rid of the 'powerful, pervasive, and long-lasting moods and motivations' of devaluation of female power, denigration of the female body, distrust of female will, and denial of women's bonds and heritage that have been engendered by patriarchal religion. As women struggle to create a new culture in which women's power, bodies, will, and bonds are celebrated, it seems natural that the Goddess would reemerge as symbol of the newfound beauty, strength, and power of women. (Christ, 1979, p. 286)

Sallie McFague explores embodied metaphors of trust and confidence in relationship, metaphors from everyday existence. In their adaptation she avoids tired clichés and quickens new life in tired-bones.

But models of God as mother, lover, friend, and healer suggest a different vision of existence. It is one of mutuality, nurture, self-sacrifice, fidelity, and care for the oppressed and vulnerable. In such a vision, delight in the other, not domination of the other, is central. If such a vision of an alternative way of being in the world is to be effective, it must take place not only within the academy but also and primarily among ordinary people who will begin to talk to and about God with new metaphors and models. (McFague, 1982)

Dorothee Sölle, in an article entitled 'Mysticism, liberation and the names of God', expresses the fact that there are numerous ways in which liberation theology has understood its general mandate of freedom from oppression. Her choice is grounded in the anti-authoritarian disposition she finds within mysticism that confounds the excesses of rational dictates.[3] In the tradition of Meister Eckhart she declares:

> The important thing is that existential experience ... within mystical understanding of God is more important than doctrinal teachings; inner light is more valid than ecclesiastical authority; certainty of God and conversation with God are more important than belief in God or rational acceptance of God. (Sölle, 1981, p. 181)

Elisabeth Schüssler Fiorenza prefers to understand this liberation in a much more political fashion. Fiorenza will identify her whole programme as one that must be consonant with the God of the oppressed. Thus she does not offer any directly related female expressions of God, though she acknowledges male-centred language must go, and finds more resonance in a God who is actively involved with the liberation of all people. The focus of her own work is none the less the liberation of women in the image of the discipleship of equals of the early Christian community. This is undertaken in consolidation with the struggles of all displaced peoples.

> Christian theology, therefore, has to be rooted in emancipatory praxis and solidarity. The means by which feminist theology grounds its theologizing in emancipatory praxis is consciousness-raising and sisterhood. Consciousness-raising makes theologians aware of their own oppression and the oppression of others. Sisterhood provides a community of emancipatory solidarity of those who are oppressed and on the way to liberation. (Fiorenza, 1975, p. 616)

This preferential option for the oppressed is a necessary ingredient in Fiorenza's feminist hermeneutics, and she would go so far as to insist that acceptable interpretation of the scriptures is possible only when one adopts such a hermeneutics from below (Fiorenza, 1981, p. 100). Whether such a unilateral stance of a political nature need be advocated in a feminist agenda as the only stance for the interpretation of scripture is debatable. Elsewhere (Joy, 1990), I have argued that temperamentally some women are attracted to more psychologically related 'revisionings' of God rather than political activism in the name of the God of the oppressed. There is need of concerted work on both fronts, where neither effort sees its mandate as exclusive.

Judith Plaskow supports an ongoing feminist impetus within a Jewish community that is already in the process of change. Such a discussion, Plaskow declares, can only develop against the backdrop of the understanding of the Jewish community which itself continues to evolve in its appreciation of feminist interpretations of the three foundational articles of Torah, Israel and God.

> As I see it, the goal of a Jewish feminist approach to God-language is to incorporate women's Godwrestling into the fullness of Torah by finding images that can communicate and evoke the experience of the presence of God in a diverse, egalitarian, and empowered community of Israel. (Plaskow, 1990, p. 122)

Apart from new examples of God-talk being used by women in Jewish ceremonies, Plaskow also discusses the idea of God as co-creator, a God with whom we collaborate in nurturing life. While Plaskow has strong reservations about wholesale adoption of pagan goddesses and obviously cannot endorse Christocentric models, she sees her work as part of a concerted effort by many religious feminists to repudiate all forms of male-centred imagery and practice.

Such theological explorations, at once diverse and tentative, are the poetic probes as it were, searching new domains and scouring the debris of male-identified forms for expressions that may relate to women's wily wisdom.[4] It will be impossible to discuss all these proposals in particular, but I wish to focus on certain philosophical concerns that are pertinent, such as dualism, relativism and essentialism.

Theology has always been something of a hybrid project. The respective claims of Athens and Jerusalem have needed continuous delicate renegotiation with changing philosophical paradigms and their associated anthropologies. And while theology has invariably affirmed that the nature of the Divine ultimately is beyond all human approximations, it has nevertheless constantly sought to reconcile biblical proclamations with human insights. Accreditation of the metaphorical and symbolic nature of these insights (dependent as they are upon human experience), and of the conceptual framework that validates them, has, until this century, been the prerogative of men. Consequently, it is no surprise that women now find the whole enterprise compromised and not particularly relevant to their mode of existence. Thus, the question emerges as to what are the changes in contemporary philosophy that render it possible for women to articulate their awareness of God in ways they feel do not compromise their integrity.

It is ironic that this feminist reparation is being undertaken at a time in contemporary scholarship when other movements, such as postmodernism, are questioning the existence of an autonomous self. As a postmodern paradigm within the philosophical climate, deconstruction questions the very foundations of philosophy itself.[5] Within religion, this movement has been appropriated in a particular way, where the undermining of foundations is linked with the death of God. In particular, the deconstructive element in its Derridean mode is heralded by Carl Raschke with apocalyptic fervour: 'Deconstruction within theology writes the epitaph for the dead God' (Raschke, 1982, p. 27). Mark C. Taylor is equally extravagant in his claims:

> The death of God ... marks the loss of the stable centre that had been believed to be the basis of unique individuality and the ground of transcendent selfhood. ... For the solitary self, inscription within the infinite play of word spells death. (Taylor, 1984, pp. 134–5)

So it would seem that by unmasking the pretensions of the Enlightenment claims of reason to certainty, deconstruction simultaneously corrodes any foundational basis for ideal types, such as God or personhood. Words and meaning are no longer linked irrevocably. The resultant instability can then be interpreted in two ways. The pessimistic reading portrays its effects as the dissolute abandonment of all standards of coherence and morality. A second and more buoyant reading understands this challenge to absolutist notions of truth as a necessary remedy to the human propensity to impose rigid structures on things which are essentially indefinable. The resultant infinite play of the word need not necessarily imply the end to all speculation about God or our own identity. John Caputo describes this change in his own optimistic version of deconstruction conceived of as radical hermeneutics:

In the end radical hermeneutics does not lead us back to the safe shores and terra firma; it leaves us slowly twisting in the wind. ... It is the play of the mystery which metaphysics is intent on arresting, and it is in order to reopen that play, to get the police off its back, that we undertake radical thinking. (Caputo, 1987, p. 267)

And it may well be that the domain of theology, as mystics of the *via negativa* have insisted, is that of the unfathomable mystery that will always evade human attempts at definition. And this is what it should mean to be at play in the fields of the Lord. Nevertheless, it seems that one needs to tread warily in this treacherous territory to avoid simplistic reductions to either a rampant relativism or a reactive essentialism. Rather than embracing either extreme, what is needed, as Caputo notes, is a radical hermeneutics that always subjects the received tradition to scrutiny. Such a stance no longer automatically assumes an implicit trust in the dictates of reason and humanity, nor a dogmatic faith in its objectivist and empirical base. Two women scholars have recently introduced notions of such approaches to the feminist agenda, but with different emphases. Their ideas were not listed in the examples above, as their postmodern interventions are somewhat at variance with most other feminist discussions of God. It is now time, however, to consider their proposals.

In a lengthy discussion of Rosemary Ruether's opus, Rebecca Chopp (1989a) draws attention to a discrepancy in Ruether's work. Chopp sees Ruether's summons to new visions and vistas as weighted down by assumptions of a modernist nature that entail universal presumptions, e.g. equality. This, Chopp feels, is especially evident in Ruether's ideal of 'full humanity' which she states is an imposition of an outmoded world-view. Chopp believes that women's unique experiences lead to an interrogation of this ideal, as much as they question the very nature of experience itself. Ruether's call to create a new order must relate, in Chopp's opinion, to new forms as well as to new content. It must avoid the use of such abstract androcentric standards as have always obscured or eliminated women's perspective. Thus Chopp recommends a paradigm shift away from modernist views of universal equality which rely in turn on Enlightenment conventions of reason and progress (and which sustain Ruether's programme).

Chopp's own response is a foray into certain postmodern themes, specifically that of discourse analysis (after Michel

Foucault) and rhetoric (see Chopp, 1989b). But she wishes to join this study of word usage with a theology of praxis. To achieve this, she identifies God as Word. Her melding of theory and practice thus promotes the liberating word/Word as that which must be proclaimed by theology to effect the transformation of obsolete structures and practices, both intellectual and practical. Integral to this project of rejuvenating the socio-symbolic order is the delineation of a feminist perspective. In this view the word/Word which has been proclaimed historically has not come to fullness because of its exclusion of women from access to its various forms of discourse. As a result, for the word to be effective today, it must acknowledge the voices on the periphery, the voices of the excluded, of the oppressed, particularly those of women. (Julia Kristeva (1981) and Luce Irigaray (1981), two contemporary French women, have influenced Chopp greatly on the marginality of women's words.) It is here, in its banished form, that feminist discourse can locate itself in tactics that disrupt the status quo. Allied with a deconstructive discrediting of masculine-identified ideals of an ideological nature, a women-conscious word, sensitive to neglected nuances, can create different ways of seeing and doing. For Chopp, God, as the Word of relationship, communion and communication, resides in this continuing redemptive reordering of human constructs. The new order is thus not proclaimed in the name, or in the manner, of modernist principles, but by its destabilization of the established system. This disruptive intervention could in no way be called a new interpretation of God, but it marks a subtle reappropriation of a traditional understanding of Word/word within a deliberately provocative postmodern context.

It is from this perspective and its reappraisal of modernism's tenets that any appeals to women's experience also become suspect. For these appeals could merely indicate a similar dualist and exclusivist bias to that which women have criticized in men. Merely to inject the notion of women's experience does not of itself change the subject/object dichotomy implicit in most empirical models. This is the problem detected by Sheila Greeve Davaney (1987). Davaney describes what she deduces to be assumptions of timeless truths made by Elisabeth Schüssler Fiorenza, Rosemary Ruether and Mary Daly that are merely female reversals of the androcentric models they proclaim to reject. The solution that Davaney prescribes is that these women should become conversant with the postmodern paradigm that informs much of

contemporary philosophical thought. In particular, she recommends the nihilism and relativism that she discerns informing the
thought of Michel Foucault. Such a move, Davaney declares,
would release women scholars from any need to postulate any
models of God other than a perspectival one. The sole criteria
for evaluation would become pragmatic grounds of effectiveness
and appropriateness. Neither women's experience nor God need
to be absolutized as they would be in traditional substantive metaphysics. But Davaney also seems to support an agenda that would
reduce any God-image or symbolic representation to a figment of
human imagination.

If these objections are valid, the identities that women are
today constructing for themselves, as well as the concomitant God
prototypes, are being seriously challenged. And perhaps the only
consolations left to counter these sceptical tendencies are the
nostalgic reveries or future projections of utopian scenarios. But
though there are many feminists who are sympathetic to postmodernism's endorsement of the fragmented and marginal status
of women as the locus of subversive strategies of resistance, other
feminists are suspicious of this account. They see women as
merely reactive and still confined by the current vogue of male
intellectual fashions, incapable of independent creative activity.
Sandra Harding, for one, voices her misgivings:

> It is premature for women to be willing to give up what they never
> had. Should women – no matter what their race, class or culture
> – find it reasonable to give up the desire to know and understand
> the world from the standpoint of their experiences for the first
> time? As several feminist literary critics have suggested, perhaps
> only those who have had access to the benefits of the Enlighten-
> ment can 'give up' those benefits. (Harding, 1987, p. 189)

But the dilemma remains. How are women today to understand themselves and establish a secure basis from which to take
constructive action against past and present injustices? And how to
revitalize God imagery and language? Should women necessarily
subscribe to the principles of whatever is the fashionable theoretical postulate? Should they automatically follow the dictates of
male-established norms of reflection, be they metaphysical, empirical
or postmodern? How are women to stake their claims and avoid
the pitfalls of relativism or essentialism? This is an extremely
complex question and one that needs a more detailed examination

than is possible here. My own thesis is that in the face of this postmodern erosion of the nature of women's experience, and the resultant instability of any categories such as race, class and gender (which can establish the grounds for a liberationary praxis), a significant contribution can be made by hermeneutics.

It is not that hermeneutics is absent from the work of either Ruether or Fiorenza. Both have adapted this method to their own procedures, though neither of them explicitly delineates a philosophical grounding for their work. Both recognize that the starting point of any such hermeneutic enterprise is human experience – in this instance, women's experiences. As Ruether (1985a: p. 113) states: 'Women's experience explodes as a critical force, exposing classical theology, including its foundational tradition in scripture, as shaped by male experience rather than human experience.' For both, the initial emphasis is naturally on a hermeneutics of suspicion in the guise of a historical-critical feminist interpretation. Here, scholars use a women-focused lens to investigate not just scripture, but other writings of the past and present, to reclaim a heritage that has been denied them. This is not a naive adoption of experience *tout court*, but a balanced awareness that any experience is always historically conditioned. In Fiorenza's words:

> Recognizing its sociopolitical location and public commitment, a feminist biblical interpretation must therefore utilize historical-critical methods for the sake of presenting an alternative interpretation of biblical texts and history for public scholarly discussion and historical assessment. In order to do so, we must develop a hermeneutics of suspicion to be applied both to the contemporary scholarly historical discourse and to that of the biblical writers. The feminist hermeneutics of suspicion understands androcentric texts as selective articulations of men often expressing as well as maintaining patriarchal historical conditions. (Fiorenza, 1984, pp. 107–8)

One consequence of locating these political and/or theological presuppositions inherent in male-dominant interpretations is a call for a heuristic recovery of models of female modalities of being and expression that have been thereby excluded. This task of reclamation encourages a regeneration by way of a hermeneutics of restoration, of latent possibilities of meaning.

> We must seek instead heuristic models that explore women's historical participation in social-public development and their efforts

> to comprehend and transform social structures. It is not 'biological' sex differences but patriarchal household and marriage relationships that generate the sociopolitical inferiority and oppression of women. (Fiorenza, 1984, p. 109)

It is obvious that neither Ruether nor Fiorenza believes there is an essential form of womanhood, but that behaviour is a result of cultural and historical circumstances. Though they both discuss women's experience and women's interpretations of scripture, they are not absolutizing these specific stances. They make very clear the respective positions on which they stand, aware that these will be subject to modification with the passage of time and further critique. With such a standpoint, it is difficult to see how Davaney's charge of reverse hierarchy can hold. For, in contrast, within the framework of a feminist hermeneutics, a hermeneutic circle is established which incorporates our present self-understanding in a way that overcomes the subject/object split. Each movement of recovery of the past leads to a new discovery of who we are and what we can be; this recuperation in turn leads to a larger base from which to make richer discoveries of an erased history. And so a cycle of recovery/discovery, grounded in the present, but incorporating both past and future, evolves. This in no way implies identification by osmosis with all women, but it introduces a critical consciousness and appreciation of women's specific struggles in history and solidarity with them.

> To recover biblical history as memory, and remembrance as history for women, does not mean abandoning critical historiography but deepening a critical understanding of historical inquiry, conceiving of historiography as a memory and tradition for people of today and tomorrow. We participate in the same struggle as our biblical foresisters against the oppression of patriarchy and for survival and freedom from it. We share the same liberating visions and commitments as our biblical foremothers. We are not called to 'empathize' or to 'identify' with their struggles and hopes but to continue our struggle in solidarity with them. (Fiorenza, 1984, p. 115)

Obviously, we have come a long way from the days when the hermeneutic circle was considered as simply the reciprocal relation of the parts and the whole in any act of understanding of a text (Palmer, 1969, p. 118). Nevertheless, even this restricted understanding of hermeneutics had ushered in the awareness that meaning was contextually and historically bound. This relatively unsophisticated approach has since been refined by Hans-Georg Gadamer and Paul Ricoeur.[6] Ricoeur specifically contends that the hermeneutic circle bridges the gap between explanation and understanding – those objective and subjective poles that had long proved stumbling blocks in any attempt to account for the way we act in the process of knowing. And the circle thus defined is not a vicious one, because both epistemology and ontology become subsumed in a more comprehensive act of experience of knowing and being, that in its very nature recognizes the reciprocal nature of our own ongoing relationship to the world. This hermeneutic appreciation of existence was introduced by Heidegger, but modified by the further refinements of Gadamer and Ricoeur.

It is on the basis of such an understanding of hermeneutics that I feel a response can be offered to Chopp and Davaney. As perceived today, hermeneutics encourages the scrutiny of implicit prejudgements that underlie all thinking. It makes no pretence to a neutral objectivity. It acknowledges the grounding of thinking in our lifeworld and establishes the fact that, depending on the situation, variables such as race, class and gender obviously need to be taken into account. In this sense, there can never be any universal attribution of women's behaviour or needs, or any assumptions as to the homogeneity of female experience. In hermeneutics, allowance is made for women to speak from their own experience, without resorting to unsubstantiated generalizations. All this occurs within an overarching acceptance of continuous critique and correction of the contents and methods one employs. This in turn presumes many different approaches by women seeking both to understand and to evaluate their lives. Such an approach appears to avoid the extremes of both relativism and essentialism that hover around postmodernism and its remedies.

It is in this sense, too, that part of Chopp's objections to Ruether's modernist values can be met. It could be acknowledged that Ruether's perfunctory recognition of hermeneutics as method does not take into account the need to question not only the structures of culture but the discourse that is used to sustain them. Incorporation of such a critique not only into the movement of suspicion but also into a process of self-examination does allow for a more detailed and subtle analysis of the socio-symbolic order – including the presuppositions of reason and method. Ruether may not wish to make such a move herself, but it is not impossible to build such checks and balances into a hermeneutic approach so that it is as much a critical self-reflective process as it is a method of evaluating texts .and ideals received from tradition.

There are also some further questions that need to be posed to both Chopp and Davaney. Though Chopp has sought to depict a proclamatory praxis of Word, her use of Foucault as well as Kristeva and Irigaray who question any comprehensive position, would seem to disallow her merger of Word and word. Foucault's theory of radical heteronomy cannot sustain the praxis that Chopp advocates to achieve a universal ideal of a redeemed and liberated humanity. And the French feminists, while they will allow subversive tactics to undermine structural hierarchies and biases, believe in multiple and fragmented identities. In Kristeva's work especially, this non-sexually specific identity, though it succumbs neither to masculine nor feminine essences, remains indeterminate and ineffectual in its ability to connect with the very praxis that Chopp requires.

A final observation needs also to be made with reference to Davaney's citation of Foucault as a proponent of nihilism and relativism. It may well be that the work of early Foucault, particularly in his genealogical studies, can be considered nihilist in the tradition of Nietzsche (see Deleuze, 1986). But in his later writings, starting with his volumes on *The History of Sexuality* (Foucault, 1986), Foucault makes a decisive turn towards an understanding of a project of the self that is distinctly hermeneutical. Foucault still rejects any notion of a founding subject or an autonomous self, but focuses on a subject who attempts to articulate life as an aesthetic expression. This is achieved by an ongoing negotiation and critical evaluation of all social norms in the name of cultivating a distinctive persona. Thought and experience, in this perspective, must never harden into dogmatic or universal pronouncements (Foucault, 1988, pp. 3–16). Foucault's project can be understood as similar to that of hermeneutics. Davaney has ignored this hermeneutic position in both feminist theologians and Foucault, yet I believe it is the hermeneutic method and its concomitant mode of pluralism that furnishes the key to a coherent method as women seek to reformulate theology. A nihilistic interpretation, as promoted by Davaney, is only one way of reading deconstruction. The other constructive form is the previously noted radical hermeneutics of Caputo. This approach interrogates all and revels in creative possibility without abandoning a context where evaluation of the most appropriate action can occur. Such a context in our present intellectual climate is one of pluralism.

And it is not as if pluralism, as a position, has been ignored by feminist scholars in religious studies. In situating her own option within a diverse spectrum of possibilities, Rosemary Ruether states:

> Feminist theology needs to be seen as a network of solidarity between many feminist communities engaged in the critique of patriarchalism in distinct cultural and religious milieux, rather than one dominant form of feminism that claims to speak for the whole of womankind. So I state that it is from a Western Christian context that I speak of patriarchal and feminist theologies. (Ruether, 1985b, p. 710)

Elisabeth Schüssler Fiorenza endorses this declaration while at the same time indicating the inherent plurality of theologies.

> There exists not one feminist theology or the feminist theology but many different expressions and articulations of feminist theology. These articulations not only share in the diverse presuppositions and perspectives of feminist studies but also function within the frameworks of divergent theological perspectives, such as neo-orthodoxy, evangelical theology, liberal theology, process theology, and various confessional theological perspectives. (Fiorenza, 1984, p. 3)

Lest these views be thought of as simply female indulgence, David Tracy has also articulated the pluralistic nature of theology itself:

> Theology, in fact, is a generic name not for a single discipline but for three: fundamental, systematic and practical theologies. Each of these disciplines needs explicit criteria of adequacy. Each is concerned with all three publics (the larger society; the academy; the church). Each is irrevocably involved in claims to meaning and truth. (Tracy, 1981, p. 31)

Pluralism, thus conceived, allows that there can be divergent perspectives and methods that can inform a topic or discipline. Yet this is not, as some critics imply, an invitation to unrestrained relativism. It is only if one holds the ultimate ideal as an absolute truth, which one then attempts to apply to all human experience, that relativism is to be feared. Advocates of such a single cohesive system of knowledge are loathe to acknowledge the impact of ideas such as those of Thomas Kuhn, who has well illustrated that, even within the sacrosanct domain of science, incommensurable paradigms often coexist and overlap without undermining the credibility of the discipline (Kuhn, 1970). One paradigm may replace another, as the Copernican did the Ptolemaic, to be in turn superceded by a Newtonian world-view. Or, they may mutually qualify each other, as do structural and phenomenological analyses of experience. But such different paradigms in the theoretical domain are but a faint reflection of the diversity of competing viewpoints that are happily (albeit unreflectively) subsumed in an individual existence. It is the nature of the hermeneutic enterprise to admit such divergencies by presupposing that variant readings are possible. But none of this implies a free-for-all abdication of standards.

In philosophy, as elsewhere, there are audiences that mediate the numerous claims to knowledge. Hermeneutics provides for the fact that, though there may be differing interpretations, some may be better than others. The debate as to which is the more appropriate interpretation occurs in the public domain, usually within a community of one form or another. With regard to theology, David Tracy has depicted the different audiences of the church, the academy and the public sphere in *The Analogical Imagination* (Tracy, 1981, pp. 28–31, 79–82, 233–41). The process of arbitrating meaning may even be protracted over centuries, and it is possible that no definitive answer ultimately emerges. There is constant overlap, and people may appropriate disparate elements of the many intersecting models and forms of discourse. This is how the fabric of knowledge is constituted, and an ongoing hermeneutic cycle can take into account the multiple strands that compose it. Women are just beginning to enter this intellectual ferment and their contribution as regards both form and content will have profound consequences.

There will always be competing interpretations among these explorations and tentative depictions of meaning in both scientific and humanistic fields. And there will always be discipline-specific guidelines for evaluating these interpretations.[7] But these disciplinary debates are never isolated from the general cultural context. Hence, any feminist hermeneutics gains momentum as part of a gradual cultural shift to acknowledge the critique of feminism. At the same time, in allowing for the historical and cultural circumstances, hermeneutics admits that all experience is always already contextualized. So I believe that the work of Ruether and Fiorenza (who specifically mention hermeneutics) and of other women adventurers in divine speculation (who implicitly apply hermeneutic premises) can be situated within a widened hermeneutic vista. It is here that hermeneutics moves beyond method to incorporate a form of knowing and being. The resultant delicate, or not so delicate, manoeuvring need not be seen as one further chapter in the unfolding saga of modernism, but as a vibrant and intense inquiry by women who now submit all modes and methods of knowing (even their own) to stringent inspection. Whether or not this involves a new revelation, as Mary Daly espouses, it none the less appears that a watershed in consciousness has been reached as far as the needed contribution of women to the structure of knowledge is concerned.

But among women themselves, one final problem remains. What is to be made of the appeal to experience that underpins the whole enterprise of feminist hermeneutics? For there are some, like Mary Daly, who declare that there is a distinctly female way of interpretation, and not simply an historically conditioned position. Perhaps the most problematic aspect of such idealizations is the figure of the Goddess. The question that needs consideration, and one that fosters extremely heated debates, is whether such claims always entail an essential ahistoricism. Ideally it would seem that it is crucial for women to move beyond the dilemmas of dualism and of reverse discrimination that arise as a result of claiming quintessential Goddess-inspired qualities. Perhaps what is needed is a more discerning awareness of what it means to use loaded terms such as essentialism in this context. For, as Diana Fuss notes:

> It is certainly true that there is no such thing as 'the female experience' or the 'Black experience' or 'the Jewish experience' ... And it seems likely that simply 'being' a woman, or a Black, or a Jew (as if 'being' were ever 'simple') is not enough to qualify one as official spokesperson for an entire community. (Fuss, 1989, p. 117)

Yet it cannot be denied that such claims of a universal nature can have tactical importance in battles for political and social rights. They can also energize those who might otherwise remain inarticulate and isolated. To mitigate any deadlock that results

from arguments between proponents of the essentialist and con-
structionist positions Fuss recommends that each side take into
consideration the internal discrepancies and political allegiances
of the respective options. What this amounts to is that, rather
than persisting in prolonged abstract argumentation, specific
situations and motivations always need to be considered. Such
a stance does not exclude that certain attitudes may be regarded
as appropriate for women in definite cases. Once again, however,
decisions on such matters should be left to the woman concerned
and not be imposed from without.

This controversy could be seen merely as a rehash of the
nature/nurture dispute in a different guise, but more specifically it
introduces the problematic that plagues women's studies between
generalizations (such as race, class and gender) and particular-
ization. The consensus that is emerging favours acceptance of
both perspectives, for without guiding principles, specific instances
tend to evaporate into random occurrences. Generalizations, on
the other hand, without reference to actual events, invite in-
tolerance of diversity. The trick is to keep the two forms of
description on dialogue within a system of checks and balances,
so that one is never privileged at the expense of the other. This
introduces a type of hermeneutic circle whereby constant interaction and review is fostered between competing viewpoints of
such artificial constructions and distinctions as the abstract and
the concrete, the universal and the particular, or the subject and
the object. Such a procedure, grounded in the practical realities
of the lifeworld, holds in check the excesses of relativism and
essentialism which seem an inevitable stumbling block in any
discussions of women and identity.

It is in this context that I believe the sensitive issue of the
Goddess can be broached. Rosemary Ruether (1986) has been
particularly critical of its ahistorical and romantic tendencies,
arguing that what is crucial is a clarification of the role of myth
and history in contemporary appropriations of divine imagery.
Ruether none the less acknowledges that what is occurring in
any reinterpretation of God imagery is a selectivity and radical
recontextualization of the past in the light of present predica-
ments. Now it seems to me that this is what Carol Christ recommends in her own adaptation of Goddess characteristics:

Though nourished by ancient symbols of Goddesses from around
the world, women's imagination is by no means subject to the

authority of the past. Instead, modern women joyfully discover what is useful to us in the past and reject what is not. We understand that many symbols of the Goddess have come down to patriarchal cultures, and, using feminism as a principle of selection, we reject those aspects of ancient mythologies that picture Goddesses as legitimators of the power of men. (Christ, 1987, p. 154)

Christ's emphasis is not so much on the fact that the Goddess needs historical verification, but on its force as an image of emerging power for women today. It authenticates strength in ways that have been absent from the accepted attributes of women. This adaptation of the Goddess then has profound psychological significance for some women in that it can graphically portray experiences and qualities that they feel they are reclaiming as their own. Undoubtedly, there will be literalisms and ill-informed historical claims, as well as unsubstantiated generalizations, but it is the psychological attributes that are of primary importance in this process. Consequently, I believe that its context of evaluation should lie more in the domain of psychological constructs, in place of Freud's oedipal romance and Jung's archetypal mythic depictions of psychic maturity and wholeness (where masculinity reigned as the basis of the interpretative schema). In this manner, though such a preference is not to all women's tastes, it can take its place in the spectrum of options available in the contemporary pluralist climate.

Not all objections are thereby met, particularly for those women who wish to visualize the Divine within the historical context of a revelation and a scriptural tradition. And it is here that problems of the constitution of a canon and correlation occur. But it has not been my intention to assess the theological aspect of these issues in accord with traditional rubrics. Yet even in this connection, from a hermeneutical perspective there is a need for all parties to recognize that, within the interpretative cycle, discriminating judgement is always being exercised. This distillation of the past is taking place in the light of changed circumstances, of needs and perspectives that were unavailable or even unthinkable in previous eras. Our visions, then, need to be both humble and daring, infused with the appreciation that there are always possibilities as yet unrealized. We are as much creatures of an unlimited future as products of a 'revisioned' past.

It may be that in the divine scheme of things the sex of God is irrelevant. There are even some feminists of an activist persuasion who claim the issue is a red herring. And it may well be the time, as Mary Daly (1973, pp. 28–33) observes, to conceive of God as 'Be-ing', (emphasizing the 'process'), rather than thinking of God in terms of idolatrous anthropomorphisms. But as Judith Plaskow (1991, pp. 124–5) relates, the resistance generated by attempts to introduce feminine modalities of God language indicates a sensitive nerve has been touched. Thus, it seems to me that, from a tactical position, it is as necessary today to discuss the sex of God, as it is to agitate for female rabbis, ministers and priests. Ideally, the present structures need major modifications in practice as well as in theory, but political interests suggest the expediency of such immediate and contentious stratagems as feminine God-language.

But my own feeling is that for a time there should be a moratorium on theoretical pronouncements as to the death of God, the relativist nature of all knowledge, etc. From a feminist perspective, such theoretical postulates exclude women from a scene to which they have just gained access and where they need time/space to give expression to their experience.

We need to be aware that we are imbedded in concrete reality addressing issues of vital concern to the lives of everyday women. Texts and expressions within a hermeneutic framework are always open to revision. At the same time, we need to be aware that all knowledge is provisional, or, as McFague admits, we can never hope to capture the ultimate in metaphorical or conceptual formats. We need time for women to mull over the complex and multiple areas that comprise their lives, being, doing, thinking in an atmosphere of mutual support and critique. Such collaboration is needed if feminist scholars are going to add their contribution to the fabric of knowledge.

In this time of creative investigation, I feel it is appropriate to allow women scholars to try on/out many diverse modes of thinking and expression in their relation to what they consider sacred. It is for this reason that I believe a period of strategic pluralism is necessary as women explore the ramifications of the experiences they are thematizing and reviewing. This process, in so far as it is occurring within a community of women scholars, marks the first time that such a breadth and wealth of of shared experience is available for investigation. Premature closure of constructive debate to establish who has the most legitimate basis, the most politically correct stance, or the most conclusive argument is, at this stage, counter-productive. For too long women in religion, as well as in society itself, have been denied their voice. Their experiences have been regarded as insignificant. Orthodoxy, or getting it right, should be the least of our concerns. Proving ourselves to the establishment should not be a high priority. Let us live in creative flux, in vibrant (if not necessarily harmonious) dialogue for some time to come.

Notes

1 For an example of this type of debate see Young (1990).
2 In this regard, while I can acknowledge and support the attempts of native American, African American, Chicana, Asian and African women to conduct their own investigations and discussions of the Divine, I do not feel qualified to speak on their behalf on this topic.
3 See other articles that explore this dimension in *The Feminist Mystic*, Giles (1986).
4 My thanks to that wicked woman, Mary Daly, for such whimsicality (in the best sense of the word).
5 For a good basic introduction to deconstruction see Norris (1988), and for a more detailed study of the work of Derrida see Norris (1987).
6 For a good introductory survey of the history of hermeneutics see Palmer (1969) and especially pp. 162–217 for the work of Gadamer. Perhaps the most accessible work for the ideas of Ricoeur can be found in Ricoeur (1976). More specific essays by Hans-Georg Gadamer are found in *Philosophical Hermeneutics* (Gadamer, 1976, pp. 1–104).
7 See Ricoeur (1976, pp. 78–9) for a discussion of forms of validation within the hermeneutic tradition.

References

Caputo, J. 1987: *Radical Hermeneutics*. Bloomington: Indiana University Press.

Chopp, Rebecca 1989a: Seeing and naming the world anew: the works of Rosemary Radford Ruether. *Religious Studies Review*, 15, 1, 8–11.

Chopp, Rebecca 1989b: *The Power to Speak: Feminism, Language, God*. New York: Crossroad.

Christ, Carol 1979: Why women need the goddess: phenomenological, psychological, and political reflections. In Carol Christ and Judith Plaskow (eds), *Womanspirit Rising: A Feminist Reader in Religion*, San Francisco: Harper & Row, 273–87.

Christ, Carol 1987: Symbols of Goddess and God in feminist theology. In *Laughter of Aphrodite*, San Francisco: Harper & Row, 135–59.

Daly, Mary 1973: *Beyond God the Father*. Boston, MA: Beacon.

Davaney, Sheila Greeve 1987: Problems with feminist theory: historicity and the search for sure foundations. In P. Cooey, S. Farmer and M. E. Ross (eds), *Embodied Love*, San Francisco: Harper & Row, 79–95.

Deleuze, Gilles 1986: *Foucault*. Ed. and trs. S. Hand. Minneapolis: University of Minnesota Press.

Fiorenza, Elisabeth Schüssler 1975: Feminist theology as a critical theology of liberation. *Theological Studies*, 36, 4, 605–26.

Fiorenza, Elisabeth Schüssler 1981: Toward a feminist biblical hermeneutics: biblical interpretation and liberation theology. In B. Mahan and L. D. Richison (eds), *The Challenge of Liberation*, Maryknoll, NY: Orbis, 91–112.

Fiorenza, Elisabeth Schüssler 1984: *Bread Not Stone: The Challenge of Feminist Biblical Interpretation*. Boston, MA: Beacon.

Foucault, Michel 1986: *The History of Sexuality: The Care of the Self*, vol. 3. Trs. R. Hurley. New York: Random.

Foucault, Michel 1988: *Politics, Philosophy, Culture: Interviews and Other Writings 1977–1984*. Ed. A. Sheridan. New York: Routledge.

Fuss, Diana 1989: *Essentially Speaking*. New York: Routledge.

Gadamer, Hans-Georg 1976: *Philosophical Hermeneutics*. Berkeley: University of California Press.

Giles, Mary E. (ed.) 1986: *The Feminist Mystic*. New York: Crossroad.

Gray, Elizabeth Dodson 1988: Eden's garden revisited: a Christian ecological perspective. In P. Altenbernd Johnson and J. Kalven (eds), *With Both Eyes Open: Seeing Beyond Gender*. New York: Pilgrim Press, 24–57.

Harding, Sandra 1987: Conclusion: epistemological questions. In S. Harding (ed.), *Feminism and Methodology*, Bloomington: Indiana University Press, 181–90.

Irigaray, Luce 1981: This sex which is not one. In E. Marks and I. de Courtivron (eds), *New French Feminisms*, New York: Schocken, 99–106.

Joy, Morny, 1990: Equality or divinity: a false dichotomy. *Journal of Feminist Studies in Religion*, 6, 1, 9–24.

Kristeva, Julia 1981: Woman can never be defined. In E. Marks and I. de Courtivron (eds), *New French Feminisms*, New York: Schocken, 137–41.

Kuhn, Thomas 1970: *The Structure of Scientific Revolutions*. Chicago: University of Chicago Press.

McFague, Sallie 1982: *Metaphorical Theology: Models of God in Religious Language*. Philadelphia: Fortress Press.

Norris, Christopher 1987: *Derrida*. Cambridge, MA: Harvard University Press.

Norris, Christopher 1988: *What is Deconstruction?* London: Academy Editions.

Palmer, Richard E. 1969: *Hermeneutics*. Evanston: Northwestern University Press.

Plaskow, Judith 1990: *Standing Again at Sinai: Judaism from a Feminist Perspective*. San Francisco: Harper & Row.

Raschke, Carl A. 1982: The deconstruction of God. *Deconstruction and Theology*. New York: Crossroad, 1–33.

Ricoeur, Paul 1976: *Interpretation Theory: Discourse and the Surplus of Meaning*. Forth Worth, TX: Texas Christian University Press.

Ruether, Rosemary Radford 1983: *Sexism and God-Talk: Toward a Feminist Theology*. Boston, MA: Beacon.

Ruether, Rosemary Radford 1985a: Feminist interpretation: a method of correlation. In Letty Russell (ed.), *Feminist Interpretation of the Bible*, Philadelphia: Westminster Press, 111–24.

Ruether, Rosemary Radford 1985b: The future of feminist theology in the Academy. *Journal of the American Academy of Religion*, 53/54 (December), 703–13.

Ruether, Rosemary Radford 1986: Feminist spirituality and historical religion: renewal or creation – 1985–6 Dudleian lecture. *Harvard Divinity Bulletin*, February–March, 5–11.

Sölle, Dorothee 1981: *Mysticism, liberation and the names of God. Christianity and Crisis*, 22 June, 179–85.

Taylor, Mark C. 1984: *Erring: A Postmodern A/theology*. Chicago, University of Chicago Press.

Tracy, David 1981: *The Analogical Imagination*. New York: Crossroad.

Young, Pamela Dickey 1990: *Feminist Theology/Christian Theology: In Search of Method*. Minneapolis: Fortress Press.

6

The Return of the Goddess: Psychoanalytic Reflections on the Shift from Theology to Thealogy

Naomi Goldenberg

I borrowed the title 'The Return of the Goddess' from a series of radio documentaries about feminism and religion produced by the Canadian Broadcasting Corporation.[1] The title describes the direction of much of the work being done by the scholars, artists, and religious leaders who are making a new place for women in contemporary religious thought. Some of the women who are doing this often call themselves witches or members of the sisterhood of the Wicca. They are engaged in founding alternative religions which place the Goddess at the centre of worship (see, for example, Budapest, 1979, 1989; Starhawk, 1979). Others are working within traditional religious denominations to champion the use of female symbols to refer to God (see Olsen 1983). Still others are interested in finding and elaborating female images of divinities within the fields of psychology, literature, art, and history.[2] Instead of naming themselves 'witches', these last two groups identify in a more general way with what is usually called the women's spirituality movement. The efforts of all such women are making the return of the Goddess a definite cultural event – an event which religious leaders, theologians, and scholars of religion are beginning to notice.

Eventually, theology and each disciplinary specialty within religious studies – history of religion, sociology of religion, philosophy of religion, and psychology of religion – will have to face 'the Goddess' and to encounter the 'thealogy' that reflection on her is creating.[3] This essay is my effort to approach thealogy as a feminist scholar of the psychology of religion. I want to begin to assess the impact of the Goddess movement from the perspective of psychoanalytic theory.

In addition to explaining how analytic thought can be used to understand the Goddess, I also intend to show how the Goddess movement can illuminate certain trends within psychoanalysis. To accomplish this dual purpose, I will concentrate first on four tendencies that I see as common to both ways of thinking. I suggest that anyone who thinks in the terms of either contemporary psychoanalytic theory or of the Goddess movement is urged: (1) to focus on the past as a central source of meaning; (2) to focus on female images of power and desire and therefore to deconstruct central images of patriarchal authority; (3) to describe the individual as formed within the context of a community; and (4) to recognize fantasy as a key structure of 'rational' thought.

These basic similarities between psychoanalytic theory and avant-garde religious feminism seem to point to an even larger movement in Western thought – a movement which, I think, turns the traditional Platonic world-view inside out. I will discuss how both modern analytic theory and ancient Goddess mythology present the same alternative to Plato after I explain my reasons for considering these two ways of thinking as very much alike.

The branch of psychoanalytic theory which is most relevant to feminist thealogy is object relations theory. This highly influential offshoot of earlier Freudian theory developed in Britain out of the work of analysts such as Michael Balint (1958), W. R. D. Fairbairn (1966), Melanie Klein (1975a, b), and D. W. Winnicott (1978, 1979). Object relations theory is usually contrasted to the classical approach to psychoanalysis, which is often termed 'instinct theory' or 'drive theory'. Instinct theory depicts the person as an individual, a separate being who is motivated by the vicissitudes of certain basic 'drives' which are believed to be inherent in the human organism. In contrast, object relations theory stresses the interconnectedness of people. To an object relations analyst, a person is always seeking relationships with 'objects' – that is, with people – with whom a shared world of feelings and activities can be constructed. In general, then, object relations theory focuses more on the human being in relationship to others, while instinct theory is more concerned with the psychodynamics of human subjects thought of as more or less discrete entities (see Greenberg and Mitchell, 1983).

Another difference between the approach of object relations and that of instinct theory, is that object relations tends to reach further back into childhood. Classical Freudian analysis had been chiefly interested in the human being after the age of five. In contrast, object relations theory began to stress the developmental significance of infancy and very early childhood. Contemporary object relations theorists conceptualize nearly every aspect of a person's behaviour and character against the background of the earliest beginnings of her or his life.

Looking to the Past in Both Goddess Religion and Psychoanalysis

Object relations theory's intense interest in the deep past is, in broad terms, quite similar to that of the contemporary Goddess religions. Both psychoanalysis and the new thealogies involve participants in an extensive reflection on what happened long, long ago. In psychoanalysis, an individual's preverbal past is judged to be most important. In Goddess religion, emphasis is placed on the collective prehistoric past.

For both philosophies, a sense of connection to the past is cultivated for the purpose of heightening involvement in the present. In the case of Goddess religion, this focus on the past is used to confer a sense of reality and legitimacy on contemporary women's experience. Books about Goddess mythology provide women with a compendium of female passions and sensibilities. The myths are used to call attention to the complexity of female experience and to dignify that experience by revealing its ancient roots. Thus, to a large degree, Goddess religion pursues meaning in the way that Mircea Eliade (1959) describes in his work on myths of 'eternal return', which confer meaning on the present by recalling ancient stories related to the foundation of culture.

In addition to using stories and images of goddesses to acquaint women with the deep background of their psychological lives, the Goddess movement relates the present to the past through its use of rituals marking the progression of time. Observing major and minor sabbaths tied to the four seasons and to the two solstices and equinoxes keeps alive a sense of connection to nature's recurring pattern of change. Similarly, attention to the phases of the moon links daily life to a monthly cycle of repetition. Present time is thus given weight and significance by explicitly linking it to seasonal and astrological timelessness.

It is probably correct to say that psychoanalysis, particularly as it has been elaborated by object relations theorists, places an even greater value on the redemptive value of connection to the past than does Goddess religion. All analytic theory aims at learning to see more about the past in the psychological structures of the present. No event is ever seen as determined wholly by present circumstance or by motives for a future end. In analysis, the present is largely a *fiction* of the past. The present is a formation or a construction of the past in the sense of the Latin root of the word 'fiction' (*fingere*), meaning 'to form'.

It was Freud (1953–74, vol. 7, p. 222) who first said that the finding of every object is actually a refinding of it. Object relations theorists interpret this idea to mean that all adult loves and all adult hates are tinged with memories of earlier loves and hates. In fact, a large part of all experience is considered to be a melange of imitations or reactions to what went before. One way in which psychoanalysis increases a person's sense of meaning in life is by making her or him more aware of how the past is being repeated in the present. Therapy results in an increased breadth of response to what went before. The past is never really surmounted; instead, it is lived out in other ways. Thus psychoanalysis, like Goddess religion, participates in the myth of the eternal return through its ritual recall of history and by its stress on experiencing the deep past as alive in the seemingly flimsy present.

There are great differences between how the two philosophies approach the past. Analysis consists of formal, elaborate reflection on one person's personal past. In contrast, Goddess religion is a more diffuse effort to re-animate an earlier, pagan, collective connection to the natural world. Nevertheless, both philosophies look back in time for the purpose of healing the present. Neither has a strategy based on the promise of a utopian future in a 'new world' imagined to be radically different.[4] There is no redemption expected to come in the form of a saviour, or as a promised land, or from the benefits of scientific progress. For both thealogy and psychoanalysis, there is only the rather modest hope of improving life through reflection on the past. They have a common orientation toward making the world a better place – an orientation which differs significantly from most contemporary forward-looking approaches to human salvation.

Female Prehistory and the Deconstruction of the Phallus

Even more significant than their shared reverence for the deep past is the fact that both thealogy and object relations theory agree on what, or rather who, is the most important part of the past. Object relations theory departs from classical analytic theory by replacing Freud's keen interest in the father with an intense preoccupation with the mother. Like the Goddess movement in religion, object relations theory places a woman at the beginning of the universe and thus champions a shift from an interest in male symbols to a focus on female ones. Both ways of thinking pose a challenge to the importance of the father.

By stressing those ignored or suppressed portions of collective religious history which refer to female figures of power, thealogy chips away at the monolith constructed in patriarchal history. Even if particular facts or arguments about the history of Goddess worship are disputed, the work of writers such as Merlin Stone (1976), Charlene Spretnak (1981), Savina Teubal (1984), Marija Gimbutas (1989), and others loosens the male monopoly on religious power. To teach that Judaism and Christianity arose out of pagan cultural contexts which granted women a great deal of prominence, certainly in their mythologies and possibly in their hierarchies, is to teach that Judaism and Christianity had political motives for their early rejection and denigration of female imagery. This approach to religious history makes it possible for many people to see female imagery living on in dominant traditions. Women are there. Things female are there. But they have been inverted or cloaked in order to be appropriated by male phallic history and mythology.

According to hypotheses framed by researchers into Goddess religion, Yahweh grew to power as a jealous God whose followers smashed the icons of those who worshipped female divinities tied to nature. Gradually, holidays which were once understood as marking the seasonal cycles of 'mother earth' became joined to accounts of male triumphs. The Exodus story obscured tales of the goddesses and their festivals of spring. The winter solstice became identified with a military victory instead of with the birth of the child of the Goddess. A harvest celebration thanking the mother deities for food became an occasion to read a male God's commandments.[5] As Christian symbolism became popular, Jesus replaced all the sons and lovers of the goddesses. He urged his followers to place more value on male words than on those 'paps which gave thee suck'.[6] In later centuries, a male clergy nearly succeeded in erasing the contribution of Christian women from recorded history.[7] Complete submission to male authority became the only appropriate role for women. All the deities that re-presented the great Goddess – the independent, often dangerous virgins and the lusty, powerful mothers – were reduced to one Virgin Mother, whose most celebrated utterance is 'Let it be done to me according to thy Will (Luke, 1: 38).[8]

The Goddess movement proposes that sexual politics have formed the traditional religious myths of Western culture. Because Goddess sympathizers suspect that patriarchal symbols rest on a stratum that both suppresses and appropriates a female prehistory, they are led to question all the important rites and images of the dominant faiths. They wonder if the bar mitzvah might not be the glorified male counterpart of a ceremony marking the onset of menstruation (Bettelheim, 1962). They feel empathy and curiosity toward denigrated graven images such as the golden calf. They dare to ask just what was so awful about Jezebel, Vashti, and Lilith (see Gendler, 1976; any issue of *Lilith*). They look at the Father, Son, and Holy Ghost and see another trinity – Diana, Luna, and Hecate.

This awareness of a possible female background to the symbols and customs of male power creates psychological distance from those symbols and customs. By raising the suspicion that solid male institutions are not all they have seemed or, rather, are more than they have seemed, Goddess ideology loosens the grip of masculine symbols upon the contemporary imagination. Both the facts and the fantasies of the Goddess movement function to crack the edifice of patriarchy by encouraging the emergence of suppressed patterns of language, visions, dreams, and theories.

I find a similar subversion of male discourse and symbols in the work of certain female theorists of psychoanalysis. Melanie Klein writes that the male fear of castration is actually derived from earlier anxiety about the disappearance of the mother's breast. Klein (1975a, p. 48) thinks that each infant sees the breast as a part of his or her own body – a part that sometimes vanishes to cause great discomfort. The male child transfers this early experience of bodily loss to his feelings about another physical protrusion, his penis. Similarly, Klein (1975b, p. 199) believes that when penis-envy occurs in women, it leads back to a desire to possess the mother's breast. Thus, for her, the power behind the symbol of the penis in adulthood is explained by the earlier importance of the breast.

More recently, Luce Irigaray (1985a, b) presents another theory to account for the intense male fear of castration. She suggests that the idea that a part of the body might be lost forever has its origin in the severing of the umbilical cord. Since a connection to the mother is lost when the umbilicus is snipped off, the cutting of the cord at the beginning of every life is traumatic. This event might well underlie all fears about the loss of pieces of the body. Irigaray's theory implies, I think, that for men, the penis may be the only way back to mother once the umbilical cord has been cut. While women have the option of closely identifying with their mothers, men's only hope of return lies in the penis. Since patriarchal culture restricts the ways in which men may be like their mothers, the penis becomes overvalued as the sole masculine tie to femininity.

The work of Melanie Klein and Luce Irigaray deconstructs the penis – that primary symbol of male domination. Their theories arouse the suspicion that the fabled organ might derive its power by evoking a connection to mother. Is phallic bravado a cover-up for the fact that castration has already occurred? Does it disguise the fact that the path to the mother – via the umbilicus and the breast – has already been cut off? The male compulsion to praise the penis is everywhere in men's writing. It appears in trashy novels such as those of Mickey Spillane, in better novels such as those of Norman Mailer, and in great theoretical works such as those of Sigmund Freud and Jacques Lacan. Could this unflagging interest have its root in the deep male desire to reconnect with the mother – a desire which expresses itself in a glorification of the only organ which can lead back to her?

By pointing to a female background behind the prominent male icons of both religion and psychology, the Goddess movement and object relations theory work to displace the father from his domination of the symbolic order. Both bodies of theory express and accelerate the slow erosion of male authoritarianism in Western culture.

A Shared Vision of the Human Being in Community

Another similarity between Goddess religion and object relations theory is that both stress the dependence of human beings on their communities. Unlike much patriarchal philosophy, which emphasizes individualism and self-determination, Goddess religion and object relations theory teach that people are created in large part by their relationships.

For object relations analysts, the focus on human life in community derives from the significance which the theory places on infancy and early childhood. Babies or young children simply cannot exist without the constant care and supervision of at least one adult, who is usually a woman. A baby is thus never a solitary being. D. W. Winnicott calls attention to the mother–infant pair by insisting that 'there is no such thing as a baby' (quoted in Greenberg and Mitchell, 1983, p. 197). Margaret Mahler takes the fusion of mother and child to absurdity by referring to a child's mother as a personified environment. 'The environment ... extremely overanxious, consulted one doctor after another', Mahler (1946, quoted in Greenberg and Mitchell, 1983, p. 282) writes.

These two famous quotations dramatize one of the central tenets of object relations theory – namely, that the life experience of human beings is determined in large part by other human beings. Although this interdependence is most apparent in early life, the theory maintains that it is also true of adulthood. Joan Riviere describes our mutual construction of one another in adult life in this way:

> We tend to think of any one individual in isolation; it is a convenient fiction. We may isolate him physically, as in the analytic

room; in two minutes we find that he has brought his world in with him, and that even before he set eyes on the analyst, he had developed inside himself an elaborate relation with him. There is no such thing as a single human being, pure and simple, unmixed with other human beings. Each personality is a world in himself, a company of many. That self, that life of one's own, which is in fact so precious though so casually taken for granted, is a composite structure which has been and is being formed and built up since the day of our birth out of countless never-ending influences and exchanges between ourselves and others. ... These other persons are in fact therefore parts of ourselves. And we ourselves similarly have and have had effects and influence, intended or not, on all others who have an emotional relation to us, have loved or hated us. We are members one of another. (Riviere, 1955, pp. 358-9, as quoted in Brown, 1966, p. 147)

To Riviere, being human means existing *in situ*, that is, in a nexus of relations with people past and present. She suggests that a truly autonomous person can exist only in theory – in an imagined parenthesis which excludes the animating context of history and emotions. Her words are an eloquent description of an object relations view of human nature: 'We are members one of another.'

There are several feminist theorists who are saying much the same thing as the object relations analysts. Human beings, say these theorists, are constructed in large part by their social, political, economic, and linguistic circumstances (see essays in Harding and Hintikka, 1983). Thus, as Naomi Schemen (1983) phrases it, 'questions of meaning and interpretation [in psychology and philosophy] cannot be answered in abstraction from a social setting'. This stress on the social context of experience actually extends the perspective of object relations theory which sometimes concentrates too narrowly on the social world as seen from a baby's perspective. To psychoanalysts, mother is the social context of baby, while to feminist theorists, mother and baby are both embedded in a bigger world. Object relations emphasizes the infant's immediate human environment, while feminist theory tries to understand the larger social conditions which make each particular human environment what it is. This exploration of the social world which constructs mothering is motivated by the feminist project of understanding women's experience in order to both learn from that experience and affect it for the better. From its early beginnings, feminist theory has been concerned with articulating the ways in which human lives, particularly women's lives, have been structured by the external world. 'The personal is political' was an early slogan that has held true in feminist thought since the early 1970s. The 'personal', say feminists, is an artificial construct which should never be thought of as radically separate from public life. All spheres of human activity are related.

The Goddess movement, like object relations theory in particular and feminist theory in general, is concerned with expanding awareness of the conditions which make lives what they are. Thealogy, however, focuses on some other, nonhuman aspects of the context of life. The Goddess movement takes seriously the ancient pagan perception that human life is part of a larger web of life which includes all of nature. Like the ecology movement, thealogy sees human life in a dynamic planetary context which is determined by the state of the water, the soil, and the air. The entire earth is conceptualized as the body of the Goddess and thus is sacred. No part of the ecosystem is separate from her, and thus no part of the material world is considered secular or profane. Starhawk, an eminent thealogian, describes the Goddess as existing in the complex connections of the entire universe. 'Each individual self', she writes, 'is linked by ties of blood and affection to the coven, which in turn is a part of the larger human community, the culture and society in which it is found, and that culture is part of the biological/geological community of Planet Earth and the cosmos beyond, the dance of being which we call Goddess' (Starhawk, 1982, p. 418).

I suggest that the mutual concern of psychoanalysis and thealogy with articulating the context of human life arises because both philosophies centre around the image of a powerful woman in the past. Since every human life begins in the body of a woman, the image of a woman, whether thought of as mother or as Goddess, always points to an early history of connectedness: Mother-*mater*-matter-matrix. 'Woman' is the stuff out of which all people are made. In the beginning was her flesh, and, after the beginning, she continues to suggest human historicity, to suggest human connection to and dependence upon the outside world. It is this deep memory of birth union, I think, which turns any serious reflection on women into a reflection on the interconnection of human beings with each other and with all the things which make up the body of the world. It is pre-birth experience and post-birth mothering which destine feminist theory to expand awareness of the context which supports everything human.

At a basic level, the image of woman is the image of human context – the image of human connection to the world. Object relations theory limits the image to mother and thus theorizes context somewhat narrowly as the mother–infant relationship. Thealogy extends the image to deity and thus envisions context more grandly as the planet as a whole. Both derive their insights into the matrices that support human life from an image of a woman-in-the-past. Classical Freudian psychoanalysis with its focus on an often absent *paterfamilias* and traditional religion with its focus on a father in heaven could never inspire similar reflection about the complex contingency of human existence.

Agreement that the Basis of Thought Lies in Fantasy

One aspect of the human context upon which both thealogians and analysts agree is fantasy. Both groups understand fantasy, or wish, as constituting the primary matrix for all mental processes.

In witchcraft, the cultivation of wishing pervades almost every practice. Goddess religion can often appear as 'wish-craft' because it teaches women to use spells and rituals to express their hopes, ambitions, and desires. Much of the effectiveness of these 'magical' practices can be explained by their ability to focus the mind and to mobilize willpower. Witches feel that a goal which can be visualized in detail is more likely to be a goal which can be reached. Thus they concentrate on representing wishes symbolically either in the form of physical objects such as amulets and talismans or in the choreography and incantations of ceremonies and rituals.

In addition to employing fantasy in religious practice, thealogians also use it to 'do thealogy', that is, to theorize about the Goddess. Sometimes the idea of a matriarchy in the past is put forward as a wish about history – a desire to be realized in the present and future. Thealogians are fond of quoting these lines of Monique Wittig from *Les Guérillères*: 'There was a time when you were not a slave, remember. Try hard to remember. Or, failing that, invent.' The wisdom of the words lies in the recognition that belief in a state of beneficence that existed in the past is an idea which empowers in the present. Wittig recommends that an invented past can be substituted for a remembered one. After all, she implies, faith is simply a very strong wish.

Some thealogians realize that their research into the past is motivated by their desire to improve women's lot in the present. 'Most writers on contemporary Goddess religion, womanspirit or Witchcraft cite the past to offer a historical basis for the present traditions,' Starhawk writes. But then she adds:

> I am not going to do that here. Historical points are always arguable, and while the past may serve us with models and myths, we need not look to it to justify the re-emergence of the feminine principle. Whether or not women ever ruled in matriarchies, women are taking power today. Whether or not contemporary Witchcraft has its roots in the Stone Age, its branches reach into the future. (Starhawk, 1982, pp. 415–16)

Starhawk, like some others, understands that for any living religion, the importance of the past lies in how it is used in the present. She knows that her religion, just as all others, is based around wishes and hopes for power, comfort, influence. and justice.

Object relations theorists share the conviction that wish and fantasy are central to human enterprise.[9] Instead of separating 'reality thinking' from 'fantasy thinking', as did Freud and many of his followers, object relations analysts conceive of fantasy as the basis or context of all thinking.[10] What is felt to be real in the inner, psychic world, they say, tends to be what is created in the external world. Fantasy is seen as creating the blueprint of a life.

Much to their credit, object relations theorists do not often take this idea to ridiculous lengths such as blaming the victim of a crime for wishing its occurrence. They do, however, use the idea of unconscious fantasy to explore character structure, ambition, and creativity. According to object relations theorists, people build their 'real' worlds of work, friends, and family to correspond to their deepest inner expectations. These analysts therefore, like many witches, see the entire external, human world as something constructed upon a stratum of internal fantasy.

Unlike the witches, object relations analysts do not believe that willpower can control fantasy.[11] To the object relations analyst, the structure of a person's fantasy life is laid down in infancy and early childhood. Paula Heimann (1952, quoted in Grosskurth, 1986, p. 331) states the general position succinctly: 'The earliest experiences lay the foundations for the type of response to people and events; those who have learned in infancy that frustration and anxiety can be quickly removed approach life with an optimistic attitude, and are capable of recovering from disappointments.' In object relations theory, a person's general attitude expresses the parameters of fantasies which have been sketched from the time of earliest infancy – a time when satisfaction depended on forces entirely outside each baby's control. Thus, to psychoanalysts, a person's attitude, inner world, and fantasy life are greatly influenced by her or his early environment and by the caregivers who shaped that environment. Analysts believe that a basic change in fantasy expression occurs only if something, such as analysis, effects a change in psychic dynamics. To them, fantasy is too much a product of personal history to be seriously influenced by the rituals and spells employed by the Goddess worshippers.

Even though the analysts and the witches disagree about the malleability of fantasy, attitude, and expectation, they both maintain that the inner world of anticipation and wish is the basis of all human thought and action. Consciousness and directed rational thought are considered to be relatively superficial phenomena which derive from older, more encompassing unconscious structures.

I think these four parallels between Goddess religion and object relations theory have a significance beyond the particular disciplines which have so far addressed them. If the ways of thinking discussed here become more typical, not only of psychological and theological discourse, but also of other branches of study, then Western thought in general will become more embodied and more contextualized. The serious inclusion of women in any system of thought fosters reflection that is grounded in both the physical body and in the body politic. This focus on human contingency and historicity is in direct contrast to the way the Platonic theory of forms has structured most Western theology and philosophy.

The idea that the best things about the world are somehow not a part of the world extends far beyond Plato. It exists in the work of philosophers like Hegel, who attributes influence to entities such as the Spirit and the Absolute. It exists in the work of analytic psychologists such as Jung, who derives the motives of human behaviour from immaterial essences called archetypes. And it exists in religions such as Christianity, which places responsibility for the existence of the world in the hands of a God who exists apart from the world. Such philosophies, such psychologies, such religions will undergo radical change if they are pressured to discard the belief that the world is constructed by disembodied abstractions.

As women become more and more central to all branches of Western thought, the belief in transcendent entities will become less and less tenable. This is true, I suggest, because the transcendent, the immaterial, and the metaphysical is actually the embodied, the physical, and the female. It is the exclusion of things female from philosophy, psychology, and theology which has allowed these disciplines to construct notions of an abstract presence which creates the world and then controls it. To include women means to recognize the physical contingency of all thought and all creation.

Ancient mythology illustrates the fact that the world does indeed begin with a woman and that it is the memory of her which inspires later creative thought. Consider the *Enuma Elish*, the ancient Babylonian epic of creation. In the poem, the hero Marduk kills the monster Tiamat and forms the world from her body. The heavens, the stars, the seas, the rivers, and the land all begin as parts of her. A woman's body is the body of the world. Creative action in the world is depicted in the poem as aggressive use of a mother's body. Mother and world are presented as identical.[12]

The object relations work of Klein and Winnicott agrees with the cosmology of the *Enuma Elish*. Klein believes that infants experience their first acts of exploring the world as aggression against their mothers. In contrast to Klein, Winnicott (see 'Transitional objects and transitional phenomena' in Winnicott, 1978, pp. 229–42) places much less stress on aggression as an early motive force. He thinks that babies become more involved with the world in direct proportion to the degree that they extend the sense of being with the mother to the greater environment. Winnicott considers the first objects (such as blankets and teddy bears) which stand for mother as 'transitional' objects. These objects, like mother, are felt to be both part of the child and part of the external world. In his view, culture, art, and religion are elaborations of transitional objects – constructions arising from the early sense of being able to use the world in the way that mother was used.

Thus, in object relations theory as well as in some of the earliest Western mythology, human experience of the world as well as all reflection on it is understood as based on the early tie to a woman. The Platonic search for the immaterial, original world of disembodied forms is an inversion of the real quest in which all humans have been involved since babyhood – that of extending their physical, psychological, animal presence into the material world. The quest is motivated more by a desire to re-experience and elaborate a union with matter, with mother, than it is to escape the embrace of the physical world. Plato has it backwards; the search for the wholly transcendent is, historically and psychologically, the search for the remembered state of union with the wholly immanent.

In Greek mythology, the image which tells the truth (psychologically and historically) about the human drives to explore the world and to create culture is that of the Muses, the nine daughters of Olympian Zeus and the Titaness Mnemosyne, Memory. The Muses are said to inspire mortals with their voices. They sing to those they love and bestow talents which make these humans happy, wise, and respected.

Surely the image of the Muses is derived from infancy and early childhood. This is the time when the sound of a woman's voice means nearly everything to nearly everyone. It signals the arrival of food, of warmth, of comfort, and of entertainment. She is heard before she is seen and that sound, because it is linked with the anticipation of good things to come, sparks the infant imagination. A woman's voice focused the attention of most babies in ancient Greece just as it focuses the attention of most babies in the contemporary world. No wonder that the Muses, the primary image of inspiration in Western thought, always work their magic through female voices (see Bion, 1967).

Object relations theory and ancient mythology both insist on the connection between the memory of the ties to a woman's body and the human desires to explore, to theorize, and to conceptualize the world. The Platonic tradition denies this connection by denigrating what is merely physical, by claiming that all knowledge is motivated by bodiless forms. The centuries-old tendency to exclude women from arenas of learning called 'higher' is probably a social dramatization of this denial. Women and matter have been repressed in our intellectual traditions when, in truth, they are at the origins of all reflection.

That which has been repressed is now returning. The contemporary focus on women in all areas of creative thought – in all domains of the Muses – means that the sources of thought itself will become clearer. This is the real significance of the return of the Goddess. When theology becomes thealogy, the metaphysical comes home to the physical.

Notes

This essay first appeared in Naomi Goldenberg's (1993) book *Resurrecting the Body: Feminism, Religion and Psychoanalysis* (New York: Crossroad).

1 This five-part *Ideas* series, written and narrated by Merlin Stone, was first aired in February 1986. The modern Goddess movement was surveyed from the time of the publication of Stone's (1976) book to the present.

2 See, for example, a discussion of the Goddess with reference to psychology in Bolen (1982), and in Downing (1984); to literature in Broner (1978); to art in Chicago (1979); to history in Stone (1976); and to theological thought in Christ (1987), and in Plaskow and Christ (1989).

3 *Thealogy, the logos of thea,* the Goddess, is surely a more appropriate term to refer to this new religion than is the word *theology,* which denotes an exclusively male God, *theos.* See Culpepper (1987).

4 For an account of how the images of witch and sorceress can be used to imagine new behaviour in this world, see Cixous and Clément (1986).

5 Although his book is not about Goddess religion *per se*, Sherwin T. Wine's (1985) *Judaism Beyond God* provides a good summary of important feminist ideas about patriarchal religious holidays. See especially pp. 151–78.

6 See, for example, the passage in Luke 11: 27, 28. It is interesting to contrast the various translations of this passage: for example, the *New English Bible* translation says: 'While [Jesus] was speaking thus, a woman in the crowd called out, "Happy the womb that carried you and the breasts that suckled you!" He rejoined, "No, happy are those who hear the word of God and keep it." ' See also Rosemary Ruether (1975, p. 59).

7 See Elisabeth Schüssler Fiorenza (1983). Fiorenza believes that a feminist reconstruction of Christian beginnings is essential to empower women in their struggle against patriarchal oppression (p. xx). She thinks that concentrating on the apostolic tradition obscures the contributions of women to the early Church (p. 69). As an example of how this patriarchal version of history can be supplemented to include women, see her chapter entitled 'The early

Christian missionary movement – equality in the power of the spirit', pp. 160–204.

8   See also Marina Warner (1976), *Alone of All Her Sex: The Myth and Cult of the Virgin Mary*. Warner argues that the image and iconography of Mary subsumes that of several goddesses in the Graeco-Roman pantheon – for example, Artemis (p. 280), Aphrodite (p. 279), Athene (p. 304), Hera (p. 267), and Persephone (p. 273).

9   Object relations theorists use 'phantasy' to refer to unconscious 'fantasy'. 'Fantasy' is given various interpretations and definitions in psychoanalytic literature. I am using the term broadly to refer in a general way to imagination, imaging, and so forth.

10 See Rycroft (1968: 42–60), and Isaacs (1948). Freud's attitude towards so-called fantasy thinking is discussed extensively by Judith Van Herik (1982) in *Freud on Femininity and Faith*.

11 On the contrary, psychoanalysis sees willpower as playing a role in the repression of fantasy.

12 *Enuma Elish*, iv. 101
He shot therethrough an arrow, it pierced her stomach,
Clave through her bowels, tore into her womb:
Thereat he strangled her, made her life-breath ebb away,
Cast her body to the ground, standing over it [in triumph].

135
He rested, the lord, examining her body:
Would divide up the monster, create a wonder of wonders!
He slit her in two like a fish of the drying yards,
The one half he positioned and secured as the sky ...

vi. 1
[Therein] traced he lines for the mighty gods,
Stars, star-groups and constellations he appointed for them:
He determined the year, marked out its divisions,
For each of the twelve months appointed three rising stars.

5
Having established the rules for the [astronomical] seasons,
He laid down the Crossing-line to make known their limits:
And that none should make mistake or in any way lose speed
He appointed, conjointly with in, the Enlil – and Ea – lines.

9
The great [Sun-]gates he opened in both sides of her ribs,
Made strong the lock-fastening to left and right:
In the depths of her belly he laid down the *elati*.
He made the moon to shine forth, entrusted to him the night.

53
He placed her in position, heaped [the mountai]ns upon it ...
Made the Euphr[ates] and Tigris to flow through her eyes.

(From 'The Epic of Creation', in *Documents from Old Testament Times*, ed. and trans. D. Winton Thomas (1958, pp. 10–11).)

References

Balint, Michael 1958: *The Basic Fault*. London: Tavistock Publications.
Bettelheim, Bruno 1962: *Symbolic Wounds, Puberty Rites, and the Envious Male*. New York: Collier Books.
Bion, W. R. 1967: A way of thinking. In W. R. Bion, *Second Thoughts: Selected Papers on Psycho-Analysis*. New York: Jason Aronson, 110–19.
Bolen, Jean Shinoda 1982: *The Goddesses in Everywoman*. Los Angeles: J. P. Tarcher.
Broner, E M. 1978: *A Weave of Women*. New York: Holt, Rinehart & Winston. (1980: Bantam Books.)
Brown, Norman O. 1966: *Love's Body*. New York: Random House.
Budapest, Z. 1979: *The Holy Book of Women's Mysteries*, 2 vols. Oakland: Susan B. Anthony Coven No. 1.
Budapest, Z. 1989: *The Grandmothers of Time: A Woman's Book of Spells, Celebrations, and Sacred Objects for Every Month of the Year*. San Francisco: Harper & Row.
Chicago, Judy 1979: *The Dinner Party: A Symbol of Our Heritage*. Garden City: Doubleday.
Christ, Carol 1987: *Laughter of Aphrodite: Reflections on a Journey to the Goddess*. New York: Harper & Row.
Cixous, Hélène and Clément, Catherine 1986: *The Newly Born Woman*. Trs. Betsy Wing. Minneapolis: University of Minnesota Press.
Culpepper, Emily Erwin 1987: Contemporary Goddess thealogy: a sympathetic critique. In Clarissa W. Atkinson, Constance H. Buchanan and Margaret R. Miles (eds), *Shaping New Visions: Gender and Values in American Culture*, Ann Arbor: UMI Research Press, 51–72.
Downing, Christine 1984: *The Goddess: Mythological Representations of the Feminine*. New York: Crossroad.
Eliade, Mircea 1959: *Cosmos and History: The Myth of the Eternal Return*. Trs. William R. Trask. New York: Harper & Row.
Fairbairn, W. Ronald D. 1966: *Psychoanalytic Studies of the Personality*. London: Routledge & Kegan Paul.
Fiorenza, Elisabeth Schüssler 1983: *In Memory of Her: A Feminist Theological Reconstruction of Christian Origins*. New York: Crossroad.

Freud, Sigmund 1953–74: *The Standard Edition of the Complete Psychological Works of Sigmund Freud*, 24 vols. Ed. James Strachey. London: Hogarth Press.

Gendler, Mary 1976: The restoration of Vashti. In Elizabeth Koltun (ed.), *The Jewish Woman*, New York: Schocken Books, 241–7.

Gimbutas, Marija 1989: *The Language of the Goddess*. San Francisco: Harper & Row.

Greenberg, Jay R. and Mitchell, Stephen A. 1983: *Object Relations in Psychoanalytic Theory*. Boston, MA: Harvard University Press.

Grosskurth, Phyllis 1986: *Melanie Klein: Her World and Her Work*. Toronto: McClelland and Stewart.

Harding, Sandra and Hintikka, Merrill B. (eds) 1983: *Discovering Reality: Feminist Perspectives on Epistemology, Metaphysics, Methodology, and Philosophy of Science*. Dordredht: D. Reidel.

Heimann, Paula 1952: Certain functions of introjection and projection in early infancy. In Susan Isaacs, Melanie Klein and Joan Riviere (eds), *Developments in Psycho-Analysis*, London: Hogarth Press, 122–68.

Herik, Judith Van 1982: *Freud on Femininity and Faith*. Berkeley: University of California Press.

Irigaray, Luce 1985a: *The Speculum of the Other Woman*. Trs. Gillian Gill. Ithaca: Cornell University Press.

Irigaray, Luce 1985b: *This Sex Which is Not One*. Trs. Catherine Porter. Ithaca: Cornell University Press.

Isaacs, Susan 1948: The nature and function of phantasy. *International Journal of Psycho-Analysis*, 29, 73–97.

Klein, Melanie 1975a: *Love, Guilt, and Reparation and Other Works, 1921–1945*. New York: Delacorte Press.

Klein, Melanie 1975b: *Envy and Gratitude and Other Works, 1946–1963*. New York: Delacorte Press.

Lilith: A Quarterly Magazine. New York: Lilith Publications.

Mahler, Margaret 1946: Ego psychology applied to behavior problems. In N. D. C. Lewis and B. L. Pacella (eds), *Modern Trends in Child Psychiatry*, New York: International Universities Press, 43–56.

Olsen, Carl (ed.) 1983: *The Book of the Goddess: Past and Present*. New York: Crossroad.

Plaskow, Judith and Christ, Carol 1989 (eds): *Weaving the Visions: New Patterns in Feminist Spirituality*. New York: Harper & Row.

Riviere, Joan 1955: The unconscious phantasy of an inner world reflected in examples from literature. In M. Klein (ed.), *New Directions in Psychoanalysis*, New York: Basic Books.

Ruether, Rosemary Radford 1975: *New Woman/New Earth: Sexist Ideologies and Human Liberation*. New York: Seabury Press.

Rycroft, Charles 1968: Symbolism and its relationship to the primary and secondary processes. In Charles Rycroft, *Imagination and Reality*, New York: International Universities Press.

7

Religion and Magic in the Modern Cults of the Great Goddess

Donate Pahnke

The General Preliminary Understanding of Religion and Magic

The general understanding of religion and magic is shaped by Christian theology and the older sciences of religion that emerged from it. There was a strong striving for a sharp differentiation between 'religion' and 'magic', which could be attributed to two main aspects: on the one hand the wish of being able to scientifically classify empirical religious phenomena; on the other hand to the simultaneous need of preserving and defending one's own 'higher' religion against the others – above all, the non-literate religions. This traditional, ideologically bound position led to a differentiation between 'religion' and 'magic' in which the main difference between the two was based on the thesis of a distinction in the power-relation between deity/the sacred and humans. Whereas the religious person would submit him/herself to the deity/the supernatural, the magic person placed him/herself above this power. In the first case, sovereign power-exercise is attributed

to the deity; in the second case to the human.[1] In the words
of Friedrich Heiler (1961, p. 27) 'Magic is profane, a piece of
power, a sovereign domination of the magical powers, an inter-
change of potencies and agents like an alchemist who works with
substances in his laboratory. Magic is characterized by a complete
absence not only of naivety, but also of awe. The magician stands
above the powerful object, the religious person below it.'

This theological differentiation between 'religion' and 'magic'
went to an extreme form by describing all other religions as
'magic' in the name of Christianity (cf. Biezais, 1978, p. 22); to
know the latter would alone suffice to understand all other religious phenomena in the world.[2] Such an ideological hierarchiza-
tion of religious phenomena finds its culmination in evolutionistic
development-theology where Christianity is similarly taken as the
measure of all other religions. All are according to their nearness
or distance to the Christian religion, or at least to monotheism,
classified as more or less magic pre-stages. Such classification
was used by Fowler (1981) and Oser (1984) for the development
stages of the individual, and by Bellah (1964) and Döbert (1973)
for the development of society. In today's science of religion there
are attempts to avoid these differentiations between religion and
magic, arrived at through ideologically and religiously grounded
evaluations; now one mostly proceeds from an essential identity
of 'religion' and 'magic' (Biezais, 1978). Nevertheless, the traditional evaluative connotations of the terms remain effective –
consciously or unconsciously – not only among the general public
but also in the science of religion. It is at least strongly to be
doubted that any suggestion of renaming the science of religion
as 'science of magic' would have any prospect of succeeding.

While the newer science of religion pleads on the one hand for
a non-distinction between 'religion' and 'magic', it adopts on the
other hand – when endeavouring the 'identification' of a religion
– the traditional focus on the relations of power and authority
within a religious system. Thus at the 1985 IAHR Congress in
Sydney the question 'What constitutes the identity of a religion?'
was answered by Hubert Seiwert with reference to the exercise of
power in a religious system which finds expression in the system
of norms of the respective religion and in the source or sources
of authority on which the system is founded (Seiwert, 1986). It
is true that this statement presents a considerable advantage over
traditional definitions, because by referring to the norm-giving
authority (which can be a godhead, ancestors, a scripture, a

prophet or similar) 'religion' as well as 'magic' can be considered. But this statement has a weakness because it functions only as long as there exists within the system examined a clear cut, identifiable and collectively recognized norm-giving authority. For investigations of non-authoritarian religious systems it is less useful.

Here lies exactly the problem with feminist spirituality where no such collectively admitted authority can be found. Neither do the followers of feminist spirituality speak of such a generally binding norm-giving power. Nor can it be clearly discerned within the relevant literature. Does this circumstance – the non-ascertainability of a norm-giving authority – now mean that feminist spirituality cannot be considered a religious system, or a religion? Or is perhaps the identity of a religious system constituted by more than the recourse to a norm-giving authority, in particular if this religious system has essentially more 'magic' to offer than 'religion' (according to the traditional criteria of distinction)?[3]

In answering this question I would first like to describe in which way feminist spirituality authors deal with the terms 'religion' and 'magic' themselves and then at the end again talk about the scientific classification of these terms.

Religion and Magic in Feminist Spirituality

With the term 'feminist spirituality' I adopt the self-description of all those new feminist Goddess communities which do not only refer to matters of faith, but also to political and scientific articulations.[4] Within this field there exists a rather large disagreement as to the use of 'religion' and/or 'magic' for one's own theory and practice. This disagreement is, in my opinion, closely connected with the traditional definitions of these terms, which are indeed not only used on the scientific level, but are also thoroughly anchored, together with their evaluating connotations, in every-day consciousness and within common linguistic usage.

An example of German usage (Heide Göttner-Abendroth)

I would like to discuss this problem with reference to the researcher of matriarchy and leader of the Hagia Academy for Critical Matriarchal Research and Experience, Heide Göttner-Abendroth, who is well known in Germany and who has re-

Table 7.1 Heide Göttner-Abendroth's distinctions between patriarchal and matriarchal cult systems

Patriarchal cult system (example of Western catholic Christianity)	Matriarchal cult system
1 Monotheism with exclusiveness pretension.	A threefold great Goddess who includes all others, with many names.
2 The godhead is something distant, high, extraneous, transcendent. *Creator* of heaven and earth and man.	The godhead is near, present. The Goddess *is* the world, heaven and earth, *is* Me.
3 Large institution, state-religion.	City- and place-religion; locally different variations.
4 Churches, minsters, cathedrals.	Sacred places outdoors, temples.
5 Unity and severe hierarchical order.	Multiplicity with certain hierarchical order.
6 Male priestly caste with a basic monopoly for sacred actions.	Priestesses and priests/kings. Monopoly only for exercise of the most sacred rites (e.g. sacred marriage).
Priests – laymen.	Priestesses – laypersons (?)
Priests are interpreters and mediators of the relation God-man.	Priestesses and Heroes – men are performers of the relation Goddess (female principle) – Heroes (male principle).
7 Dogmas.	No dogmas (?)
8 Repressive moral code with commandments and prohibitions.	Authoritative moral code with commandments and prohibitions.
9 Subordination and obedience to God.	Integration and obedience to the natural laws.
10 Political imperialism and mission.	No imperialism, no mission.
11 Linear comprehension of time and cult.	Cyclic-spiral comprehension of time and cult.
12 Repetitive character. Spiritual experiences of the founders are tried to be repeated.	Present character, with reflection on the tradition. Spiritual experiences are central.
13 Sacred actions as rite whose meaning hardly seems experienceable.	Sacred actions are magic in the sense of correspondence with (nature-) events.

Table 7.1
(*Cont'd*)

14 Dualistic view of world:	Holistic view of world:
(a) heaven and earth are divided	(a) heaven and earth are one
(b) man and woman are basically and completely different	(b) man and woman are different aspects of the one
(c) man stands above nature	(c) wo/man is part of nature
(d) God – devil	(d) the Goddess is good as well as evil
(e) body – spirit	(e) body plus spirit
(f) life – death – the beyond.	(f) life – death – survival in the sense of rebirth.

peatedly discussed 'religion' and 'magic' in her work (Göttner-Abendroth, 1980, 1982, 1988). It is notable that with Heide Göttner-Abendroth there is a clear contradiction in her use of these two terms. While in theory she refers to Goddess cult forms of matriarchy definitely as 'religion' ('Matriarchal religions in myth, fairy tales and poetry', Göttner-Abendroth, 1980), she refuses to apply this term to the spiritual activities of her own coven: 'But is *matriarchal spirituality* not something like a new religion? It is not. It is even the complete opposite to what is called religion, and its practice is a radical practical critique of religion' (Göttner-Abendroth, 1984, p. 171, original emphasis).[5] For, as her reasoning runs: '*Religions* are structures which typically did not arise before patriarchal societies' (Göttner-Abendroth, 1984, p. 171, original emphasis). On the one hand 'religion' is thus equated by Göttner-Abendroth with patriarchal religion, as is done by other feminist authors (e.g. Jannberg, 1983; Mies, 1984), but on the other hand it is none the less still used as an historical-systematic term.

As Heide Göttner-Abendroth's books are widely distributed and discussed within the German language area, I would like to take a closer look at her distinction between patriarchal and matriarchal religion. For this purpose I have taken definitions from her papers[6] and set them next to each other in table 7.1 to show how, according to Göttner-Abendroth, patriarchal and matriarchal religions differ.

After the matriarchal cult system has been defined, at least for the spiritual practice of her own coven, as the opposite of 'religion', Göttner-Abendroth writes:

> In this sense *matriarchal spirituality* is not a religion ... If it is about the goddess within, it is not about an almighty, omniscient super-mother in heaven, a counterpart to god the father, but this term means no more – and no less – than the spiritual capacity within each single woman herself, which expresses itself harmoniously *altogether* with the totality of intellectual, emotional, physical capacities. (Göttner-Abendroth, 1984, p. 171)

And this is not even a question of 'religion' but of 'magic'. 'In the magical-artistic rites we spontaneously create, it is less a rigid Weltanschauung which expresses itself, but individual experience' (Göttner-Abendroth, 1984, p. 172). However, Heide Göttner-Abendroth is conscious of the inevitable reproach of naively regressing to the cultural stages of humankind which have long been overcome. Thus she adds in defence of the also politically understood matriarchal spirituality: 'And this attitude, I think, as it is humanitarian and biophilic, is rational through and through, namely reasonable in the furthest sense of reason' (Göttner-Abendroth, 1984, p. 172). This last quotation already sounds rather different from the traditional understanding of 'magic': 'magic' is no longer an expression of an irrational-omnipotent attitude of human power *over* nature and the supernatural, but rather an expression of an attitude of solidarity and inclusiveness *within* nature and the supernatural.

On the whole one can say that within the German language area the term 'religion' is mostly used by feminists in the way of Heide Göttner-Abendroth when it is about the historical and current whole of the myth and rite of Goddess cults. They are called 'religion' on this level to make clear that they are (at least) equivalent to other religions. Yet as on the personal-practical level great value is put on the differentiation from patriarchal religions, the characterization of the individual and collective spiritual *practice* of today's women is mostly termed magic. Also frequently used is the popular pun *Magie* = *M*atriarchale Ener*gie* (magic = matriarchal energy).

An example of English usage (Starhawk)

The same procedure is also used in the English language as one can see in the texts of Starhawk, which have also become very popular in Germany. In the historical-systematic classification Starhawk talks about witchcraft as the 'ancient *religion* of the great goddess', whereas for the description of ritual practice she mostly uses the term 'magic' (Starhawk, 1979, 1982).

Starhawk's feminist comprehension of 'magic' does not limit itself to the characterization of spiritual practice alone, but like Heide Göttner-Abendroth and many other authors, she goes far beyond that: 'magic' determines the relation within the interaction of the triangle individual–society–religion as a whole, wherein now, instead of the exercise of power-over, it is rather about the gaining of power-from-within. Starhawk (1982, p. 13) defines 'magic' as 'the art of changing consciousness at will'. Furthermore she explains: '*Magic* is another word that makes people uneasy, so I use it deliberately, because the words we are comfortable with, the words that sound acceptable, rational, scientific, and intellectually correct, are comfortable precisely because they are the language of estrangement' (Starhawk, 1982, p. 13).

To cancel this estrangement, which characterizes the current desolate situation of the world and especially that of women, is the concern Starhawk ascribes to the term 'magic'. This concern relates to the private as well as to the political sphere for 'the heart of magic is a paradox: consciousness shapes reality; reality shapes consciousness' (Starhawk, 1982, p. 13; see also Starhawk, 1984, p. 32). While 'magical' techniques and behavioural attitudes thus change individual consciousness, there are – at least partially – new political realities created which on their part can again initiate processes of consciousness-raising, and so on. Connecting an intellectual political consciousness, stamped by Marxist and critical theory, with various old and new esoteric techniques of consciousness-extension, Starhawk thus creates a practical synthesis called 'magic' which is above all about the perception and the (re-)establishing of energy connections, connections which not only affect the individual, but also interhuman dimensions between person and nature, between the everyday world and the supernatural world.

Theoretical and practical consequences

In this understanding 'magic', in stark contrast to the traditional definitions quoted earlier, is not just about the domination, the power-over the supernatural, but about the mental–psychical–physical fitting-into the flow of energy which passes through every living reality and which feeds and reveals the power-from-within. In this way 'magic' becomes a synonym for the personal and collective way of transformation from 'estrangement' to 'immanence' (see Starhawk, 1984 for detail). This way of transformation could theoretically also happen without the concrete superstructure of a certain mythology or theology but it needs in practice, according to Starhawk, the symbol system of the Goddess for making experiences and ways of interaction communicable among each other. In this sense 'magic' could be called the fundamental connecting Weltanschauung and life-practice of feminist spirituality, whilst the 'religion' of the Goddess goes beyond by representing a mythical-theological superstructure. But it is not absolutely expected that this superstructure will necessarily be subscribed to by each participating person. Whether a person connects herself with the symbol of the Goddess and how she does so, remains the individual's concern within feminist spirituality. She could as well work with even any male god or be completely atheistic, as is indeed frequently the case in practice. Which godhead is individually revered is by no means unimportant, but it is not decisive. In fact, I have repeatedly met women who call themselves witch as well as Christian, Buddhist or other at the same time, and who do not consider simultaneous membership of different religious systems as contradictory at all. Of course there are also certain individuals within feminist spirituality who enjoy a rather high degree of authority as authors or teachers though none of them is comparable to the *absolute* authorities of Jesus or Buddha. Indeed until now every ever so timid attempt to present oneself as an authoritative religious founder has been quickly met with some distancing.[7] It is certainly not exaggerated to say that, considering the strongly distinctive distrust against the pretensions of divine or human authorities, feminist spirituality might even be described as an anti-authoritarian religion. The affiliation to feminist spirituality is not primarily expressed through the belief in the Goddess or in a mythical superstructure, nor through formally joining a movement or denomination, nor by following a prophetic authority, but its determining characteristic is the decision for a life-practice of 'magic' as the art of changing consciousness and reality at will.

Summary: Final Remarks

Undoubtedly feminist spirituality is a religious system. Its history, mythology and ritual practice are variously documented, its followers form a manifold living scene (for a summary, see Pahnke, 1991, ch. 4). Nevertheless a theoretical classification is not so easy because feminist spirituality struggles against the established categorizations of the study of religion (*Religionswissenschaft*). Some categories for the classification of feminist spirituality can be suggested:

1 It is a *feminist* system; i.e. here (contrary to almost all other subjects studied by the science of religion) a stronger value is put on the life and experience of women than that of men. This requires rethinking one's approach, because in the usual androcentrically established tradition of the science of religion there is little experience of researching feminism in theory and practice.
2 It is a *non-hierarchical* system, i.e. searching for the God/priest/individual stratifications, so familiar within Western culture, remains unproductive.
3 It is an *anti-authoritarian* system, i.e. the attempt to link the identity of this system with a certain collectively recognized, norm-giving authority fails.
4 It is a *counter-cultural* system, i.e. values and terms are completely differently handled to what is familiar to academics from elsewhere.

The last point concerns particularly the irritation caused by the use of the terms 'religion' and 'magic'. One of the most difficult problems of the science of religion concerns the adoption of the terms we are working with; nearly without exception these come from the language of the religions themselves. The evaluating connotations of the original use has frequently been transferred to the academic use of these terms. Thus the science of religion adopted the higher evaluation of 'religion' and 'magic' in its self-assessment. Within spiritual feminism, as I have shown by two examples, the term 'religion' is in a fairly contradictory way on one hand rejected (religion = patriarchal religion), but on the other hand it is reclaimed for one's own purpose (matriarchal religion, witches' religion). The term 'magic' has, in opposition to its common usage, nearly totally positive connotations, but is in its contents completely transformed and revalued. 'Magic' is no longer regarded as power-over the 'magical powers', but as power-from-within from and with those powers. It is the peculiarity of the transformation of the meaning of these terms that

the Western researcher does not meet them as a religious phenomenon of any far-off exotic culture, but as an expression of
members of the *same* culture to which the researcher belongs
him/herself. So it raises at the same time a question about the
language used in research. We have to note that in parts of our
own culture exactly those terms which are constitutive for our
work as academic researchers of religion have become ambivalent
and fragile and we will not be able to ignore this fact.

Moreover, the meaningful linking of the terms 'religion' and
'magic' with the process of human or divine power-exercise, as
it has been and is done by Christian theology as well as by
feminist spirituality, makes clear that the use of these terms com-
prises at the same time an explosive political dimension, because
both sides have extremely contrary ideas about power and its
right use. This is also a problem we must not avoid as academic
researchers of religion if we want to continue using these terms.

The theoretical insight that at the metalevel no distinction can
be made between religious and magical phenomena does not at
all lead to the result that these terms do not continue to exist
simultaneously in academic texts. I therefore consider it absolutely
necessary that we gain consciousness of the intended or un-
intended potential political consequences of our academic use of
language. For by using the terms 'religion' and 'magic' – and by
using them with very particular connotations – we take our own
position within the conflict between traditionalism and feminism,
whether we are conscious of it or not.

Notes

1 Cf. entry *Zauberei* (which is synonymously used with *magic*) in the
   Kirchenlexikon der kath. Theologie und ihrer Hilfswissenschaften,
   vol. 12, Freiburg 1901, p. 1870ff. Entry *Magie* in *Sacramentum
   Mundi* vol. 3, Freiburg 1969, p. 317ff; *Magie* in *Religion in
   Geschichte und Gegenwart* (RGG) vol. 4, 3. Aufl Tübingen 1960,
   p. 595ff; Entry *Religion* in *RGG*, vol. 5, 3. Aufl. Tübingen 1961,
   p. 961ff, especially 'IV B. Theologisch', p. 976ff. *Religion* in *Sacramentum Mundi*, vol. 4, Freiburg 1969, p. 164ff. *Religion* in *Staats-
   lexikon*, vol. 4, 7. Aufl. Freiburg 1988, p. 792ff. All these definitions
   refer to men as subjects of action, very seldom to women.
2 'Wer diese Religion nicht kennt, kennt keine, und wer sie samt ihrer
   Geschichte kennt, kennt alle.' ('Who does not know this religion,

knows none, and who knows it together with its history, knows them all.') A. von Harnack, cited in C. Elsas (1985, p. 259).

3 I would not like to enter the never ending debate about defining religion, but I keep in mind Seiwert's statement which is so self-evident at first glance. For a systematic examination of feminist spirituality, I consider the approaches of Kippenberg (1983) and Antes (1979) more promising, though not unproblematic, supplemented by epistemological reflections like those of Harding (1986) or Meyer-Wilmes (1990). For a general assessment of feminist spirituality within the esoteric scene in Germany cf. Pahnke (1989).

4 I have pointed this out elsewhere (Pahnke, 1991). 'Spirituality' is used here in the sense of more recent language usage, not in the sense of the catholic philosophical tradition.

5 Translation of all Heide Göttner-Abendroth quotations are by the author of this essay.

6 Especially Göttner-Abendroth: Kalliope – das Epos der grossen Symbole, in Göttner-Abendroth (1988). Also the title 'Du Gaia bist Ich. Matriarchale Religionen früher und heute' in Pusch (1983).

7 This remark concerns disputes around and with, for example, Heide Göttner-Abendroth, Judith Jannberg, and Zsuzsanna Budapest.

References

Antes, Peter 1979: 'Die Religionswissenschaft als humanwissenschaftliche Disziplin. *Zeitschrift für Missionswissenschaft und Religionswissenschaft* (ZMR) 63, 275–82.

Bellah, Robert 1964: Religious Evolution. *American Sociological Review* 29, 358–74.

Biezais, Haralds 1978: Von der Wesensidentität der Religion und Magie. *Abo Akademi*, 55, 3, 7–25.

Budapest, Zsuzanna 1979/80: *The Holy Book of Women's Mysteries I and II*: Los Angeles: Susan B. Anthony Coven no. 1. (German: *Herrin der Dunkelheit, Königin des Lichts. Das praktische Anleitungbuch für die neuen Hexen.* Freiburg. 1987.)

Döbert, Rainer 1973: *Systemtheorie und die Entwicklung religiöser Deutungs-systeme.* Zur Logik des sozialwissenschaftlichen Funktionalismus, Frankfurt: Suhrkamp.

Elsas, Christoph 1985: Selbstverständnis/Forschungsdisziplinen/Methoden der Religionswissenschaft. In Jürgen Lott (ed.), *Sachkunde Religion II*, Stuttgart: Kohlhammer, 253–82.

Fowler, James 1981: *Stages of Faith: The Psychology of Human Development and the Quest for Meaning.* San Francisco: Harper & Row.

Göttner-Abendroth, Heide 1980: *Die Göttin und ihr Heros.* Die matriarchalen Religionen in Mythos, Märchen und Dichtung, München: Frauenoffensive.

Göttner-Abendroth, Heide 1982: *Die tanzende Göttin.* Prinzipien einer matriarchalen Ästhetik. München: Frauenoffensive.

Göttner-Abendroth, Heide 1984: Matriarchale Ästhetik, ein ganzheitlicher Prozess. In Rüdiger Lutz, *Frauenzukünfte. Ökologbuch 3*, Weinheim: Beltz, 166–75.

Göttner-Abendroth, Heide 1988: *Für die Musen.* Neun Essays. Frankfurt: Zweitausendeins.

Harding, Sandra 1986: *The Science Question in Feminism.* Ithaca: Cornell University Press. (German: *Feministische Wissenschaftstheorie*, Hamburg, 1990.)

Heiler, Friedrich 1961: *Erscheinungsformen und Wesen der Religion.* Stuttgart: Kohlhammer.

Jannberg, Judith 1983: *Ich bin eine Hexe.* Erfahrungen und Gedanken. Aufgeschrieben von Gisela Meussling. Bonn: Edition Die Maus.

Kippenberg, Hans 1983: Diskursive Religionswissenschaft. In B. Gladigow and H. G. Kippenberg (eds), *Neue Ansätze in der Religionswissenschaft.* München: Kösel, 9–28.

Meyer-Wilmes, Hedwig 1990: *Rebellion auf der Grenze.* Ortsbestimmung feministischer Theologie, Freiberg: Herder.

Mies, Maria 1984: Tantra – Magie oder Spiritualiät? *Beiträge zur feministischen Theorie und Praxis*, 12, Köln: Eigenverlag, 82–98.

Oser, Fritz and Gmünder, Paul 1984: *Der Mensch. Stufen seiner religiösen Entwicklung.* Ein strukturgenetischer Ansatz, Zürich: Benzinger.

Pahnke, Donate 1989: Postmoderne Religion: Ökologisch, magisch, weiblich? In Peter Antes and Donate Pahnke (eds), *Die Religion von Oberschichten*, Marburg: Diagonal Verlag, 243–56.

Pahnke, Donate 1991: *Ethik und Geschlecht.* Menschenbild und Religion in Patriarchat und Feminismus, Marburg: Diagonal Verlag.

Pusch, Luise (ed.) 1983: *Feminismus. Inspektion der Herrenkultur.* Frankfurt: Suhrkamp.

Seiwert, Hubert 1986: What constitutes the identity of a religion? In Victor Hayes (ed.), *Identity Issues and World Religions*, Bedford Park: The Australian Association for the Study of Religions, 1–7.

Starhawk, 1979: *The Spiral Dance: A Rebirth of the Ancient Religion of the Great Goddess.* New York: Harper & Row. (German: *Der Hexenkult als Ur-Religion der Grossen Göttin. Magische Übungen, Rituale und Anrufungen.* Freiburg. 1983.)

Starhawk, 1982: *Dreaming the Dark. Magic, Sex and Politics.* Boston: Beacon Press. (German: *Wilde Kräfte. Sex und Magie für eine erfüllte Welt.* Freiburg. 1987).

Starhawk, 1984: Bewusstsein, Politik und Magie. Ein Aufruf zum Handeln. In Rüdiger Lutz (ed.), *Frauenzukünfte. Ökologbuch 3.* Weinheim: Beltz, 32–40.

8

Spirituality, Consciousness and Gender Identification: A Neo-Feminist Perspective

Felicity Edwards

The purpose of this essay is to offer an outline of neo-feminist spirituality (which is by no means for women only), to trace its relations to consciousness and gender identification and to indicate its wider implications in terms of justice, peace and global sustainability. Neo-feminist spirituality is best understood in its evolutionary setting, where it is assumed that the cosmos is not static and complete but dynamic and evolving, and that at least part of the goal of cosmogenesis, biogenesis and the rise of humankind is that human persons should be able to actualize their full humanity. It is also assumed that the mark of the fully human person is the integral practice of love (as in Jesus, but also, for instance, the great compassion, *mahākaruṇā*, of Buddhism). What is entailed is a new and higher type of consciousness based on, but transcending, our present normal level of awareness. It manifests itself as self-giving (love) rather than the customary self-centredness which misinterprets how things are and reacts to the other out of fear.

The origin of this present understanding of neo-feminist spirituality is in the work of the American catholic philosopher and theologian, Beatrice Bruteau, who uses particularly the terms 'neo-feminine consciousness' and 'participatory consciousness'. In the main sections of this essay I am drawing largely upon her insights, with full acknowledgement to her and with the strong conviction that she is right. Bruteau is an established exponent of the thought of both Pierre Teilhard de Chardin in the West and Sri Aurobindo in the East, and draws particularly on the work of the former, as I do myself in the application and elaboration of Bruteau's thought. Such application and elaboration is an exercise to which, happily, in the preface to her undated collection of previously published essays, she invites all who find her ideas attractive.

The context of neo-feminist spirituality links with the way the question of gender and religion is now being raised as part of a unique, critical situation, which, instead of being merely local or national, is correctly described as global. It is global particularly because networks of intricate interdependencies are being recognized at every level, across the planet. Contemporary physics recognizes that the world is a web or network of complex interrelationships and this principle applies not only to the physical world but to the human, social and personal worlds also. We are grasping the fact that interrelationships shape existence (cf. Schaeffer, 1990, p. 67), and that the world we have is the world we are having to take responsibility for making. And it is also becoming clear that there is a direct relationship between social justice and environmental sustainability. In fact the overall global crisis which has to be contended with is such that, unless a high degree of social justice is rapidly implemented, it is all too possible that our earth will be unable to escape from its present crash-course towards self-annihilation. Injustice and oppression can all too easily be terminal; all people and all things are interconnected. It is, however, the nature of crises not only to threaten with diminishment and death but also to present unique opportunities for transformation and transcendence. Rodger Walsh, who is a transpersonal psychologist and Western Theravada Buddhist, suggests that this present global crisis may be seen as a potential 'evolutionary catalyst' (Walsh, 1985, p. 83) challenging us to ever deeper and more significant personal and social transformation.

What I am suggesting, *inter alia*, in this essay is that social justice and environmental responsibility, on a scale global enough to avert planetary holocaust, are dependent on a significant evolutionary shift to the next level of consciousness in a significant number of human beings. Neo-feminist spirituality addresses precisely this shift, doing so particularly in its context of the necessary breakthrough in the present social structures of domination and subservience which so seriously vitiate so much of human life. Here the link is drawn with gender identification, as well as with psychological and systemic racism. For gender polarization, male/female, engendering male dominance and female subservience, has become linked with racial domination, according to a logic which clearly emerged in the history of psycho-social development. Indeed the gender paradigm might be said to operate, often in the unconscious layers of the psyche, as a model for the racial. Further, we need to be realistic about the fact that conditioning in the deep levels of the psyche cannot be changed on command. It is no good telling people that they must love each other and be compassionate to one another; consciousness must change.

An earlier version of this paper was published in 1989 in *The Journal of Theology for Southern Africa*, having been written for the Southern African context where its theme applies *par excellence*. In that version I suggested that if gender and race could be transcended in Southern Africa, if we who are aware of the possibilities could just begin to do this, not only would it generate peace and viability in the Southern African region but it would also be a considerable contribution to the global advancement of human evolution. Now, in 1993, I am even more confident of the validity of this suggestion. Holographic theory confirms what the mystics of the past knew experientially, as a felt sense, that what happens in any one part affects the whole.

Sexual Polarization and the Denigration of the Feminine

In previous papers (Edwards, 1981, 1984) I have argued for what I called holistic feminism, positing the mutual complementarity of male and female, masculine and feminine. But now, taking into account some of the processes by which human consciousness and social structures have evolved, it has become clear that there is much more here than I had previously imagined. Femininity and masculinity certainly are polar concepts representing complementary aspects of human beings. But as Bruteau (1977) points out, what is crucial is how the 'axis of polarity' is delineated and used contexually.

In the ancient pre-classical world and in early Hebrew culture there was no notion of splitting up the human person into constitutory elements of body and soul. A person was one whole. Later, particularly as Orphic influence impinged on classical thought, the human person came to be viewed dualistically as made up not so much of complementary, but rather of mutually opposed elements: body and mind (or body and spirit, or body and soul). Such dichotomizing was harmful enough to human wholeness and to the understanding of liberation, for it was thought that it was the soul or spirit that was to be liberated from the body. But when the body/mind dualism became assimilated to the already existing female/male dualism of the classical world, the repercussions for women were disastrous and far-reaching. Women came to be identified with matter, the body and sensuality, while the association of the male was with spirit, mind and purity. The body (feminine) was perceived as dragging down the soul or spirit (masculine), contaminating its moral integrity and preventing its liberation back into the world of pure spirit (cf. Ruether, 1972).

This anti-feminine, anti-body, world-negating interpretation was generally accepted without question by the Church Fathers and came to be built into Christian theology. There was nothing 'Christian' about it. In fact it was grossly anti-incarnational and a prime example of culture suppressing an integral part of the gospel. As body was inferior to spirit, so woman was inferior to man, and as the body had to be subordinated to the mind, so the woman had to be submissive to man. This became the generally accepted pattern in the West. Christian missionaries spread it to the colonies of the Western empires and it is still part of our world-view today, charged as it is with the harmful psychological attitudes that accompany the perceptions of superiority and inferiority. And then the female/male polarity became popularly ingrained in people's minds such that female is to male as weak is to strong, passive to active, dark to light, and so on. These polarities have become a major part of the paradigm according to which persons are perceived and valued, and according to which social structures operate, with the resultant deep-seated, often unconscious discrimination against those who are not male. All too easily racial differentiation became subsumed into this female/male polarity, with consequently dehumanizing discrimination against people who are not white. A new perception is urgently needed, one that corresponds to fact and which values all people in their totality, rather than being so dangerous a distortion of the truth.

A New Perception of Sexual Polarity

To bring about change we have to re-form our perception of the human person, and indeed of being. For while the *polarity* between masculine and feminine is an energizing reality of a kind, we do not have to go along with the popular (and false) *polarization* between female and male, black and white. We can choose to re-image sexual polarity, to experience it differently. There is the option of relating to one another with a different kind of consciousness which is at the same time a new level of spirituality.

Contrary to the popular dichotomization (male, strong; female, weak, and so on) there is the established fact that both masculinity and femininity coexist in each person. It is a matter of both/and, not either/or. Both masculinity and femininity need to be integrated and lived. Realizing this, we are then able to make the deliberate move of selecting a different and more appropriate axis than the strong/weak, dominant/submissive one, to envision the masculine/feminine polarity co-existing in and between all. The orientation of the male/female axis needs to be such that polarity is recognized as the dynamic it is, without this leading to polarization and the consequent perception of superiors and inferiors. So crucial is this to our well-being, our evolutionary future and our liberation that Bruteau states uncompromisingly that, 'A significant future will not be born until the orientation of the axis itself has been shifted' (Bruteau, 1977). Her suggestion is that the orientation of the axis be perceived between, for instance, the specialized and the general, the analytic and the intuitive, and between the focused and the holistic.

The significance of this new orientation of the axis is that it does not impute value to one pole over the other. We all have both masculine consciousness which is specialized, analytical and focused, and feminine consciousness which is general, intuitive and holistic. There is then no question of one being stronger or weaker than the other. The differences are important of course, but the point is that since neither pole is more valuable than the other, neither has connotations of superiority or inferiority.

Unconscious and Conscious Evolution

Bruteau, like Teilhard de Chardin in the West and Sri Aurobindo in the East, has a clear sense of human evolution towards an ever higher order, beyond mental consciousness and into the spiritual or supra-mental. Regarding the physical body, we humans have prob-ably evolved as far as we are going to; physically we have peaked. Evolution is now at the level of human awareness (cf. Bruteau, 1980, p. 124). Jung affirmed that it is our destiny to create more and more consciousness, which is another way of expressing it.

What is more, evolution up to humanity has proceeded *un-consciously*, more or less along the lines set out by the Neo-Darwinian microbiologists et al. From the present stage on, however, evolution will have to proceed *consciously*, for we, the evolvers, are self-conscious or reflexively conscious beings, con-scious of being conscious. To progress now we need to know what the options are and then freely, responsibly and consciously to opt for transformation. Opting for greater awareness (or higher consciousness) means simultaneously moving into the fuller, deeper dimensions of personhood for which we are destined. The responsibility for making what Teilhard calls 'the grand option' (Teilhard de Chardin, 1969), opting consciously into the ongoing evolutionary process, is encapsulated in his frequently quoted dictum, 'We are evolution'. Rodger Walsh spells it out: in the present global crisis, seen as catalytic, we are challenged 'to relinquish our former limits and be and become and contribute all that we can' ... and to 'choose, both individually and collec-tively, conscious evolution' (Walsh, 1985, p. 85).

Masculine Consciousness as Evolutionary Advance

At the present stage of evolution masculine consciousness is the norm. It is most valuable and women operate with it as well as men. Frequently a woman is valued only if she can operate like a man, with masculine consciousness, in 'a man's world'. With masculine consciousness the societal structures are patriachal, authority being imposed from above downwards. The beings making up the society each find their identity in, and as, their own ego, perceiving themselves and one another as separate, isolated individuals, each outside and apart from the other. In the West particularly, the goal of being 'an individual' is frequently set up as the highest that can be attained.

Prior to the rise of this masculine mode, human consciousness was different. Not a great deal is known of this very ancient period but it is thought to have been a time of strong group consciousness, or co-consciousness. This is to say that there was much less distinction between self and other, and people would identify themselves primarily in unity with the group or tribe. Membership of the group was what conferred meaning, and life would have been concretely experienced and integrated in terms of the tribe and its common myths and rituals. In parenthesis, it is significant that today's adolescents and teenagers, who have not yet reached full egoic individuality, tend to find their identity in their peer group and have to dress, behave and think the same as the others in the group, or else they do not belong. This looks very much like a parallel between ontogenesis (development of the person) and phylogenesis (development of the human race).

In this period prior to analytic, logic thinking, it was emotions, feelings and psychic sensitivity which predominated and characterized the general consciousness. Here, also, fertility was of primary importance, and women rather than men stood for and symbolized the fertility that would ensure the continuance of the group and its supply of livestock and crops. In this ancient period then, the prevailing consciousness was feminine and Bruteau (1977) calls it 'palaeo-feminine consciousness' to distinguish it from the neo-feminist consciousness which will characterize the now dawning, post-masculinized, post-egoic stage.

An important point that Bruteau makes here is that neo-feminism is not simply a recovery of all that the previous feminism (palaeo-feminism) stood for. To go back to the old feminism as some contemporary feminists wish to do, is regressive, or retrogressive, rather than evolutionary. It is the task of neo-feminism as it arises now evolutionarily on the other side of masculine consciousness, to take over and express the best of both the earlier feminism (like its strong sense of interconnectedness, concreteness and unity) and of the masculinism current today (like its clear incisive, rational thought processes). In this, neo-feminism is different from the present masculine age which took over little of the earlier feminism and indeed represents a repudiation of much of it. But in that case the rejection of the palaeo-feminine modality was an important evolutionary advance which at the time was necessary and appropriate.

Typical of masculine consciousness is to work by separating and excluding, so that the awareness becomes increasingly focused, sharp and concentrated. As developments unfolded and the world of human experience became larger and much more highly complex than the original tribal environment, it was necessary to make ever finer distinctions, to separate out and categorize according to perceived characteristics. So this masculine type of consciousness was just right to render the world manageable, to put it in order and to get control of it. Bruteau points out how such focused consciousness would have encouraged the cultivation of the kind of psychological attitudes which would continue and reinforce the focusedness – in other words, it has positive survival value – and thus masculine qualities and virtues that went with it also came to be highly valued. Among the latter are the ability to organize society to one's own advantage, and the motivation to dominate other groups of which one is not a part. Once these attitudes were established, egoic consciousness may be said to have evolved. At the same time it was this masculine consciousness that led to the development of modern science and technology which was, for all that may be said against it, an important and necessary stage in evolutionary advance.

Masculine Consciousness and Injustice

Masculine consciousness operates particularly by analysing, selecting and separating. From the world of experience which is fundamentally an interconnected whole it abstracts that part in which interest lies at the time, and it focuses on that to the exclusion of all else experienced. This perceptual strategy is extremely useful for grasping and working with details and was definitely an advance on the diffuse co-consciousness of the palaeo-feminine era, where awareness was predominantly of the whole and its patterning, but was much less conscious of distinctions and categories. But when masculine consciousness has selected and focused on one valued characteristic or feature, it tends not only to ignore but to disvalue or negate all other values (cf. Bruteau, 1977).

Interestingly, the way we have recently begun to do theology *contextually* is a significant indication of the shift away from masculine consciousness. Masculine-style theology tended to operate by abstraction, focusing on particular selected areas and excluding all else. The area of interest, now a concept, would be removed to the ivory tower, the monastic cell or the air-conditioned office, there to be worked on according to (usually) Aristotelian logic. Being cerebral, working with concepts to the exclusion of concrete reality, is typical of masculine consciousness. Contextual theology, by contrast, is much more in the neo-feminist mode, where none of the incisive rationality of masculinity is lost, but where there is, as much as possible, the constant emphasis on the experience of the whole and on the interconnectedness of everything happening. This means being in touch with concrete event, process and structure, with historical and cultural reality, with socio-economic factors and so on, as well as with ideational and conceptual influences.

Bruteau suggests that at least a possible source of social injustice may be traced to the working logic of this typically masculine consciousness as it inexorably moves through abstraction and negation, and she gives the following example (Bruteau, 1977): (1) if, for instance, *sharpness* is the characteristic selected as of interest, all other qualities of the object in question (colour, origin, etc.) are screened out, excluded, negated; (2) all sharp objects are seen as belonging to one category or class, and are perceived as different from objects which are *not-sharp*; (3) unsharp objects are negated, rejected, not used; (4) sharp objects are prized over against not-sharp ones and so emotions become involved, approval being given to the sharp object and scorn to the non-sharp one; (5) next, the person who owns or is associated with the sharp object comes to be highly regarded while the person with the opposite association is scorned; (6) finally, as all sharp objects are seen as comprising a category or class, so all persons possessing them come to be perceived as a class. The class itself, now a social class, comes to be honoured and those belonging to that class expect to receive privileges which are totally unrelated to the sharpness of implements. They proceed to scorn other members of the society not of their class and to dominate them. Bruteau (1977) aptly calls this 'the error of misplaced abstractness'. While abstraction is useful where it is appropriately applied, it is not only an enormous mistake but also a serious injustice to relate to concrete persons in terms of abstracted categories. This is an extremely important and relevant point. With this perceptual and moral error the domination paradigm is set up and both 'inferiors' and 'superiors' tend to go along with it, more or less unconsciously supporting the system. But persons are not abstractions. They are concrete. Bruteau points out cogently that so long as society at large persists in using abstractions as criteria of the value of persons, it is psychologically impossible not to go on perpetrating injustice.

To overcome injustice our perception, our awareness, has to change so that instead of perceiving persons in terms of abstractions we perceive them in their concreteness, and experience all reality and all people in their interconnectedness – which is, of course, the view of reality presented by contemporary physics, as well as being what we are endeavouring to do in contextual theology. In Bruteau's thesis it is precisely this movement forward into neo-feminine awareness, that brings liberation, both for those who are unjustly discriminated against and who all too easily support structural injustice by behaving with resigned submissiveness, and for those who perpetuate injustice and claim privilege. There is no escaping the fact that the dismantling of the domination paradigm of social relations involves a qualitative leap forward in consciousness.

This explains why it is that if women try merely to replace men, as is the strategy of some 'hard' feminists, this simply perpetuates the domination paradigm, with a different group doing the dominating and no real advance being attained. They are simply buying into a masculinized system. It explains also why replacing one governing regime by another would not necessarily deal with the dehumanizing effects of domination and injustice.

The Alternative

Clearly the argument of this essay hinges on the question as to what precisely enables this evolutionary breakthrough, this transformation, this new and higher level of consciousness. Bruteau finds the origin of it in what she terms the Holy Thursday Revolution (Bruteau, 1980: 125). This she sees as the achievement of Jesus in dismantling the structures of domination and submission, to which his disciples, like everyone else, subscribed. He did this by refusing to accept it at all – or perhaps, as I would prefer to suggest, by accepting it and transforming it in himself, as he seemed to do with all evil. In any case, what he did was to replace it, in action, by an altogether different way of being and way of perceiving. John 13 tells of the event where he, the Lord (the *Dominus*), washed the feet of his disciples in what was not so much a condescending reversal of roles as the deliberate destruction of the paradigm of domination. When Peter protests, Jesus responds by saying: 'Unless I wash you, you cannot have a part [*meros*] in me, you cannot participate in me.' And he had previously alerted them: 'You know that the rulers of the Gentiles lord it over them, dominate them ... It shall not be so among you', linking this with his own liberating role as Son of Man who came 'not to be served but to serve and to give his life as a ransom for many' (Matt. 20: 25–8).

The group comprising Jesus and his disciples was to be perceived no longer as consisting of superior and servants, but of friends participating in one another. In this way Jesus replaces domination by participation, and later that night at supper he dramatized the giving of himself for, and into, them. Here is the alternative – a totally different paradigm of relationship: *mutual participation*. The image Jesus gives of himself as the vine of which the disciples (or learners) are the branches, triggers the awareness of his new 'mutual selfhood' (Bruteau, 1977), and this is reinforced as he says that they, his friends (not servants), are *in* him and he is *in* them.

This is definitely a new level of consciousness, awareness of others not as separate, as is our normal (masculine) perception of how things are, but awareness rather of mutual indwelling. Bruteau (1977) calls this 'participatory consciousness', and the new paradigm of social relationships which replaces domination and submission she terms 'the communion paradigm' (Bruteau, 1980, p. 128 ff).

Neo-Feminist Spirituality as Participatory Consciousness

In Bruteau's thesis (Bruteau, 1977) participatory consciousness is the essence of neo-feminism. Its principal features and effects are the following.

The value of persons

There is the point already alluded to, that in contrast to masculine consciousness which values persons on the basis of abstracted qualities and hence tends to treat them as if they were abstractions, neo-feminist awareness relates to the person as a whole. It appreciates the whole concrete existence of the person within the reality of all the person's relationships: it is holistic. Most importantly, it values each person equally. Neo-feminism also uses, where appropriate, the masculinist perception of qualities and abilities, and for practical purposes, like getting a job done, people can be ranked with respect to these. Some people are better at some things than others. But this will be done within neo-feminist participatory awareness which is much wider and fuller than masculinist focused selectivity, and so the person will be perceived as a person, a whole within the whole, rather than being valued solely in terms of the abstracted attribute under consideration.

Affirmation of others, rather than negation

Masculine consciousness distinguishes 'this' from 'that', and negates whatever is not selected for focused interest. This is useful and neo-feminism will utilize that ability where appropriate. But unlike the masculinist mode, in neo-feminist awareness these distinctions are not extrapolated such that I identify myself as not being you, and vice versa, which ends up as mutual negation. Instead, identity is established by mutual affirmation. This engages and activates a quite different type of energy, positively affirming the other and seeking the other's good, giving oneself away and receiving from the other affirmative, life-giving energy. This is loving one another as Jesus loves us, the very actualization of his being in us and of our being mutually in him and in one another. This is participatory consciousness, the integral practice of love. In this my identity is no longer exclusively encapsulated within the skin-defined boundary which I would otherwise experience as separating 'me' from 'the other'. In this larger, expanded state of awareness my boundary is enlarged to include the other, and others; and then, of course, the other is not other all (Bruteau, 1983; 58). This unity is the unity of the mystical body which is the ground of our mutual participation and the reality of our *koinonia*.

It is important to see that in this unity there is no question of personal uniqueness being swamped, absorbed or dissolved.

Rather, as Teilhard de Chardin was fond of saying, 'unity differentiates'. Participatory consciousness establishes me as more truly myself, not less (cf. Bruteau, 1980, p. 130).

A *new perception of selfhood*

When masculine consciousness abstracts attributes and properties, and identifies people according to these, it is looking from the outside and the people so identified are being regarded more as objects than persons. Teilhard speaks of this as 'tangential' energy relations, the relating of outside to outside which characterized the earlier stages of evolution, and is as objects are related to each other, exterior to exterior. But in perceiving our self in terms of a collection of attributes we are in fact dealing with a pseudo-self, for this listed collection of characteristics and roles is not what we deeply and existentially are. Thomas Merton effectively inveighs against this false self, saying that it is no more than a mask and an illusion. In terms of neo-feminist consciousness he is certainly right, for experiencing oneself conceptually in terms of roles and attributes blocks access to who one really is. The deep existential self is profoundly different from the superficial or pseudo-self. It is known in living experience, in the present, rather than at the level of concepts abstracted by the mind. Words cannot contain it. It is what Bruteau (1977) calls 'a luminous aliveness', and 'awareness of being vitally an "I" ... an indefinable being who is sheer life-energy', and in this consciousness others are similarly perceived. This is what Teilhard spoke of as 'radial energy', that which flows and radiates from our deep, transcendent centre outwards, 'a spring welling up to abundant life'. This is spiritual experience; it is moving evolutionarily beyond masculinist consciousness, which is mental, conceptual consciousness *par excellence*, to the level of spirit. Spirit is beyond or above or deeper than the ego developed in the separatizing masculinist mode. This mutual participation is infinitely energizing and the energy available is of quite a different order to the self-seeking motivation that comes from the ego competing against other egos to get to the top.

Secondly, this is spiritual experience because it reflects, as we humans are able, the intra-Trinitarian relations as each person of the Trinity is who he is, as he gives himself into the others. Thirdly, it is spiritual experience because, as transcendent, it also underlies, subserves, applies to all life, such that the cosmos is perceived as a dynamic interconnected whole in which every whole within the whole is in connection with the Source whom we call Father. Only in connection with the Source, with the Spirit of God, can one recognize this.

Bruteau is careful to distinguish this existential perception of 'I am-ness' as an intuitive insight, as being quite different from the gut feeling which many swear to today as being their access to what is true and right. Gut feelings are, by definition, perceptions on the existential level that are unaccountable, not understood, and as such they belong to the level of palaeo-feminine consciousness, remnants of which are still operative in us and into whose archetypal patterns our behaviour sometimes lapses. By contrast, neo-feminist consciousness, epitomized in this luminous, radiant aliveness, the perception that 'I am I insofar as I am in you' (Bruteau, 1980, p. 129) has all the incisive clarity and rationality of masculine consciousness, along with the holistic inclusiveness of the feminine. This identifies it as a definite advance in the evolution of consciousness, and to live this way is to love.

Notes

This essay is based on a paper published in the *Journal of Theology for Southern Africa* vol. 66, March 1989, under the title, 'Neo-feminist spirituality: an evolutionary perspective'. The essay was revised in 1993 and is published here with permission.

References

Aurobindo, Sri 1963: *The Future Evolution of Man*. Pondicherry: Sri Aurobindo Ashram.

Bruteau, Beatrice 1977: Neo-feminism and the next revolution in consciousness. *Cross Currents*, XXVII, 170–82. (Also published in *Anima*, Spring 1977.)

Bruteau, Beatrice 1980: Freedom: 'If anyone is in Christ that person is a new creation'. In F. A. Eigo and S. E. Fittipaldi (eds), *Who Do People Say I Am?*, Pennsylvania: Villanova University Press, 123–46.

Bruteau, Beatrice 1983: The living one: transcendent freedom creates the future. *Cistercian Studies*, 18, 1, 42–58.

Edwards, Felicity 1981: The doctrine of God and the feminine principle. *Journal of Theology for Southern Africa*, 37, 23–37.

Edwards, Felicity 1984: God from a feminist perspective. In W. S. Vorster (ed.), *Sexism and Feminism in Theological Perspective*, Pretoria: University of South Africa Press, 36–57.

Ruether, Rosemary Radford 1972: *Liberation Theology*. New York: Paulist Press.

Schaeffer, J. 1990: The liberation of creation. *Ecumenical Review*, 42, 1, 61–7.

Teilhard de Chardin, Pierre 1969: The grand option. In P. Teilhard de Chardin, *The Future of Man*. London: Collins, Fontana, 39–63.

Walsh, Rodger. 1985: *Staying Alive: The Psychology of Human Survival*. Boston and London: Shambala, New Science Library.

Part II

Empirical Investigations

Introduction

Ursula King

The empirical investigation of religious life and practice yields many new perspectives and research results when gender differences are fully taken into account. However, gender-sensitive inquiries also raise many new problems in acute form. This is well brought out in Kim Knott's account in chapter 9 where she addresses the vexed question of what is the most appropriate methodology for empirical work in religious studies when undertaken from a feminist perspective. What is the methodological inheritance of women scholars in religion who want to do research on women's religious rituals, roles and experience in different religious traditions? Is the scientific study of religion, as practised and conceptualized so far, inimical to a critical feminist perspective? Do we have to seek the reconceptualization of the entire field of religious studies where most research has remained at a general, non-gender specific level until now? Knott touches on these questions when she interrogates herself about the inadequacy of established, so-called 'objective' research procedures on entering into new research relationships when studying a local Hindu temple, a new religious movement or young Asian women in Britain. Her account deals not only with methodology but describes a personal research journey which involves new insights and experiences and raises ethical issues about the responsibility of the researcher. The rich texture of her work leads her to formulate some important points regarding future research on women and religion, and her recommendations express a commitment to process rather than results alone.

My own contribution in chapter 10 takes up further the issue of female scholarly identity, already raised in Knott's paper. Women scholars in religion have few role models to follow but the development of their individual and group identity suffers from the additional constraint that the past contributions of women to the study of religion are not acknowledged in the official histories of religious studies. I give some examples from conferences and encyclopaedias and discuss three British women pioneers in the modern study of religion to which quite a few examples from other countries could be added. Rediscovering the voices of women in the study of religion provides a rich terrain for historical research today.

The need for a continuous hermeneutics of suspicion directed towards established histories and textbooks is not only evident in the history of religions but applies equally to Christian theology and its foundational writings, whether produced by the so-called 'Church Fathers' or by medieval writers. In her survey of recent women's studies of the Christian tradition in chapter 11, Kari Elisabeth Børresen shows how the critical category of gender transforms our understanding of God, men and women. She underlines the importance of comparative research and stresses the pioneering nature of women's scholarship on the Christian tradition and its importance for a more fully developed understanding of human genderedness.

A rich field of empirical data is provided by the last two chapters which deal with women in contemporary African and Japanese religions. As very little or no work at all is available on these in standard books on women and religion, these chapters represent pioneering contributions at the level of description while at the same time touching on some of the theoretical issues raised in other chapters of the volume.

A growing interest in new religious movements exists today but few are the studies which give attention to women in new religious movements. Rosalind Hackett is particularly interested in the power of women in the new independent churches in Africa and her chapter (chapter 12) examines the presence of different women founders and women leaders, and the general membership and participation of women in new religious movements in Africa today.

The last chapter, by Marilyn Nefsky, discusses the traditional place of women in Japanese religions, that is in Buddhism, Confucianism and Shinto, and includes a brief discussion on women in contemporary new religions and in popular religious practice in Japan. Such examination demonstrates the powerful forces of patriarchy which mostly are still fully in place, especially in Japan. At the level of popular religiosity, Japanese women are deeply involved in religion, but only the future can tell whether religion will also bear the seeds of liberation for them.

Encompassing both empirical and theoretical perspectives, the different contributions to this book show each in their own way how the new insights of gender inquiry – in this case primarily focused on female gender – produce a new sensitivity and consciousness which leads to many new research investigations and results. Attention to the importance, meaning and differences of gender are now transforming and enlarging the field of religious studies whereas the results of gender critical studies in religion also make a valuable contribution to the further development of more inclusive gender studies.

9

Women Researching, Women Researched: Gender as an Issue in the Empirical Study of Religion

Kim Knott

It is the vexed question of methodology, 'the theory and analysis of how research does or should proceed' as Sandra Harding (1987, p. 3) puts it, that I wish to address in this essay.[1] Women have been busy studying women and religions, critiquing religious systems for androcentrism, challenging scholars for their sexism. How far have we gone in religious studies in investigating either the tools of the trade or the general principles for using them? In the past, women's religious experiences were, by and large, invisible. This is still true in many studies. What produced this? Do women scholars, when they do their work of researching and writing about women, do something different? Do they use different principles and tools? Most of us work with an awareness of the need to focus on women's experiences so long ignored, but is this the only difference? If not, what are the others, and how can they be explained? Do they constitute a new methodological approach, and, if so, how does it stand in relation to the methodological inheritance of religious studies?[2] Women in other disciplines have made considerable progress in attempting to answer these questions in their own fields, in sociology, anthropology, literary theory, philosophy, the biological sciences, and feminist theology.

First, however, I have to reinvent the wheel for myself as I believe we all have to in matters methodological. It simply will not do to be told what one is doing or ought to be doing when conducting one's research. This was a mistake I made in the past and I hope not to do it again. As Werblowsky (1975, p. 145) wrote: 'Some of the best methodological clarifications come not from *a priori* legislators but from active researchers stepping back for a moment, putting some distance between their nose and the grindstone, and asking themselves what exactly they and their colleagues have been and are doing, and how they should best proceed.' Readers should not expect 'the best methodological clarifications' in what follows, but only some observations and reflections on a research journey, in particular on one involving the practical methods of ethnography and interviewing.

In recent years I have become increasingly concerned about my integrity as a researcher with regard to my feminism and my methodological inheritance: the 'scientific study of religion'.[3] Reflections on this inevitably had consequences for my work, particularly my ethnographic fieldwork and writing. I have always been interested in how I was doing my research and why I was doing it that way. Frequently, I wondered if it was a 'good' and 'sound' way. Was it ethically and politically justifiable? I wondered if what I was doing was what I was taught I should do, and if I wasn't, why wasn't I? Should I change my ways?

In order to consider these questions more seriously, I pursued several strategies:

(a) I made changes in my use of traditional methods, trying particularly to find a satisfactory interview procedure and different ways of writing up my research.
(b) I recorded on tape a methodological autobiography: my reflections on the research projects I had undertaken, memories of my thoughts and feelings during them and my present interpretation developed with the benefit of hindsight.

(c) I undertook some interviews with women colleagues, friends and students who were engaged in fieldwork, particularly in the field of religious studies.

(d) I read extensively feminist reflections on methodology from a range of disciplines.

The question of personal and intellectual honesty became one of my particular concerns in relation to all stages in the research process, and I was interested to see how others had tackled this issue.

This essay will focus initially on my research journey, illustrated with reference to the methodological autobiography mentioned above. This will be supplemented by comments made by other women researchers reflecting on comparable experiences. The final section will offer a more analytical assessment of central issues in relation to wider debates in the feminist literature. A bibliography of the works by writers with whom I have felt myself to be in dialogue is included, though I have not discussed their contributions explicitly in this paper.

Reflections On Our Research Journeys

I wish to begin with a quotation:

> In the same way as a scientist tries not to influence the results through the interruption of unnecessary human factors, so the observer must act as a medium, despite the constant pressure of his background and personality. In this way, he would, as nearly as possible, elucidate the religious practices and ideas of the group he studies in terms of their value for the society from which they stem. Obviously, the end product could not be a completely 'true' account of what went on and what it meant. But, taking into account the two translations through which the material must pass, from believer to observer and from observer to reader, this scheme would hopefully represent the nearest possible approximation.

This rather conventional and sexist passage was the product of my own pen, writing, in 1977, for an MA essay on the role of the observer in religious studies. It represents me articulating what I felt was expected of me, what I felt was academically correct.

In my recent methodological autobiography, I recorded the following about that early training:

> We learnt about the objective science of religion, being an observer, laying one's own beliefs on one side, being aware of the things within oneself that were affecting the methods one was employing and the way one was interpreting the material – but we were concerned particularly with *not* interpreting the material, if we could possibly not do so. That is to say, we were schooled very much in the tradition of understanding the material and describing it, but not explaining it in the sense of giving some overt outsider's interpretation of what was going on. The account that we were to present was the believer's own account uncontaminated by theoretical interpretations that did not come from that account ...
>
> So that was where I got my basic schooling in the science of religion, and I think that had a major impact on the way in which I pursued all sorts of things, not just research, but all sorts of human relationships in my own life, in the sense that I got well-practised, through research, through the methodological principles of doing it, in laying on one side my views about things, and I learned to be a good listener. (Knott, 1990, p. 1)[4]

This is where I started my research journey and, from here, I went out 'into the field'; I began an investigation into the local Indian Hindu community.

From the beginning this produced interesting situations which caused me, as both a woman and a trained student, to reflect on the research process. On the first visit to the Hindu temple, I went with a friend, which:

> was good because it gave support on one's first ethnographic visit, but also – him being a man – he was the person who was focused upon in the research setting. That is to say, the pandit, who we were talking to and who was explaining to us about Hindu ritual, talked directly to my friend even though he knew that I was the one doing the study. In addition, he made it quite clear, during the interview, what he thought about young women and their moral conduct. I can't remember the details of it, but certainly he thought that young unmarried women should be virgins ... (Knott, 1990, p. 2)

Another factor of the research which ensued from my gender in these early days was my identification with the women of the

community, though they were often not the people who interpreted Hinduism for me. Nevertheless, I sat with them, ate with
them and played with their children. I felt most comfortable
doing this, and, indeed, it was expected by everyone that I would
do so. Also, being a women meant that 'I wasn't treated as "the
great researcher", I wasn't put on a pedestal or asked to do
public speaking' on behalf of the community as many of my male
colleagues were (Knott, 1990, p. 2).

Some of the women researchers I have interviewed recently made
similar points from their own experiences. One woman found it
both a hindrance and a help being accompanied by her husband
on research visits. It brought her additional respectability, but he
became the focus of attention in the interview setting. As a married
woman with children, she, like several other women I asked,
found these social roles useful in establishing a working relationship with women and men, young and old. The women felt they
were seen as non-threatening. One, who had interviewed young
women, said: 'They talk to you like a mother ... a mother figure,
but not how they would talk to their own mother.' Women researchers who were not mothers sometimes felt at a disadvantage,
particularly in situations where they were working cross-culturally
with other women. It seemed that their lack of experience in
motherhood made them alien to some. One referred to herself as
'neuter'.

Most of the women felt very positive about their gender in
relation to the research process, one seeing it as a vehicle for
access to disadvantaged social groups, several seeing it as a way
in to gleaning more personal information, less 'facts and figures'
about people. One saw femaleness as less confrontational: the
male researcher 'sets his face' and is more assertive, thus setting
up a more aggressive power relationship, especially with other
men. All the women felt they were good at blending in, getting by
unnoticed in many fieldwork situations, just as I had done when
researching local Hindus.

During this early period of research, I would say I had no
problem in keeping my own beliefs on one side, in accordance
with the principles of scientific phenomenology which I had been
taught, but I did have other problems with the methodological
baggage:

Sometimes one was beset by questions like 'how should I answer
this person's enquiry about my own religious background?', for

example, or 'should I do what this person has asked me to do?', 'should I be of service in this way or will this in some way contaminate the field?'. So ethical questions arose from the beginning, and I would say that one answered those in a very *ad hoc* way, whatever seemed best at the time, bearing in mind all the possible things, although I certainly never properly wrote them up in the end ... Whereas in another context we might say, 'What are your guts telling you about this situation?', you never let your guts tell you anything in a fieldwork situation, or [at least] that it is never formally done, although of course all the time you were doing things as a result of what you were feeling. But you were never allowed to acknowledge that in any way. (Knott, 1990, p. 3)

I had understood the phenomenological approach to be a relatively simple one of bracketing oneself and one's own beliefs, separating them from the field of inquiry. The theory sounded straightforward. However, putting it into practice often meant both resisting being oneself in the research situation and pushing to one side unexamined qualms and anxieties. One could hide behind the phenomenological approach, resist responsibility and openness. One could also miss the chance to learn useful things from one's feelings. In other interactional situations, including, for example, counselling, group work, training and management practice, one's feelings are seen as valuable assistants in the process of information gathering and relationship building. At the time I felt that I was a bad phenomenologist because my thoughts and feelings kept making their presence felt. Either I had badly misunderstood the phenomenological approach itself or its exponents had failed to convey its principles and practices to me in such a way as to train me to function as a researcher with integrity and self-confidence.

I should not be too hasty, however. Integrity in research comes through experience, not merely through reading good books on the subject. In terms of my own journey, I must now skip some stages. Some time after my doctorate I undertook research on the Hare Krishna movement, a new Hindu sect. This work forced me to enter into a dialogue with members – and with myself – on questions of spiritual truth, and subjectivity and objectivity, not least of all because here was a group with an active mission to people of my own age and type. Looking back at this period, I recorded that:

one cannot separate oneself off from the research that one is doing ... The costs to oneself are very great. How can they not be? All human relationships have the potential to be transforming. Why should research relationships be any different? (Knott, 1990, p. 6)

It was at this time that I began to gratefully acknowledge the personal growth that came as a result of fieldwork where I had previously tended to see the impact on my personal feelings as a sign of my weakness, a failure to be a successful medium for the messages of others. Other women researchers I have spoken to also had interesting insights on this issue. One saw her research with older women as 'not just an intellectual journey, but a personal journey as well'. Another said, 'I get a lot out of doing interviews. They can challenge you and make you think about your own philosophy ... and they can affirm you in your own experiences.'

The Hare Krishna research also made me think hard about the final production of a research essay or book. Whose is it? Whose agenda does it represent? How much consultation should one seek before publishing it, and how much notice should one take of comments made about it? What lessons can be learnt about power, even about oppression, from this exercise? Working on the Hare Krishna movement taught me a great deal about the need to represent a multiplicity of experiences. In relation to women's roles, for example, some devotees had taken on board very traditional Indian views of women's role; others had adopted a qualified-feminist view which could be held in conjunction with Hindu Vaishnavism. And critics of the movement, of course, had expressed a variety of modern Western views, some feminist. I had a responsibility to make sense of these many voices, to fit them together with my own.

But it was very challenging because I was very unwilling to give up my feminist interpretation, but couldn't and wouldn't always have stated it because of wanting the believers' views to come across. But I was unwilling to give it up as a way of seeing the world and a way of explaining roles and past experiences ... But obviously, it's not adequate for understanding Hare Krishna women and their location and perspectives on that location because other interpretations have to come into that. And that was very interesting, dialoguing with people on those many perspectives ...

and seeing that those perspectives were discrete and represented many voices. Hare Krishna women, for example, would try to answer questions about Western feminism in the context of their own viewpoint. They would say, for example, that Hare Krishna women could do any job, that men will share work in the home. So that was, in effect, an answer to Western feminists' questions about the true role for women. So all those voices were already in dialogue within the movement, irrespective of whether I was there. (Knott, 1990, p. 8)

We were all aware of the differences of viewpoint, sometimes trying to negotiate these, sometimes to express their contradictory nature. But I was aware of my own impact and agenda, and theirs, and the differences and similarities between these, and had to take care to write all these into the final account (Knott, 1987). It represented an attempt to deal with the issue of poly-vocality.

To move on now, a major project in recent years, using interviewing rather than ethnography as such, was work on the place of religion in the lives of young Asian women in Britain (Knott and Khokher, 1993). This involved understanding the context and, as far as possible, the production of young women's views about religion. I tried to achieve this through the interview process, by asking particular questions, creating an appropriate setting, and using a quasi-counselling style. As usual, the re-search was interdisciplinary in nature and proceeded somewhat anarchically. The way I set up this project was derived from my previous experiences in research and by my thoughts and views at that time about the research exercise, human relationships, women, power and spirituality. Not everything that I did was intentional, however. Some things happened by design; other things by accident or serendipity.

One issue which became important to me during this project was reciprocity.

You want people to have an opportunity to speak about what they want to speak about, what they are interested in, and what they view as important – just to have their lives seen as interest-ing and central – but you have to offer yourself in doing that. You can't just expect that people will be willing to speak about themselves without knowing who you are, without also being free to ask you questions. It has to be reciprocal. And it has to be that from the beginning. You can't just do that at the end. ...

And if that was damaging to the research then it would just have to be damaging because I saw that responsibility as more important than actually extracting the information. You can only legitimately extract information on the basis of an honest relationship, as far as you can have one as a researcher and an informant. And if you don't have that relationship of honesty, where you have spoken about yourself or allowed questions to be asked about yourself, then the person is giving of themselves without knowing how that information might be used or whatever, and that is dangerous and could lead to all sorts of misuse and abuse. (Knott, 1990, p. 10)

So, at the beginning, space would be given for inquiries and, at the end of our time together, a further opportunity would be presented for questions and comment, queries and curiosity. As I saw it, this was a vital part of managing the research relationship. It was not friendship, as some researchers have suggested. It was, admittedly, temporary and conditional; but, as far as I could make it so, it was also reciprocal and just.

'The important thing, as I saw it, was not just getting the information, but was the doing of the process' (Knott, 1990, p. 11). The means of research seemed as rewarding and worthwhile as the ends. Interviewing could be enjoyable and fulfilling for both parties. The relationship and the opportunity for disclosure, for most of those interviewed, could be seen as a legitimate part of the informal research contract. Often we think of the end result as the purpose of the research process, the monograph, the bringing to the public eye, through the academic enterprise, of a particular community, a particular viewpoint: 'I'm going to write it up as a book.' But, very often, the participant community or individuals cannot recognize themselves in a final product in which the authorial voice, however self-consciously reticent or fair, has control. It is important then for the process itself to have value.

For this to be true in my own work, it was necessary to leave open the possibility of unexpected and unaccountable topics coming up in the interview. It was not possible to know in advance how a subject like religion – with its attendant themes of death, divine judgement, family practice and tradition, and personal spirituality – would affect each person. Flexibility and a degree of courage in being willing to deal with sensitive personal matters were required. I do not wish to claim too much for this kind of interviewing process, but I saw it as offering, in some cases, an element of healing as well as opportunities for self-disclosure, experimentation with ideas and opinions, and a listening and uncritical ear.

There is one further research experience, this time related particularly to the task of writing up fieldwork, which I wish to mention in relation to my research journey. In 1989, I was asked to rework and bring up to date a previously unpublished paper I had worked on five years before on a low-caste Gujarati community in Leeds. I thought this would be relatively simple: undertaking several new interviews; updating some facts and figures. This did not prove to be the case. For one thing, a rereading of the previous paper revealed a striking personal political orientation underpinning the basic argument. While I remained in sympathy with this viewpoint, I was struck by its covert presence in what I had seen as a straightforward ethnographical account. It forced me to accept and reflect on my role in shaping a potentially public account of a real community of which I was not a part.

My second overriding feeling was that any paper I might write in 1989 should attend further than the earlier one to a consideration of women in the community. I thought that I would simply be able to append this or add it in at some point during the course of the account. I struggled unsuccessfully to do so, and realized that this had a great deal to do with both caste itself as an institution and the way academics had written about it, focusing generally on hierarchy, occupational interdependence, public status and power. Justice to women's work and contribution could not be done if they were merely fitted into an existing debate about the historical and social location of a caste argued in somewhat conventional terms.

> The women's world that I wanted to describe somehow did not fit into the existing structure of the essay. I didn't really know what to do about that. And ultimately I realized that this was largely to do with the process of my having done research on this community. The way I'd started was one way, the way I'd finished was another. The new work, thinking more about women, did not fit into the old way of seeing this particular group. The considerations I was using latterly were not the same as those I used formerly. And these two things could not be fitted together without an explanation of that. So I had to have two pieces of work, one after the other, with an explanation [all within the same account]. And that was the only way to do justice, not only to women within this community, but also to my own academic process.

> It was very interesting because it gave one the opportunity to look back over one's research career to see the way in which not only one's view of the world but one's way of doing research actually changed: The things one was prepared to do, the questions one was asking of one's methodology ... these were different ... I didn't want my view, a view that I'd held in the mid-1980s ... to go down in history as the way the Mochis of Leeds actually are. I wanted it to be recognized that this was one story from the point of view of one woman at one point in her life which actually didn't speak to her five years later as a sound account of this community. I had to rewrite it in such a way that those things were said. (Knott, 1990, p. 15–16)

This is a further example of the way in which the academic process can be seen to have an impact on the collection and presentation of the accounts of others. Again, issues of ethical procedure had come to the fore and resulted in a transformation of my work (Knott, 1994).

Thinking about this and earlier projects has encouraged me to produce a list of general principles for myself, my own guidelines for research practice. I list them here, not because I think anyone else should adopt them wholesale, but because they illustrate how methodological reflections on our past work may be fed into the construction and practice of future projects. There are ten points and they illustrate a commitment to process rather than results alone. They are the need for the following.

1 *Feminist considerations to be applied in the choice of subject matter and informants.* This does not mean that only women should be researched, but that discernment is vital in understanding the context and relationships involved in the intended research area. This is important principally because so much research in the past has participated, often unwittingly, in entrenching women and other groups in powerless and marginal positions. Academic accounts contribute to building a public account of the world. Taking this power seriously requires a commitment to avoiding rewriting received wisdom and, instead, to opening up new possibilities.

2 *Responsibility in the structuring of the ethnographic process.* We might like a clean sheet or blank tape which might be filled with the informant's own words and thoughts, unprovoked and uninfluenced by the researcher, but, in fact, we have a responsibility to guide and structure the interview while seeking not to impose ourselves or our own views.

3   *Honesty and openness.* These should be striven for without shifting the focus from the researched to the researcher.

4   *A commitment to the experience of each and every informant, hence, an appreciation of differences.*

5   *An awareness of context.* It is important to seek to understand the political, social, cultural and economic forces at work within the research area which have an impact on researcher and researched alike.

6   *An awareness of one's own feelings and thoughts throughout, and a consideration of their role in the research as a whole.*

7   *Accountability and partnership.* It is important to explain what one is going to do with the research, making informants, wherever possible, part-owners of your account of their story.

8   *A listening ear, but also the participation of the whole self where necessary.*

9   *A willingness to be changed in the process.*

10   *An ethical and responsible attitude to the questions of power and hierarchy in the relationship between researcher and researched.* This may require, for example, discerning and perhaps serving their needs and interests, honouring their agenda and balancing it with an awareness of one's own.

Throughout, self-awareness and a realistic and balanced attitude are essential. We have suffered from too many unexamined methodological ideals in the past.

These are some of the principles that I see guiding my ethnographic work. Partly, they have been informed by the reading I have continued to do on methodology, particularly on feminist – and to a lesser extent postmodernist – responses to this. But, as I have tried to illustrate with this narrative journey, they have come out of my continuing reflections on and experience of research practice. We all do this. We could all tell a story like this one, a story demanded not just by the need to acknowledge the centrality of the author in the practice of research and production of a text, but desperately required by our students who wish to make sense of the research process, who deserve to see that it is frequently *ad hoc*, often 'unscientific', subjective while striving to be objective, painful yet challenging.

Theoretical Issues: Women Researching

Let me quote for the last time from this methodological auto-biography, though, of course, what I have missed out is probably as important as what I have kept in.

> If you see someone drowning while you're doing your fieldwork and they're part of the community you're studying, and if you're a strong swimmer, do you stand on the bank and watch them drown or do you dive in and save them? You know, fieldwork is active work, where we are in relationship with people. Questions of responsibility, ethics, politics come into those things. How can they be left on one side? They may be able to be left on one side for half of the time, but there will be occasions which come up that demand that we be ourselves in the interview situation. To try not to be, to pretend not to be, to pretend to be behind a glass screen, to pretend not to be in relationship with somebody is a vain hope and is unethical. It's like a child putting its head under a cushion and hoping you can't see it – because it can't see you! Not being ourselves is a denial of the responsibility we take in hearing this person's story, of the contract that we make with that person, of the gift that they are offering, of the time that they give. (Knott, 1990, pp. 11–12)

But, is this responsibility a legitimate part of the 'science of religion'? Not the way I learnt it, I believe. But, of course, both natural and social science are themselves continually under scrutiny with regard to questions of 'good' and 'bad' science, rationality, and subjectivity and objectivity, not least of all in feminist and postmodernist discourses. In addition, in our own field, scholars of *Religionswissenschaft* have exercised themselves on these subjects in recent decades (Wiebe, 1978, 1988; Honko, 1979; Tyloch, 1990). Attention has been focused, particularly, on the dilemma of the discipline with regard to its roots in the phenomenological approach. What is the distinction between phenomenology and theology? Are we being theological phenomenologists? Does the concept of 'eidetic vision' point both ways – depending on one's interpretation – at the crossroads of objectivity and subjective involvement? The battle for the 'true' phenomenology rages on. Recently, in response to this, some scholars have discussed the need to move towards a social scientific methodological framework for religious studies, thus moving away from the traditional but problematic arena of interpretative phenomenology (Tyloch, 1990).

There are two points I wish to make here. First, it is important to make clear the difference between a confessional approach within religious studies (which might be called theological phenomenology) and an ethical approach to tackling questions about how to do religious studies such as I am suggesting here. Such an ethical approach will no doubt be related to my view of the world and of human relationships, but this ethical approach is directed, not at a consideration or judgement of data, but the application of methods. Secondly, while I recognize the difficulties inherent in applying a phenomenological approach, I feel it would be irresponsible to run away from the challenge presented by it. As an ethnographer and interviewer, I work largely within a social scientific framework informed particularly by the practical methods of anthropology and sociology. However, the question of interpretation, the need to explain, to consider the place of subjective judgement and the value of objectivity are no less present there. Leaving phenomenology behind would not resolve the difficulties (currently some postmodernist anthropologists are expressing an interest in it themselves), because social science faces the same questions and dilemmas as the 'science of religion', the discipline of religious studies. In my opinion, it is the personal reflection of researchers on their own methodological approach and the academic debate which ensues when these approaches are aired which is of the utmost value. Different ways of working and variety of opinion seem to me healthier than the attempt to resolve the methodological argument within religious studies once and for all, thus favouring the approach of some scholars and marginalizing that of others.

It is not my intention, then, to throw out science wholesale or to reject phenomenology. Both, and the interrelationship between the two, have taught me many good lessons which I continue to apply in my research practice, though, at times in the past they served to confuse me, to make me feel guilty about my approach and churlish about how much I was willing to share as a human being in the research exchange. However, they do not permit some of the principles I outlined in the last section. This brings us to feminism, as it is that discourse which I see principally informing my current practice.[5]

Although it is important to resist pretending that all feminists think alike on questions relating to the theory and analysis of what they do (Harding, 1987, 1989), most feminists who have discussed methodology point out that what a feminist perspective offers is an awareness and critique of domination and oppression in society and the continuing operation of androcentrism and sexism at all levels. This is not just the diagnosis of a condition, but a commitment to resistance and change. This includes tackling these issues in all areas of the academic process, particularly ensuring that our epistemology and methodology do not hamper us in seeing and giving voice to women's experiences and allowing them to be the instruments of change. This also requires an awareness of the practical methods we use in our research and their relationship to the aims we have as academics and as members of society. Undoubtedly, this is a political orientation which, inevitably, has an impact on issues such as choice of subject matter, research aims, research relationships, production and use of the final product, and interpretation.

It is the issue of interpretation, I believe, which requires most careful and honest dealings and serious collegial discussion, and I can do little more than mention it briefly here. The religious studies tradition, generally, encourages a standing back from interpretation. This has been seen as a virtue by some; by others it has been criticized as an impossible idealistic stance. In my view, while it provides an important check against the unnecessary bias and self-centredness of the researcher at the expense of the experience of the researched, at times it becomes a mask behind which the researcher can hide, thus failing to recognize her place in the research process.

Despite its overtly political starting point, contemporary feminism, as I see it, offers a potential and challenging solution to the methodological problem of interpretation precisely because it recognizes difference, inequality, and the plurality of experiences.[6] At its best then, it ought to be able to facilitate the presentation of varying points of view irrespective of their nature. This, of course, has to be applied with care and rigour, or it leads to the promotion of one view above others. A feminist methodological orientation, as I see it, despite the bias the name suggests, can offer a realistic rather than an idealistic approach to questions of interpretation because it faces difficult issues of power and justice head on rather than resisting them for fear of contaminating the data. It is not its uncovering of social or political inequalities, but its general methodological principles – such as those listed in the section above or discussed in the work of Mies (1983), Stanley and Wise (1983a, b), Harding (1987), the October 29th Group (1989), and Reinharz (1992) – that are of use in this.

However, self-reflection, realism and intellectual honesty are required for its application to be successful.

Many of the principles I mentioned in relation to my own work are listed in other discussions of feminist theory and method. In those, there are also lively arguments and sometimes differences of perspective on a variety of questions from objectivity to interpretation, research objectives to use of results, power and responsibility, and the degree of friendship between those involved in the research process. It is quite clear that there can be no single feminist 'method' despite the common ground that can be found in feminist diagnoses of social situations and a shared interest in finding responsible and appropriate ways of working.

I believe that, as feminists, we would do well to stop worrying about whether we are shifting paradigms or establishing a single method or a new science (Harding, 1987; Strathern, 1987; Longino, 1989), particularly as such changes can be identified only *post factum*. This is to use benchmarks provided in the competitive world of academic life which may be of dubious contemporary value. Instead, we might continue to examine and share our processes, recognizing and learning from what we as women do and have done in our research and writing (e.g. through reading and analysing women's scholarship on religions past and present, women's ethnography, personal narratives – our own and those of the women we are studying – and women's fiction and other forms of expression). As feminists, we will continue, no doubt, to face criticism and judgement from mainstream scholarship – as strident, biased, ineffective, unscholarly, conservative or radical – because we will continue to use a variety of practical and personal methods, to elicit a range of dissonant views, to present these against a complex background of social and political conditions, with a plurality of explanations and interpretations. Very little of this will seem hygienic, neat or harmonious. This is good for two reasons. First, no one will want to incorporate it and claim it for his or her own. Secondly, human reality does not conform to these ideals. In fieldwork we need to work with the premise that there is no single version of the truth, no single method, no single interpretation, but some basic principles for good practice that are themselves personally constructed and tested, sharpened through honest discussion and wise to the impact of oppression and suppression on those researched and those researching.

Notes

1 Harding (1987, p. 2) distinguishes between the terms 'method' and 'methodology', seeing the first as 'techniques for gathering evidence', and the later as 'the theory and analysis of how research should proceed'. I have followed her usage in this essay.

2 In Britain, the discipline commonly known as *Religionswissenschaft* or the science of religion goes by the name of religious studies. This name generally signals the application of historical and/or phenomenological approaches, though many are also in dialogue with social scientific methods.

3 Since I wrote the conference paper from which this essay is derived Rita Gross, in an appendix to a recent book (Gross, 1993), has reflected on her own journey as a feminist scholar of religions. Her thoughts are of great relevance to all women working in this field.

4 This and later passages from my methodological autobiography are in 'the spoken voice' as they are transcripts from a tape recording. I have not changed the grammar or syntax to make them more acceptable for the academic ear.

5 I have focused on feminist accounts of methodology here, despite my interest in and debt to the work of some postmodernist writers, particularly in the field of anthropology. The latter work, while it helps us understand and explain many aspects of the authorial voice in the research exercise, including some aspects of power relations, does not sufficiently concern itself with the nature of inequalities in society as a whole, in the studied societies or in the academic community. It is not sufficiently con-textual (Mascia-Lees et al., 1989).

6 Early feminist approaches have been accused subsequently of a failure to observe the impact of differences, for example of class and race among women. As a result, a commitment to the variety of experiences has become an intrinsic part of contemporary feminist work.

Bibliography

Bell, C. and Roberts, H. (eds) 1984: *Social Researching: Politics, Problems, Practice*. London: Routledge & Kegan Paul.

Beteille, A. and Madan, T. N. (eds) 1985: *Encounter and Experience: Personal Accounts of Fieldwork*. Delhi: Vikas.

du Bois, B. 1983: Passionate scholarship: notes on values, knowing and method in feminist social science. In G. Bowles and R. D. Klein (eds), *Theories of Women's Studies*, London: Routledge & Kegan Paul, 105–16.

Bowles, G. and Klein, R. D. (eds) 1983: *Theories of Women's Studies*, London: Routledge & Kegan Paul.

Brown, K. McCarthy 1991: *Mama Lola: A Vodou Priestess in Brooklyn*. Berkeley CA: University of California Press.

Clifford, J. and Marcus, G. (eds) 1986: *Writing Culture: The Poetics and Politics of Ethnography*. Berkeley CA: University of California Press.

Finch, J. 1984: It's great to have someone to talk to: the ethics and politics of interviewing women. In C. Bell and H. Roberts (eds), *Social Researching*, London: Routledge & Kegan Paul, 70–87.

Finnegan, R. 1992: *Oral Traditions and the Verbal Arts: A Guide to Research Practices*. London: Routledge.

Geertz, A. 1990a: The study of indigenous religions in the history of religions. In W. Tyloch (ed.), *Studies on Religions in the Context of Social Sciences: Methodological and Theoretical Relations*, Warsaw: Polish Society for the Science of Religions.

Geertz, A. 1990b: As the other sees us: on reciprocity and mutual reflection in the study of Native American Religions. XVI Congress of the International Association for the History of Religions.

Geertz, C. 1988: *Works and Lives: The Anthropologist as Author*. London: Polity Press.

Golde, Peggy (ed.) 1986: *Women in the Field; Anthropological Experiences*, 2nd edn. Berkeley CA: University of California Press.

Gross, R. 1983: Women's studies in religion: the state of the art, 1980. In P. Slater and D. Wiebe (eds), *Traditions in Contact and Change*, Waterloo, Ontario: Wilfrid Laurier University Press, 579–91.

Gross, R. 1993: *Buddhism After Patriarchy: A Feminist History, Analysis and Reconstruction of Buddhism*. Albany, NY: State University of New York Press.

Halpin, Z. T. 1989: Scientific objectivity and the concept of the other. *Women's Studies International Forum*, 12, 3, 285–94.

Harding, S. (ed.) 1987: *Feminism and Methodology: Social Science Issues*. Milton Keynes: Open University Press.

Harding, S. 1989: How the women's movement benefits science: two views. *Women's Studies International Forum*, 12, 3, 271–83.

Hess, B. B. and Ferree, M. M. (eds) 1987: *Analysing Gender: A Handbook of Social Science Research*. London: Sage.

Honko, L. (ed.) 1979: *Science of Religion: Studies in Methodology*. The Hague: Mouton.

King, U. 1986: Female identity and the history of religions. In V. C. Hayes (ed.), *Identity Issues and World Religions*. Bedford Park: Australian Association for the Study of Religions, 83–92.

King, U. 1990: Religion and gender. In U. King (ed.), *Turning Points in Religious Studies*. Edinburgh: T & T Clark, 275–86.

Klein, R. D. 1983: How to do what we want to do: thoughts about feminist methodology. In G. Bowles and R. D. Klein (eds), *Theories of Women's Studies*. London: Routledge & Kegan Paul, 88–104.

Knott, K. 1977: The observer in the study of religions. MA essay, Department of Theology and Religious Studies, University of Leeds.

Knott, K. 1987: Men and women, or devotees? Krishna consciousness and the role of women. In Ursula King (ed.), *Women in the World's Religions, Past and Present*, New York: Paragon House, 111–28.

Knott, K. 1990: Methodological autobiography. Unpublished transcript of a recording made on 22 August 1990.

Knott, K. 1994: From leather stockings to surgical boots: the Mochis of Leeds. In R. Ballard (ed.), *Desh Pardesh: The South Asian Presence in Britain*, London: C. Hurst & Co, 214–30.

Knott, K. and Khokher, S. 1993: Religious and ethnic identity among young Muslim women in Bradford. *New Community*, 19, 4, 593–610.

Longino, H. E. 1989: Feminist critiques of rationality: critiques of science or philosophy of science? *Women's Studies International Forum*, 12, 3, 261–9.

Mascia-Lees, F. E., Sharpe, P. and Cohen, C. B. 1989: The postmodernist turn in anthropology: cautions from a feminist perspective. *Signs: Journal of Women in Culture and Society*, 15, 1, 7–33.

Mies, M. 1983: Towards a methodology for feminist research. In D. Bowles and R. D. Klein (eds), *Theories of Women's Studies*, London: Routledge & Kegan Paul, 117–39.

Millman, M. and Kanter, R. Moss (eds) 1975: *Another Voice: Feminist Perspectives on Social Life and Social Science*. New York: Anchor Books.

Oakley, A. 1981: Interviewing women: a contradiction in terms. In H. Roberts (ed.), *Doing Feminist Research*. London: Routledge & Kegan Paul, 30–61.

October 29th Group 1989: The October 29th Group: Defining a feminist science. *Women's Studies International Forum*, 12, 3, 253–9.

Okely, J. and Callaway, H. (eds) 1992: *Anthropology and Autobiography*. London: Routledge.

Personal Narratives Group 1989: *Interpreting Women's Lives: Feminist Theory and Personal Narratives*. Indianapolis: Indiana University Press.

Rabinow, P. 1986: Representations are social facts: modernity and post-modernity in anthropology. In J. Clifford and G. Marcus (eds), *Writing Culture*, Berkeley CA: University of California Press, 234–61.

Reinharz, S. 1983: Experiential analysis: a contribution to feminist research. In D. Bowles and R. D. Klein (eds), *Theories of Women's Studies*. London: Routledge & Kegan Paul, 162–91.

Reinharz, S. 1992: *Feminist Methods in Social Research*. Oxford: Oxford University Press.

Ribbens, J. 1989: Interviewing – an 'unnatural situation'? *Women's Studies International Forum*, 12, 6, pp. 579–92.

Roberts, H. (ed.) 1981: *Doing Feminist Research*. London: Routledge & Kegan Paul.

Shechter, P. et al. 1987: A vision of feminist religious scholarship. *Journal of Feminist Studies in Religion*, 3, 1, 91–111.

Shostak, M. 1981: *Nisa: The Life and Words of a !Kung Woman*. Cambridge, MA: Harvard University Press.

Shostak, M. 1989: 'What the wind won't take away': The genesis of Nisa: The Life and Words of a !Kung Woman. In The Personal Narratives Group (ed.), *Interpreting Women's Lives*. Indianapolis: Indiana University Press, 228–40.

Srinivas, M. N., Shah, A. M. and Ramaswamy, E. A. 1979: *The Fieldworker and the Field: Problems and Challenges in Sociological Investigation*. Delhi: Oxford University Press.

Stanley, L. and Wise, S. 1983a: *Breaking Out: Feminist Consciousness and Feminist Research*. London: Routledge & Kegan Paul.

Stanley, L. and Wise, S. 1983b: 'Back into the personal' or: our attempt to construct 'feminist research'. In G. Bowles and R. D. Klein (eds), *Theories of Women's Studies*, London: Routledge & Kegan Paul, 192–209.

Strathern, M. 1987: An awkward relationship: the case of feminism and anthropology. *Signs: Journal of Women in Culture and Society*, 12, 2, 276–92.

Tyloch, W. (ed.) 1990: *Studies on Religions in the Context of Social Sciences*. Warsaw: Polish Society for the Science of Religions.

Waardenburg, J. 1973: *Classical Approaches to the Study of Religion*, 2 vols. The Hague: Mouton.

Walton, H. 1990: My mother is ill: an experiment in feminist research. *Working Papers in Applied Social Research*, University of Manchester.

Werblowsky, R. J. Z. 1975: On studying comparative religion. *Religious Studies*, 11, 145–56.

Whaling, F. (ed.) 1984–5: *Contemporary Approaches to the Study of Religion*, 2 vols (Humanities; Social Sciences). The Hague: Mouton.

Wiebe, D. 1978: Is a science of religion possible? *Sciences Religieuses/ Studies in Religion*, 7, 5–17.

Wiebe, D. 1988: Why the academic study of religion?: Motive and method in the study of religion. *Religious Studies*, 24, 403–13.

10

A Question of Identity: Women Scholars and the Study of Religion

Ursula King

The study of religion has seen many changes in recent years, but it still remains deeply rooted in an androcentric framework which women scholars continue to question and challenge. This androcentrism is particularly apparent in the historiography, methodology and conceptual tools of the discipline which express the marginality and invisibility of women as both subjects and objects in the study of religion. Feminist critical consciousness is not yet an integral part of the commonly accepted horizon of religion as an academic discipline. However, many contemporary women scholars have demonstrated through their work that careful attention to gender differences significantly alters the gathering, description and analysis of data and can lead to important new directions in different academic disciplines.

To begin with some general observations, it is striking to see how far the study of religion itself is not only marginalized, but mostly invisible in women's studies courses, whether in the United States, Britain, or other European countries. The very considerable work of feminist theologians and religious scholars by and large has not been integrated into the curricula of women's studies courses nor is it taken into account in the formulation of feminist theory concerning research methodology or the restructuring of academic disciplines. One only has to consult such works as Dale Spender's (1981a) *Men's Studies ·Modified. The Impact of Feminism on Academic Disciplines* or the work by Ellen Carol DuBois et al. (1985), *Feminist Scholarship. Kindling the Groves of Academe* to become aware of the marginality of feminist work on religion within overall feminist scholarship. The book *A Feminist Perspective in the Academy. The Difference it Makes* (Langland and Gove, 1981) contains a welcome chapter by Rosemary R. Ruether on 'The feminist critique of religious studies', yet this is less concerned with theoretical issues in the study of religion as a whole than with Christian theological culture and educational praxis. More helpful methodological reflections regarding the content and form of religious studies are found in Carol P. Christ's contribution to Christie Farnham (1987), *The Impact of Feminist Research in the Academy*, entitled 'Toward a paradigm shift in the Academy and in religious studies'. Carol Christ states there: 'Though women scholars are a small minority in the field of religious studies, and feminist scholars an even smaller group, we have been very visible in recent years' (p. 62). Yet this visibility is perhaps more a North American than a global phenomenon; it has not yet sufficiently transformed either the study of religion as a discipline nor general feminist reflections on the construction and dissemination of knowledge inside and outside academic structures.

It is also somewhat misleading when Carol Christ maintains that religious studies is a relatively new academic discipline which has separated itself from a denominational context only during the past twenty-five years (Christ, 1987, p. 61). This again may primarily apply to the North American context, for it is not true of Europe where the independent study of religion has been pursued for more than one hundred years, as is amply documented by Eric Sharpe's (1986) history of *Comparative Religion* and the source material printed in Jacques Waardenburg's (1973) *Classical Approaches to the Study of Religion*. The study of religion has traditionally often been referred to as 'history of religion', understood in a wider sense, and international congresses comprising many sections concerned with the study of different religions and with methodological issues have been held since 1900 (see the list of conferences in King, 1984, p. 49). Thus the time scale of the development of religious studies is much longer than twenty-five years. The modern study of religion has developed as a comparative, cross-cultural and global field of studies during the entire course of the twentieth century, although this process has been greatly accelerated since the early 1970s. Many discussions in this field are concerned with basic conceptual issues, methodological clarifications and theory-building, as is evident from the relatively new *Encyclopedia of Religion* (Eliade, 1987). But this collaborative work, produced by a team of international scholars, also proves how much the study of religion as an academic discipline is still deeply rooted in an androcentric framework which often remains unquestioned. Many other examples of scholarly production in religious studies – articles, monographs, reference and text books – provide continuing evidence of the marginality, if not the invisibility, of women. This marginality is particularly evident in the historiography of the discipline and in current academic teaching on religion where most courses operate a 'sexism by omission' which is not overcome by instituting separate courses on women and religion.

Several women scholars, Carol Christ (1987) among others, have argued convincingly that much more is needed, namely, a complete paradigm shift in religion as a field of studies, a fundamental reorientation which will affect all data, theories, methodological discussions and basic categories, such as the understanding of 'homo religiosus', for example. Careful attention to gender differences will significantly alter both the gathering and the analysis of all data which have so far been onesidedly and androcentrically selected, as the feminist critical perspective is not yet an integral part of religious studies.

A few years ago I undertook a detailed survey of recent methodological debates in the study of religion (King, 1984). Following on from that I discussed the issue of androcentrism in my paper on 'Female identity and the history of religions' (King, 1986). More recently I have analysed the feminist challenge to religion in a book dealing with the wider issues of *Women and Spirituality* (King, 1989, 1993). These investigations provide the background and starting point for the present observations on the contribution of women to the modern study of religion. As far as I know, no historical investigation has been undertaken up to now to establish how far women writers, missionaries and scholars made a significant contribution to the rise and development of the modern study of religion. In my earlier article (King, 1986) I mentioned the examples of Hannah Adams, Lydia Maria Child, Carolyn H. Dall, Annie E. Cheney, Mrs Rhys Davids, Mrs Sinclair Stevenson, Eliza R. Sutherland from Ann Arbor and Alice C. Fletcher from Harvard (the last two belonged to the nineteen official plenary women lecturers at the 1893 World's Parliament of Religion in Chicago), but there are many more.[1] From the mid-nineteenth century onwards the teaching of religion as an academic discipline was institutionalized in several universities and colleges. One therefore has to ask how far women took part in teaching and research at an early stage or were even pioneers in the development of the discipline; how far they contributed to the study of particular religions; and how far their contributions have remained unacknowledged and forgotten.

To undertake such an investigation is not simply a matter of setting the record straight or asking 'non-questions' about 'non-data' (Christ, 1987, p. 54), as feminist scholarship must do by questioning unquestioned, taken-for-granted scholarly assumptions *of the past*, but it is also an issue of central concern for the personal and corporate identity of women scholars and students today. This sense of identity among women scholars in religion needs to be focused and strengthened as we women speak our own voices and create new agencies for the production and distribution of new knowledge whose perspectives modify the existing ethos, modes and models of scholarship. Identity is grounded in psychology; it is related to awareness, consciousness, the experience of a relational self and the larger web of the group – all much debated in feminist theory. Identity is *constructed* by using existing materials drawn from personal and collective historical experience; but thereby identity is also *constricted* within the traditional boundaries given to history so far. Women scholars are much concerned with the reversal or rearrangement of boundaries and, for the growth and maintenance of their own identities, need to relate not only to each other, but to the 'foremothers' in their fields of study.

The politics of knowledge have until very recently been entirely shaped by men. The advent of women as a group into the work and institutional structures of academic disciplines is a modern phenomenon brought about by the struggle of the women's movement to achieve the equality and education of women. Again, women arrived later in the field of the study of religion than in other fields of knowledge, and perhaps latest of all, and only very slowly, have they become visible in theology.

While women as a group of significant numbers were not present in teaching positions of religion in universities or colleges until relatively recently, there are nevertheless a considerable number of individual women who undertook and contributed to the study of religion earlier this century and even before that. But the official histories of the discipline say little of the contribution made by women writers, missionaries and academic teachers to the modern study of religion. It is important to research these data on earlier women's scholarly work, as the example of their struggles and achievements can enlarge our own consciousness, strengthen our identity as women scholars of religion, and provide additional role models and inspiration for younger women entering the discipline today.

Much research is needed to break out of the androcentric prison of religious studies. I can only offer some notes, some prolegomena to further research which needs to be undertaken in much greater detail. I shall first consider some random data about earlier women scholars, including their participation in history of religions congresses, then briefly refer to the pioneering work of three British women scholars who devoted their lives to the study of religion, and lastly analyse some articles and perspectives of the *Encyclopedia of Religion* (*ER*) (Eliade, 1987).

Women and the Historiography of the Study of Religion

The synoptic outline of the contents of the *ER* lists under 'The study of religion' as its last entry the 'Scholars of religion' who are recognized to merit a separate article in the *Encyclopedia*. Of the 142 scholars who have a biographical sketch devoted to them, only four are women: two Americans, the anthropologists Ruth Benedict (1887–1948) and Barbara G. Meyerhoff (1935–1985), and two British women, Jane E. Harrison (1850–1928), the scholar on Greek religion, and Evelyn Underhill (1875–1941), the writer on mysticism. It is surprising, if not to say extraordinary, that outstanding women scholars such as Mrs Rhys Davids (1857–1942) and I. B. Horner (1896–1981), who both made important contributions to the study of early Buddhism, do not even find a mention anywhere.

No doubt other women scholars will come to mind whose names have been overlooked. If we examine earlier histories of the study of religion, it is interesting what Louis Henry Jordan (described as 'Late Special Lecturer in Comparative Religion at the University of Chicago') observed in 1905 in his large survey *Comparative Religion. Its Genesis and Growth*. When looking at the prophets and pioneers of 'comparative religion' in the USA, he deals with only one writer, and she is a woman, Hannah Adams (1755–1832). Jordan devotes three pages to her book, *An Alphabetical Compendium of the Various Sects which have appeared in the World from the Beginning of the Christian era to the Present Day* (published in 1784, it dealt with Christianity, paganism, Islam, Judaism and deism).[2] He also acknowledges the contribution made by Lydia Maria Child's three volumes on *Progress of Religious Ideas through Successive Ages* (1855). Then he mentions three more recent women scholars, Mrs Agnes Smith, Mrs Margaret Dunlop Gibson and Miss Jane Ellen Harrison and goes on to say in his quaint style:

> It is sincerely to be hoped that the example which these industrious ladies have set, whether Mrs Adams or her more fully equipped successors, will now quite frequently be imitated, indeed, it may confidently be predicted that, under the vastly improved conditions which at present prevail, the example in question will before long be deliberately and strenuously emulated, why should not ladies of scholarly tastes, and possessed of the leisure and skill which this quest so rigidly demands, apply themselves with patience and diligence to a solution of one or more of the problems which Comparative Religion unfolds? (Jordan, 1905, pp. 149–50)

Such leisure and skill were available, albeit limited to a social elite, and it can be instructive to analyse the attendance figures at some of the earlier history of religions congresses. The Third International Congress for the History of Religions, held at Oxford in 1908 (see *Transactions*, 1908), lists a total of 599 members of whom 253 were women. The majority, i.e. 183, are listed as attending independently rather than with their husband, nor were they a majority of Oxford women, but came from different countries. This is probably a higher presence of women than can be found at many conferences on religion today. When it comes to reading papers, the situation looks different however. Out of the 132 papers given in nine sections at Oxford, only eight were by women, while twelve women acted as discussants of papers. The papers read by women were in the area of tribal religions (3), Egyptian religion (2), Bahai religion, Buddhism

(Mrs Rhys Davids), Greek religion (Jane Harrison) and Christianity (*Transactions*, 1908: vol I, p. vi–xxxii). From a contemporary perspective one can say that the large number of women present at the Oxford Congress (more than 40 per cent of delegates) did not give them a proportionate visibility or a public voice. Most women remained silent; they were present without being active participants.

Four years later, at the next Congress in Leiden in 1912 (*Actes du IVe Congres*, 1913), the proportion of women present was not as high as at Oxford. There were 59 women out of a total number of 297 participants and only two papers on tribal religions are listed as given by women in the section on 'Religions des Peuples Sauvages et Questions Générales'. A woman professor from Milan (Professor Lilly Marshall) is listed as a participant of the Congress, and so is Miss Jane Harrison.

What was the participation of women at more recent IAHR congresses? For the VIIth Congress, held in Amsterdam in 1950 (Bleeker, Drewes and Hidding, 1951) and important as the starting point for a new organizational development after World War II, the founding of the International Association for the History of Religions (IAHR), the following distribution of participants pertains: thirty-six women attended out of a total of 193 participants and thirty of these women are listed independently, in their own right. Nine women had doctorates and one woman was a professor, described as 'Miss Professor C. E. Visser' from Groningen, who presided over one session of the section on Christianity and Hellenism. The theme of the Congress was 'The mystical-ritual pattern of civilization', but the *Proceedings* contain only a summary of the programme and lectures and do not give a comprehensive list of all contributors. From these summaries the following data can be gained: out of the three plenary lectures and fifty-six papers given at the Amsterdam Congress in 1950, only two were by women, one in the section on classics (Momolina Marconi), the other in the section on Germans and Celts (Ellen Ettlinger). A 'short contribution' by Dr Maryla Falk to the section on Christianity and Hellenism is also mentioned, but no further details are given. In addition, two women chaired the meetings of one section and another Dutch woman scholar read out the paper of a Hindu scholar who was unable to attend (Mrs J. E. van Lohuizen-de Leeuw read Prof. Mahadevan's paper).

Proportionally speaking the participation by and contributions of women to the Amsterdam Congress in 1950 was not as great as it was forty-two years earlier in Oxford. Has this relative decline been reversed since then in more recent congresses of the IAHR? It is not possible to gain a completely accurate picture, as the published Proceedings of different International History of Religions Congresses follow different patterns and do not always give full information, nor can the sex of participants always be accurately identified when only initials are given for first names. Within these limitations the following information is available on the three more recent congresses.

In the *Proceedings* (Pye and McKenzie, 1980) of the XIIIth Congress, held in Lancaster in 1975, 349 participants are listed of whom thirty-six can be identified as women participants. Out of the 184 papers given in fifteen sections ten had women authors. This is a definite advance on the situation twenty-five years earlier in Amsterdam. The Lancaster Congress theme was 'The nature and destiny of man', but little initial reflection on this theme is found. The papers remained locked in an entirely androcentric perspective in treating the theme, and no attention was given to gender differences in either the arrangement of the sections, the content of the papers (with one single exception on 'Women in Greek rituals' by I. Chirassi-Colombo) or the methodological reflections.

The following XIVth IAHR Congress, held in Winnipeg in 1980 (Slater and Wiebe, 1983), remedied some of this by including the (somewhat oddly) entitled section seventeen on 'Femininity and Religion', but this has not been recorded in the published, selected *Proceedings*. The little territory gained by women, in terms of a separate section, has thus been made invisible again by being suppressed in the written record of the conference which neither lists the sections nor the names of participants, but simply consists of the text of forty-three chosen papers of which five were authored by women. However, the participants list and its supplement made available at the Congress listed a total of 548 participants of whom seventy-five can be identified as female scholars. Of the four plenary addresses one was given by a woman and of the 425 papers listed fifty were authored or co-authored by women, and women chaired a total of seventeen sessions out of the numerous sessions of twenty sections of the Congress.

The XVth IAHR Congress in Sydney (1985) returned to the earlier arrangement of sections and did not include a separate section on 'Women and Religion', nor was there a section on this theme planned for the IAHR Congress in Rome in 1990.

However, I was able to organize a panel on 'Religion and Gender' in which nineteen women scholars from around the world gave papers.[3] In Sydney some Australian women scholars organized a separate parallel meeting to the Congress, but this is barely reflected in the official *Proceedings* (Hayes, 1986) which give the text of twenty-seven selected papers of which five were by women scholars. The papers were, according to the editor, chosen from a total of 278 presentations in eighteen sections and three symposia, including the symposium on 'Women and Religion', where six presentations are listed. The total number of people registered for the Sydney Congress came to 439; of these, 100 can be identified as women, of whom about a third, namely thirty-three, were family members accompanying either husband, father or mother. Thus the number of women scholars or postgraduate students present was about sixty-seven in total. An analysis of the Congress Programme and the Book of Abstracts shows that originally 296 contributions were announced, of which twenty-one were by women, and only eight sessions were chaired by women.

For easier reference I have tabulated my findings (table 10.1) although the numbers can only be approximate, due to the ephemeral nature of some of the sources and the difficulty of identifying some of the participants. The table shows, however, that there is considerable fluctuation in the number of women participants (as well as the total number of participants) and that in terms of the percentage of papers given by women the IAHR congresses have not progressed far since the beginning of this century. It remains a source of surprise that the number of women present at the Oxford Congress (even though they mostly were not active participants) has not been reached again more recently. I had also searched for information on women giving plenary addresses, but there are few data available. (Out of four plenary addresses at the Winnipeg Congress one was given by a woman scholar.)

It would be of great interest to analyse the data on the participation and papers given by women scholars at the Annual Meeting of the American Academy of Religion, especially to investigate whether there has been a marked increase in the figures of participation since the Women and Religion section was founded in 1975. Perhaps one day an American scholar will undertake this task which I cannot pursue here. Instead, I would like to discuss three British women scholars who each have made a significant contribution to the study of religion, but have received little recognition for this beyond their own lifetime.

Table 10.1 Participation by and contributions of women to History of Religions Congresses

History of Religions Congress	Participation		Papers		Women chairing sessions
	Total	Women	Total	By women	
Oxford 1908	599	253	132	8	12
Leiden 1912	297	59	–	2	–
Amsterdam 1950	193	36	56	2	2
Lancaster 1975	349	36	184	10	–
Winnipeg 1980	548	75	425*	50	17
Sydney 1985	439	100	296**	21	8

Note: The Selected Proceedings from the IAHR Rome Congress (1990) were published too late (Bianchi, 1994) to be taken into account here. The *Book of Abstracts* available at the time of the Congress listed 384 participants, but about fifty did not attend. As far as can be ascertained, over fifty women scholars participated in the Rome Congress and gave papers.
*   In the Selected Proceedings of the Winnipeg Congress (Slater and Wiebe, 1983) 43 papers were published of which only five were by women.
** In the Selected Proceedings of the Sydney Congress (Hayes, 1986) 27 papers were published of which five were by women.

Three Examples of Women Pioneers in the Modern Study of Religion

The examples chosen are Mrs Rhys Davids, Miss I. B. Horner and Miss Jane Ellen Harrison. The first two have made important contributions to the study of Theravada Buddhism while the last was, during her lifetime, greatly renowned for her study of ancient Greek religion, but is now virtually ignored by classical scholars. The most obscure and difficult figure to research is Mrs Rhys Davids because she stood in the shadow of her husband whom she, however, survived by twenty years. It is of interest to note here that Miss Horner's first book, *Women under Primitive Buddhism*, is often quoted in contemporary writing on women and religion and so is Jane Harrison's *Prolegomena to the Study of Greek Religion*.

Let us look briefly at each of these women scholars.

Caroline Augusta Foley, usually referred to as Mrs C. A. F. Rhys Davids (1857–1942)

As far as I have been able to ascertain, no research has been done on the scholarly work of Caroline Augusta Foley Davids. In 1894, she married the Orientalist scholar Thomas William Rhys Davids (1843–1922) who in 1904 was appointed to the new Chair in Comparative Religion at the University of Manchester. In 1881 he had founded the Pali Text Society of which he remained President until his death in 1922. This office was then taken on by his wife who held it until her own death twenty years later. In his survey of 'Comparative religion at the University of Manchester, 1904–1979', Eric Sharpe (1980, p. 33) laconically states about Mrs Rhys Davids: 'She too lectured at Manchester' and in James Hastings' (1979) *Encyclopedia of Religion and Ethics* (*ERE*) she is described as 'Formerly lecturer on Indian Philosophy in the University of Manchester' (vol. 13, p. 721), but it has proved impossible to obtain more details than that. The *ERE* (vol. 13, p. 721) also lists her as a 'Fellow of University College, London' and as author of the following works: *Buddhist Psychological Ethics* (1900), *Psalms of the Early Buddhists* (1909, 1913), *Buddhism* (1912), *Buddhist Psychology* (1914), *Kindred Sayings* (1917) and other works. Caroline Rhys Davids contributed twenty entries to the *ERE* (her husband had forty entries), including the important article on the central Buddhist topic of 'Abhidharma'.

On examining the 'List of issues' of the Pali Text Society (1991) it emerges that Caroline Rhys Davids is the editor, translator or collaborator of twenty-four different publications of Pali texts, while her husband's name is associated with only a total of nine publications. Almost all Pali editions in the West have appeared under the imprint of the Pali Text Society (its 1991 catalogue lists 286 editions, translations and reference works in print) whose work has been indispensable for the foundational studies of Buddhism. However, Caroline Rhys Davids' contribution rarely ever finds any mention or appreciative comment. While there is no separate entry on her husband either among the scholars of religion in the *ER*, he is at least referred to four times (although the date of the founding of the Pali Text Society is erroneously given as 1831 instead of 1881; see *ER*, vol. 2, p. 555).

In a brief obituary on Caroline Rhys Davids by a later President of the Pali Text Society it is said that with her death in 1942:

> closes the pioneer stage of Pali studies and a scholarly interpretation of Pali Buddhism in England. In this capacity she was the co-worker and successor of her husband T. W. Rhys Davids to whom she owed her inspiration for Buddhist studies. His life-work, the editing of the Pali Canon, through the medium of the Pali Text Society, she almost concluded. ... It is not too much to say that the ideas of the educated layman about Pali Buddhism today are those put forth by Mrs Rhys Davids, and her own translations are worthy of being classed among gems of English poetical literature. (Stede, 1942, pp. 276–7)

Stede also describes her as an enthusiastic missionary of 'Gotama the man' who, however, stood alone in many of her theories. He does not give much detail about her nor does Eric Sharpe in his 1980 survey where he mentions that Mrs Rhys Davids 'became as celebrated a scholar in the area of Buddhism as was her husband' and says about her short book on *Buddhism* that it 'has still not outlived its usefulness'. Assessing what he calls the 'Rhys Davids family partnership' and its service to Buddhist studies in the West, he draws on the assessment made by G. R. Welbon (1968) in his book on *The Buddhist Nirvana and its Western Interpreters* which leads Sharpe to conclude 'that Mrs Rhys Davids comes out rather better than her husband' for the reason 'that while Rhys Davids provided Pali scholarship with many of its tools, Mrs Rhys Davids used them more skilfully'. He quotes Welbon, saying:

The present generation of Buddhist scholars ... has learned much from Mrs Rhys Davids. We no longer 'read our Buddhist scriptures like fundamentalists' ... To the extent then that she focused attention on the history and change in the Pali Canon, to the extent that she has made sophisticated textual criticism – higher and lower – an indispensable aspect of Buddhist studies, she has indeed won her battle with the 'little books on Buddhism'. (Quoted in Sharpe, 1980, p. 33)

This is the most appreciative comment on Caroline Rhys Davids found to date. The fact that she died in the middle of World War II caused a lack of comments and obituaries at the time. People who knew her have said that there 'are those who believe that she went somewhat mad towards the end of her life, and certainly some of her later views border on the unlikely, if not the insane' (personal communication). Their daughter, Miss Vivian Rhys Davids, proved unhelpful in providing material on her father (Kannangara, 1987, p. 161) and nothing is known about her relationship to her mother. If only she could have enlightened us more on the personal struggles and lack of public recognition of her mother, whose pioneering work and lasting contribution to Buddhist studies should be given much fuller attention than has been the case so far.

Isaline Blew Horner (1896–1981), usually simply listed as Miss I. B. Horner

To members of the Pali Text Society, Isaline Blew Horner will be well known, as she was President of the Society from 1959 until her death in 1981. The Society's current list of publications shows that Miss Horner edited or translated seventeen volumes of Pali texts on her own and was co-translator of another two volumes. There does not seem to exist a complete bibliography of all her works so far, but in a *Festschrift* produced for her in 1974 – a *Festschrift* for a woman scholar, a rare occurrence indeed – the figure of 200 or more articles is quoted in the biographical sketch, but only forty-three publications including book reviews are listed in a selected bibliography (Cousins, Kunst, and Norman, 1974). She is said to have occasionally lectured on Pali language and literature, but her running of the Pali Text Society almost single-handedly for over twenty years made her name practically synonymous with that of the Society.

Her interest in Buddhism was first awakened through meeting Professor and Mrs Rhys Davids at the house of a relative at the age of twelve. She later took the Tripos in Moral Sciences at Cambridge, and from 1918 onwards worked as assistant librarian and later librarian (1923–36) at Newnham College, Cambridge, during which time she wrote her first book, *Women Under Primitive Buddhism* (1930), followed a few years later by the study *The Early Buddhist Theory of Man Perfected* (1934) which in spite of 'all that has been written on these subjects since then ... have never been superseded, and they were reprinted in 1975' (Norman, 1982a, p. 53).

After those two books all her subsequent major publications were editions or translations of Pali texts, especially the six volumes of the monumental translation of the Vinaya Pitaka, the first complete translation into a Western language of the Buddhist *Book of the Disciplines*, which she began in 1938 and concluded in 1966. Her knowledge of Pali was internationally recognized and she was for many years the general reviser of the Copenhagen Critical Pali Dictionary. She also published a number of minor works including selections and anthologies of Buddhist texts in translation.

Isaline Horner travelled extensively in Sri Lanka, India, Burma and Europe. In 1964 she was awarded an honorary D. Litt. by the University of Ceylon and in 1977 by Nava Nalanda. In 1980 she was awarded the OBE 'for services to the Pali Text Society'. However, in spite of all her achievements, in the assessment of the current President of the Society:

> it is likely that future scholars will judge that Miss Horner's greatest contribution to the academic study of Pali and Buddhism lay not in her own publications, valuable though they were, but in the efforts which she made to encourage such studies. Not only did she persuade others to make new editions and translations, to replace works that were out of date ... but she enthusiastically wrote forewords and introductions to their books, and made indexes and supplied lists of parallel passages based upon her extensive reading of Pali works. Perhaps more important, she devoted her time, energy and money to the task of putting the Pali Text Society on a sound financial footing ... Miss Horner *was* the Pali Text Society, and without her it will never be the same again, but in the form in which she left it it will remain as a living memorial to her scholarship and generosity. (Norman, 1982b, pp. 147 f. and 148 f.)

As we have a commemorative volume recognizing Miss Horner's services to Buddhist studies and the Pali Text Society, she is somewhat better acknowledged and remembered than Mrs Rhys Davids, especially as Miss Horner died only relatively recently.

Jane Ellen Harrison (1850–1928)

Another important English woman scholar of an earlier generation who gained considerable prominence through her study of ancient Greek religion is Jane Ellen Harrison, former fellow of Newnham College, Cambridge, who unlike the two previous examples, shares the distinction of being one of the four women scholars in the study of religion on whom we have an article in *The Encyclopedia of Religion* (vol. 6, pp. 201–2, by A. W. H. Adkins from the University of Chicago). Apart from this article, there are a further eight references to her in the *ER* while there are none whatsoever to Mrs Rhys Davids or Miss Horner. There are also two biographies on Jane Harrison, an earlier one by Jessie Stewart (1959) giving a mere outline of Harrison's life based on her letters, and a full critical study by Sandra J. Peacock (1988), which analyses Jane Harrison's rich and tense experience, already hinted at in the subtitle 'The mask and the self', with much sensitivity and insight.

Jane Ellen Harrison, who held honorary degrees from the Universities of Durham and Aberdeen, was a prolific author who published from 1882 onwards, but made her reputation especially through three books, the massive *Prolegomena to the History of Greek Religions* (first published in 1903 and reprinted many times since), *Themis. A Study of the Social Origin of Greek Religion* (1912), and *Epilegomena to the Study of Greek Religion* (1921). Jane Harrison early recognized the importance of archaeology and especially anthropology for the study of the Greek classics at a time when other classicists concentrated exclusively on the study of literary texts. The influence of Frazer, Marett, Durkheim and later Freud and Jung is much apparent in her three important books, all of which are currently available in reprint editions (see Harrison, 1977, 1980, 1991). The *Prolegomena* contain a detailed chapter on 'The making of a goddess' and discusses the process whereby earlier matriarchal cults in ancient Greece were displaced and superseded by the patriarchal cults of the Olympian gods. It comes as no surprise that this book is often quoted by feminist writers working on the mother goddess, but one does not easily come across references elsewhere. In assessing the fate of Jane Harrison's work, Adkins (1987, p. 202) states that: 'Some of her conclusions, inevitably, are now of merely historic interest, but the subsequent development of the study of Greek religion has been profoundly influenced by her.' This concurs with what Gilbert Murray had already said in a letter of 1955:

> Jane Harrison's work was memorable. It is a little forgotten now for two reasons: first, she was a wonderful *teacher* and of course that is a quality which is forgotten when the teacher dies. Also it was all *pioneer* work; that is, it suggested new ideas and opened up new paths of research, without delaying to get the new results perfect. Few people would accept the whole of JEH's conclusions, but nobody can write on Greek religion without being influenced by her work. (Quoted in Stewart, 1959, p. xi)

The entry on 'Greek religion' in the *ER* does not contain a section on the history of its study, as is the case with other religions, but does it not seem extraordinary that Jane Ellen Harrison's work finds no mention, not even in the substantial annotated bibliography with separate sections on 'Gods and heroes', 'Myth and ritual', 'Divination and oracles', 'Sacrifice', 'Mysteries, Dionysism, Orphism' – all themes which have a central place in her work? However, Jane Harrison's *Prolegomena* are listed in the bibliography of the entry on 'Lady of the animals' where Carol Christ writes that this book 'has never been super-seded as a comprehensive reference on Greek religion with parti-cular emphasis on the prepatriarchal origins of the goddess (*ER*, vol. 8, p. 422) and two quotations from the *Prolegomena* are included in the entry on the 'Virgin goddess' (*ER*, 15, pp. 276 and 278). There is also another quotation from Harrison's book *Ancient Art and Ritual* (London, 1913) in support of the theory that art developed from ritual (in the entry on 'Poetry', *ER*, 11: 370). But why is historical memory so shortlived, especially with regard to the contribution of women? If just over thirty years ago Gilbert Murray could speak of all the pioneer work of Jane Ellen Harrison, why has she not found more than a fleeting reference in Eric Sharpe's (1986) *Comparative Religion*? Why is her contribution not chronicled among that of other pioneers in Jacques Waardenburg's *Classical Approaches to the Study of Religion* (1973; there are four references to Jane E. Harrison in Waardenburg's book, but three of these refer to citation of her by other scholars)? The reason for this can only be the androcentric perspective from which these books are written. This is a tradition still dominant in the contemporary study of religion as will become evident from a closer examination of the recently published *Encyclopedia of Religion*.

Women and the Encyclopedia of Religion

Apart from some notable exceptions the editors and contributors of the *Encyclopedia of Religion* show a remarkable lack of awareness regarding the development of feminist studies on women and religion over the last fifteen years or so. This is all the more surprising, given the strong overall North American orientation of this important reference work in the study of religion. Kitagawa's 'Foreword' (vol. 1, pp. XIII–XVI) highlights the contrast in both content and approach between the *Encyclopedia of Religion* *(ER)* (Eliade, 1987) and James Hastings' (1979) earlier *Encyclopedia of Religion and Ethics (ERE)* (1908–26). If one compares the number of women contributors to these two reference works, one can initially note a definite increase in the contributions made by women scholars in the intervening sixty years or so, but it is by no means as large as one would like to see. The *ERE* counted thirty-nine women among its 895 contributors whereas the *ER* has approximately 227 women contributors out of a total of 1,356 international scholars. The figure is as accurate as possible – some scholars' first names are listed only by their initials, and some first names are ambiguous as they can apply to either sex – but not even the publishers have been able to provide an absolutely accurate figure because there were a good many contributors whose gender was never known to them (personal communication). Thus we get a figure of not quite 17 per cent for women contributors to the *ER*, a figure perhaps not all that different from the actual representation of women scholars in academic posts in many countries.

However, feminist methodology and hermeneutics have not been made an integral part of the project of the *Encyclopedia* as a closer examination of its contents soon reveals. 'Women' as one of the themes in the study of religion are acknowledged through four columns of entries in the index of the *ER*, but these remain mostly factual-descriptive without including theoretical concerns. There is the important entry on 'Women's studies' (Constance H.

Buchanan), also cross-listed under 'Scholarship on women', but the theoretical and cross-disciplinary perspectives raised there are not applied in other entries of the *Encyclopedia*. There is an entry on 'Androcentrism' (Rosemary R. Ruether), cross-listed under 'Women in Christianity' and quite rightly so, as it restricts its discussion mostly to the Christian tradition (with additional references to 'Women's studies', 'God' and 'God in post-biblical Christianity'). There is no index reference to sexism, and the *ER* contains no article on either matriarchy or patriarchy. This is a grave omission, and also rather surprising, as the original prospectus had listed an article on 'Matriarchy and patriarchy' (Rita M. Gross); the article was submitted but rejected. In the index fourteen cross-references are listed under 'Matriarchy', whereas only two references are given under 'Patriarchy'. One of these simply refers to 'Patriarchy as prevailing religion of the world' and points back to Constance Buchanan's article on 'Women's studies', the other mentions the article on the 'Virgin Goddess' (Carol P. Christ). There is no article or even index reference to the important category of 'gender', only references to 'gender-reversed homosexuality' and to the article on 'Gender roles', which mainly deals with 'gender change' rather than with the theoretical implications of gender in contemporary feminist thought. There is also a brief reference to 'sex of God and gender roles' which sends the reader to the long entry on 'Goddess worship'. This article deals with cross-cultural and historical data (discussed by various authors) and concludes with 'Theoretical perspectives' (James J. Preston), much informed by anthropological studies. This contribution is followed by another one on 'Gods and goddesses' (Theodore M. Ludwig). There are also quite a few entries on particular goddesses in different religious traditions and cultures. The index lists several references to 'Androgynes' and 'Androgyny', but the main article on 'Androgynes' (Wendy Doniger O'Flaherty and Mircea Eliade) does not deal with the contemporary feminist treatment of this theme; reference to androgyny as wholeness and fullness of being is only found in the article on 'Earth' (Mircea Eliade and Lawrence E. Sullivan). There is a wide-ranging article on 'Feminine sacrality' (Nancy E. Auer Falk) and a long contribution on 'Witchcraft' (Maxwell Gay Marwick), but neither of these topics is linked to the contemporary practice of feminist spirituality (in fact, the index entry on 'Spirituality' mentions only '*See* Christian spirituality', as if spirituality were not a comparative topic).

It is my contention that neither the historical link between religion and the women's liberation movement in the past nor the contemporary relationship between religion and feminist theory and practice are given their due importance and space in the *ER*. There is no article on 'Feminism' although the index points to six references under this heading. The 1848 Women's Rights Convention in Seneca simply finds a brief mention, together with the Women's Christian Temperance Union and the later Women's Missionary Society and Christian Women's Action Guild in a paragraph on Victorian women's contribution to 'Christian social movements' (vol. 3, p. 449).

It seems more extraordinary, however, that the index entries on ordination, priesthood, ministry, clergy and shamanism do not make any reference to women, nor are any of these terms cross-listed under the 'Women' entry. The comparative articles on 'Ordination', 'Priesthood' and 'Shamanism' do not discuss women (there is a reference to shamanistic gender change in the article on 'Gender roles'); from studying these articles one might easily, and mistakenly, conclude that women have never been religious specialists in the past, and that there exists no lively debate about the ordination of women in the Christian churches today. There is no reference to it whatsoever in the section on 'Christian priesthood' (vol. 11, pp. 536–9) nor in the long article on the 'Ecumenical movement'. Brief mention of the ordination of women is made in the article on 'Ministry' (see vol. 9, p. 540) and the topic of 'Feminist liberation theology' is listed as a subtitle in the bibliography for the article on 'Political theology', mentioning the *Journal of Feminist Studies in Religion*, Rosemary Radford Ruether's *New Woman, New Earth* and Elisabeth Schüssler Fiorenza's *In Memory of Her* (see vol. 11, p. 407), a somewhat limited list on the topic of women and liberation theology as it does not include titles by Letty Russell or by the well-known feminist political theologian Dorothee Sölle, and other writers.

It is not only women as religious specialists, but also as ordinary practictioners of religion who are ignored. There is no reference to them in the long article on 'Popular religion' (vol. 11, pp. 442–52). The discussion of descriptive material, global structures and theoretical studies in this article does not include any attention to gender variables, as if women were not an important segment of 'the folk', 'the common people' or 'the peasants' deeply involved with the celebration, expression and transmission of religion at the popular level. (There is no reference to women

either in the much more substantial study by Jacques Waardenburg (1979), *Official and Popular Religion*).

It is not just the marginality, but the complete invisibility of
women in some of the descriptive data of the *ER* which has to be
criticized. At a more general level there is the absence of a sufficient integration of contemporary feminist scholarship and theory
in theoretical discussions pertaining to the study of religion, and
at the most general and basic level of all, there is the use of
completely unreflective and exclusive language in many articles
of the *ER*. It is still quite literally 'man' alone who is 'incurably
religious in one way or another', as is stated by Winston L. King
at the end of his article on 'Religion' (vol. 12, p. 292).

From what I have seen of the 'Contributors' Manual' sent out
earlier to the writers of the articles in the *ER*, no conscious effort
was made to avoid exclusive language. Eliade's own Preface to
the *ER*, written before his death in 1986, speaks of the contemporary 'information explosion' which demands a new presentation
of all areas of religious studies, itself informed by new methodological approaches and a more adequate hermeneutics which
make us better understand 'the mind and behavior of *homo religiosus* ("religious man")'. But nowhere among all the new developments mentioned is there any hint of new perspectives coming
from the feminist analysis of religion. There are many other criticisms one can address to Eliade's methods and theories, but
one important criticism certainly concerns the complete blindness
to gender differences at the linguistic, descriptive and theoretical
level.[4] If it was Eliade's hope, according to the comments in
Kitagawa's Foreword to the *ER*, that this work 'would imple-
ment his lifelong vision of a "total hermeneutics", a coherent
interpretive framework for the *entire* human experience' (vol. 1,
p. XV, emphasis added), then women scholars must judge this
hermeneutic as far from total, because it does not integrate their
perspective and experience. This is borne out, at the linguistic
level, by the completely androcentric perspective in which Eliade's
own words remain locked in the Preface of the *Encyclopedia of
Religion*. Speaking of the facts relevant 'for an understanding of
modern Western man', he refers to:

> that nostalgia for initiatory trials and scenarios, nostalgia deciphered
> in so many literary and artistic works (including the cinema) re-
> veals modern *man's* longing for a *renovatio* capable of changing
> *his* existence ...

... here is a great network of historical and descriptive articles, synthetical discussions, and interpretive essays that make available contemporary insight into the long and multifaceted history of religious *man* ...

To know the great variety of worldviews, assumed by religious *man*, to comprehend the expanse of *his* spiritual universe, is, finally, to advance our general knowledge of humankind. (Vol. 1, pp. XI and XII, emphasis added)

Eliade uses the inclusive word 'humankind' here, yet it makes little sense, given the fact that all other expressions are restricted to the male gender. The same exclusive language is used in the 'Introduction' by the Macmillan Senior Project Editor, Claude Conyers, who uses an interesting organic comparison between editing and gardening where, however, both the editor and gardener remain a 'he'. Conyers draws on the conceptual scheme of a garden to develop his thoughts on the creation of the *ER* which needed tending like a garden to 'let a thousand flowers bloom', 'to enchant the eye, engage the mind, and enrich the spirit' (vol. 1, p. XVII). This it does to a large measure but, alas, the garden still remains too confined as it has not given enough space to make visible the rich flowering of women.

This is not simply a straightforward conclusion on the *ER*, but it invites and challenges us to find new directions in feminist practice regarding the creation and nurturing of new scholarship so that it can be fully transmitted to the next generation. Contemporary women scholars are critiquing and reshaping the concepts inherited from male scholars, but as long as their thoughts and findings are not integrated into existing scholarly discourse, women scholars will remain muted as a group. Dale Spender (1981b), in her article 'The gatekeepers: a feminist critique of academic publishing' has clearly pointed out the dynamics of the politics of knowledge where the creation, transmission and recognition of new knowledge directly depend on academic publishing and its role in shaping a discipline and helping to define what is considered mainstream and what is marginal. As the gatekeepers of the academic world and of publishing are predominantly male, women also need to evolve their own agencies for the production of knowledge.

The research undertaken for this essay has convinced me that the identity of contemporary women scholars remains fragile and vulnerable as long as it is not grounded in an enlarged con-sciousness aware of the substantial contributions made by women scholars in the past, and as long as it is not strengthened by a better connected network of women scholars in the present which can become powerful enough to ensure the integration of feminist perspectives in all areas of religious studies. Given the exclusive onesidedness in which this discipline is still largely taught, written about and its history recorded, younger women scholars need support in finding role models for their own identity and en-couragement for the directions of their own work. To possess an inclusive sense of identity as scholars of the academic study of religion alone is not enough. As a group we also need an ex-clusive identity, an identity born out of the new consciousness of being *women scholars* of religion whose contributions, both past and present, need to be given far more visibility and prominence.

In our historical and theoretical work we have to apply a critical 'hermeneutics of suspicion' concerning the data so far found and recorded, as their perspective usually remains onesided and androcentric. This is particularly true of the historiography and methodology of religious studies, as is all too evident from the examples given here.

Notes

1   I have examined the contribution of women speakers at the 1893 Chicago World's Parliament of Religions in 'Rediscovering women's voices at the World's Parliament of Religions' (King, 1993).
2   Recently reprinted as *A Dictionary of All Religion and Religious Denominations, Jewish, Heathen, Mahometan, Christian, Ancient and Modern* with an Introduction by Thomas A. Tweed, Atlanta, GA: Scholars Press, 1992. See also Thomas A. Tweed (1992).
3   Thirteen of these scholars have contributed chapters to this book but these are not necessarily the same as the papers given at the IAHR Congress in Rome. See the Acknowledgements at the beginning of this volume.
4   For a critique of Eliade see Christ (1991) and King (1990).

References

Actes du IVe Congres International d'Histoire des Religions 1913: tenu à Leide du 9–13 Septembre 1912. Leiden: E J Brill.

Adkins, A. W. H. 1987: Harrison, Jane E. In *The Encyclopedia of Religion*, vol. 6: 201–2.

Bianchi, Ugo (ed.) 1994: *The Notion of 'Religion' in Comparative Research. Selected Proceedings of XVIth Congress of the International Association for the History of Religions*, Rome, 3–8 September 1990. Rome: 'L' Erma' di Bretschneider.

Bleeker, C. J., Drewes, G. W. J. and Hidding, K. A. H. (eds) 1951: *Proceedings of the 7th Congress for the History of Religions*, Amsterdam, 4–9 September 1950. Amsterdam: North Holland Publishing Company.

Christ, Carol P. 1987: Toward a paradigm shift in the Academy and in religious studies. In Christie Farnham (ed.), *The Impact of Feminist Research in the Academy*, Bloomington: Indiana University Press, 53–76.

Christ, Carol P. 1991: Mircea Eliade and the feminist paradigm shift. *Journal of Feminist Studies in Religion*, 5, 1, 75–94.

Cousins, L., Kunst, A. and Norman, K. R. (eds) 1974: *Buddhist Studies in Honour of I. B. Horner*. Dordrecht and Boston: D. Reidel Publishing Company.

DuBois, Ellen Carol, Kelly, Gail, Paradise, Kennedy, Lapovsky, Elizabeth, Korsmeyer, Carolyn W. and Robinson, Lilly S. 1985: *Feminist Scholarship. Kindling in the Groves of Academe*. Urbana and Chicago: University of Illinois Press.

Eliade, Mircea (ed.) 1987: *The Encyclopedia of Religion*, 16 vols. New York: Macmillan Publishing Company and London: Collier Macmillan Publishers.

Farnham, Christie (ed.) 1987: *The Impact of Feminist Research in the Academy*. Bloomington: Indiana University Press.

Harrison, Jane Ellen 1977: *Themis. A Study of the Social Origins of Greek Religion*. London: Merlin Press.

Harrison, Jane Ellen 1980: *Prolegomena to the Study of Greek Religion*. London: Merlin Press.

Harrison, Jane Ellen 1991: *Epilegomena to the Study of Greek Religion*. Edmonds WA: Holmes Publishing Group.

Hastings, James (ed.) 1979: *Encyclopedia of Religion and Ethics*, 13 vols. Edinburgh, T & T Clark. Reprint. Original edition 1908–21, index volume 1926.

Hayes, Victor C. (ed.) 1986: *Identity Issues and World Religions*. Selected Proceedings of the Fifteenth Congress of the International Association for the History of Religions. Sydney, August 18–23, 1985. Bedford Park, South Australia: Australian Association for the Study of Religions.

Horner, Isaline Blew 1930: *Women under Primitive Buddhism: Lay-women and Almswomen.* New York: E. P. Dutton.

Horner, Isaline Blew (trs.) 1975: *The Book of Discipline (Vinaya-Pitaka),* Vol. V (*Culavagga*). London: The Pali Text Society.

Horner, Isaline Blew (trs.) 1986: *The Book of Discipline (Vinaya-Pitaka),* Vol. VI (*Parivara*). London: The Pali Text Society.

Jordan, Louis Henry 1905: *Comparative Religion. Its Genesis and Growth.* Edinburgh: T & T Clark.

Kannangara, A. P. 1985: Review of *The Genesis of an Orientalist: Thomas William Rhys Davids and Buddhism in Sri Lanka* by Ananda Wickerematne. *Journal of the International Association of Buddhist Studies,* 10, 161–4.

King, Ursula 1984: Historical and phenomenological approaches to the study of religion: some major developments and issues under debate since 1950. In F. Whaling (ed.), *Contemporary Approaches to the Study of Religion.* Berlin/New York/Amsterdam: Mouton, vol. 1, 29–163.

King, Ursula 1986: Female identity and the history of religions. In V. C. Hayes (ed.), *Identity Issues and World Religions: Selected Proceedings of the Fifteenth Congress of the International Association for the History of Religions.* Bedford Park: The Australian Association for the Study of Religions, 83–92.

King, Ursula 1989: *Women and Spirituality. Voices of Protest and Promise.* London: Macmillan; New York: New Amsterdam Books. (Second edition 1993: London: Macmillan and University Park, PA: Penn State Press.)

King, Ursula 1990: Women scholars and the *Encyclopedia of Religion. Method and Theory in the Study of Religion,* 2, 1, 91–7.

King, Ursula 1993: Rediscovering women's voices at the World's Parliament of Religions. In E. J. Ziolkowski (ed.), *A Museum of Faiths. Histories and Legacies of the 1893 World's Parliament of Religions.* Atlanta, GA: Scholars Press, 325–43.

Langland, Elizabeth and Gove, Walter (eds) 1981: *A Feminist Perspective in the Academy. The Difference it Makes.* Chicago and London: University of Chicago Press.

Norman, K. R. 1982a: Miss I. B. Horner – academic achievement. *Newnham College Roll* Letter, 53–5.

Norman, K. R. 1982b: Obituary: Isaline Blew Horner (1896–1981). *Journal of the International Association of Buddhist Studies* 5: 145–9.

Pali Text Society 1991: *List of Issues.* Oxford.

Peacock, Sandra J. 1988: *Jane Ellen Harrison. The Mask and the Self.* New Haven: Yale University Press.

Pye, Michael and McKenzie, Peter (eds) 1980: *History of Religions.* Proceedings of the Thirteenth International Congress of the International Association for the History of Religions (Lancaster, 15–22 August, 1975). Leicester: Department of Religion, University of Leicester.

Rhys Davids, Mrs C. A. F. (trs.) 1917; 1922: *The Book of the Kindred Sayings*, Vol. I and II. London: The Pali Text Society.

Rhys Davids, Mrs C. A. F. (trs.) 1974: *Buddhist Psychological Ethics*, 3rd edn. London: The Pali Text Society (1st edn 1900).

Rhys Davids, Mrs C. A. F. (trs.) 1990: *Poems of Early Buddhist Nuns*. London: The Pali Text Society.

Ruether, Rosemary R. 1981: The feminist critique of religious studies. *Soundings*, 64, 388–402. Also in E. Langland and W. Gove (eds), *A Feminist Perspective in the Academy*, 1981, 52–66.

Sharpe, Eric 1980: Comparative religion at the University of Manchester 1904–1979. In University of Manchester Faculty of Theology, *Seventy-Fifth Anniversary Papers* 1979, Victoria University of Manchester (cyclostyled).

Sharpe, Eric 1986: *Comparative Religion. A History* 2nd edn. La Salle, Illinois: Open Court. First edn, London: Duckworth, 1975.

Slater, Peter and Wiebe, Donald (eds) 1983: *Traditions in Contact and Change*. Selected Proceedings of the XIVth Congress of the International Association for the History of Religions, Winnipeg, August 15–20, 1980. Waterloo/Ontario: Wilfrid Laurier Press.

Spender, Dale (ed.) 1981a: *Men's Studies Modified. The Impact of Feminism on the Academic Disciplines*. Oxford, New York: Pergamon Press.

Spender, Dale 1981b: The gatekeepers: a feminist critique of academic publishing. In H. Roberts (ed.) *Doing Feminist Research*. London: Routledge & Kegan Paul, 186–202.

Stede, W. 1942: Caroline Augusta Foley Rhys Davids. *Journal of the Royal Asiatic Society*, 267–8.

Stewart, Jessie 1959: *Jane Ellen Harrison. A Portrait from Letters*. London: The Merlin Press.

Transactions of the Third International Congress for the History of Religions 1908: 2 volumes, Oxford: Clarendon Press.

Tweed, Thomas A. 1992: An American pioneer in the study of religion. Hannah Adams (1775–1831) and her *Dictionary of all Religion*. *Journal of the American Academy of Religion*, vol. LX, 3, 437–64.

Waardenburg, Jacques 1973: *Classical Approaches to the Study of Religion*, 2 vols. The Hague/Paris/New York: Mouton.

Waardenburg, Jacques 1979: *Official and Popular Religion*, Religion and Society No 19. The Hague/Paris/New York: Mouton.

Welbon, G. R. 1968: *The Buddhist Nirvana and its Western Interpreters*. Chicago: University of Chicago Press.

In addition to the above, the Programme, Abstract Resumes and cyclo-styled Participants Lists for the Winnipeg IAHR Congress (1980), the Congress Programme and Book of Abstracts for the Sydney IAHR Congress (1985) and the *Book of Abstracts* for the Rome Congress (1990) have provided data for my essay.

11

Women's Studies of the Christian Tradition: New Perspectives

Kari Elisabeth Børresen

After my more than thirty years of research in patristic and medieval history of ideas, focusing on Christian anthropology and gender models, I have prepared an extensive review-article on women's studies of the Christian tradition.[1] This study covers 553 books and articles published since about 1970, which I have found of special value and/or of particular interest. My survey concentrates on the formative periods, from early Christianity to the Age of Reform. Results and perspectives are summarized in the present essay.

Traditional gender models of Christian doctrine and symbolism were structured in Late Antiquity, corroborated through the Middle Ages, unaffected by the Renaissance and preserved after the Reformation. Historical analysis of this ideological construction and sociological deployment is of fundamental importance for understanding both previous and contemporary Western culture, since European/North American civilization has developed with and is still shaped by the Christian tradition.

Since the early 1970s women's studies concerning the formative periods of Christianity have multiplied. In order to systematize this variety of scope and content, my review article includes the following main topics: theological anthropology, as elaborated in Greek and Latin patristics, imposed through medieval doctrine and left unchallenged by the Renaissance and Reformation; women's monasticism, emerging in fourth-century Egypt and expanding in Europe from the early Middle Ages, with decline after the thirteenth century; women writers, mostly aristocratic nuns, but in the late Middle Ages also recluses and beguines from the higher *bourgeoisie*; hagiography, where sources from lower strata of society reveal so-called popular religious culture. Women's studies of the Christian tradition provide interdisciplinary and comparative research, since doctrinal anthropology and women's writings concern the history of ideas, whereas female monastic culture and hagiography are parts of social history. The common denominator of these overlapping fields is the historical perspective, which is fundamental in humanistic scholarship.

Human Genderedness as Main Analytical Category

Contemporary women's studies presuppose a twentieth-century holistic anthropology where the human being is defined as a sexually differentiated psycho-physical entity, no longer split into male or female body and a sexless, rational soul. Nevertheless, influenced by behaviourism and Marxist epistemology women's studies, often pursued from a social sciences perspective, still makes a sharp distinction between sex as biologically determined and gender as culturally constructed. I consider this distinction a paradoxical relic of androcentrism in asexual disguise. *Sans doute* motivated by fear of male-centred sociobiology, this device is an ironic imitation in reverse of the Church Fathers' 'feminist' stratagem of including sub-male women in God-like humanity by means of a sexless *imago Dei*. In fact, the radical difference between male and female God-language is evidenced in the Christian tradition, for instance by comparing Augustine and Julian of Norwich or Hildegard of Bingen and Thomas Aquinas. The *dialogue des sourds* exposed in the letters of Abélard and Héloïse is a typical case. It follows that women's studies in religion are at the forefront of intellectual inquiry by applying human, that is male or female, genderedness as a main analytical category. This new concept is holistic in the sense of connected interaction between biologically programmed sex and socio-culturally expressed gender. Such an innovative focus on both female and male humanity corrects two basic fallacies in traditional scholarship: androcentrism, where men's experience and thought are valued as normatively human, and asexualism or the assumption that scientific performance is unaffected by the researcher's male or female genderedness.

Inculturated Anthropology

The traditional paradigms of androcentrism and asexualism correspond to basic themes in patristic and medieval anthropology. Due to the interaction between definitions of Godhead and God-like humanity, Christian gender models are verbalized in terms of socioculturally shifting anthropology. The main inculturated concepts of human God-likeness can be summarized as follows:

Androcentric monism with correlated andromorphic Godhead where the exemplary human being is male, since Adam is created in God's image (Gen. 1: 26–7a; 2, 7). According to this first doctrinal stage, valid into the fourth century, only men are considered to be creationally God-like, whereas women can achieve salvational Christ-likeness by 'becoming male' (1 Cor. 11: 7; Eph. 4: 13).

Androcentric dualism with correlated metasexual Godhead, where the sexless rational soul is created in God's image, although exemplary human maleness mirrors the excellence of an asexual *imago Dei* (Gen. 1: 27b attached to 1: 26–7a by means of Gal. 3: 28). In this second doctrinal stage, initiated in the third century by Clement of Alexandria and elaborated by Augustine to become normative during the Middle Ages, women's salvational God-likeness is backdated to creation despite their non-theomorphic femaleness.

Holistic monism with correlated male and female metaphors describing God, where women and men are defined as God-like *qua* female or male human beings.[2] This third doctrinal stage is anticipated by medieval women mystics' identification with a kenotic Christ through their vulnerable femaleness. It is important to remember that women's female God-likeness was explicitly formulated only in nineteenth century feminist exegesis, first by the Norwegian painter and female theologian Aasta Hansteen in 1878.[3] In fact, superseding the traditional concepts of male or sexless *imago Dei*, this post-androcentric inculturation has become normative only in the twentieth century. Adopted by Protestant and later endorsed by Catholic theological anthropology, it is of note that such holistic God-likeness remains unaccepted in Orthodox doctrine.

Updated God-Likeness, Outdated Typology

It is essential to observe that the first doctrinal stage, with men's exclusive God-likeness in the order of creation, survives tenaciously in traditional typology. Androcentric gender asymmetry is here transposed from the first human couple – Adam and Eve in the biblical account of Genesis – to the order of salvation. God-like Adam prefigures Christ who as new Adam and divine Redeemer is incarnated in perfect manhood. Non-God-like Eve prefigures the church/Mary, who as new Eve represents dependent and therefore gynaecomorphic humanity (Rom. 5: 14; Eph. 5: 32). These typological gender models were elaborated in the second century by Justin and Irenaeus, to persist unembarrassed by the second doctrinal stage of asexual God-likeness. In fact, the new Adam–new Eve typology remains fundamental in both Catholic and Orthodox christology, ecclesiology and mariology. Consequently, the non-Protestant majority of institutional Christendom invokes typological sexology for affirming women's cultic incapability which excludes them from priestly ordination (Børresen, 1992). It follows that by refusing to ordain women, the present deadlock suffered in Roman Catholicism results from the simultaneous upholding of two, logically irreconcilable, doctrinal tenets: second-century androcentric typology on the one hand, twentieth-century holistic God-likeness on the other.[4] To formulate this contradiction succinctly: God-like women are deemed unfit to be Christ-like priests.

Matristic Strategy

Women's studies of the Christian tradition display varied female dismantling of male-constructed barriers. The obstacles raised by theological anthropology, sexology and canon law were surmounted by many women, as made visible through their history, writings, and hagiographical accounts. The main tenets of this confrontation are men's creational priority and women's salvational parity, accepted as normative by both parties. It is important to consider that androcentric gender hierarchy is apparently accepted by all female authors whose writings are preserved within the Christian tradition. Their works were transmitted by ecclesiastical establishments and often censured, redacted or translated by male confessors and clerics. This procedure might explain why no female text challenges the axiomatic precedence of male humanity in the creational order. Nevertheless, these matristic writers demonstrate an assertive exploitation of salvational advancement. From the perspective of Late Antiquity women's redeemed equivalence results from God's enhancement of creationally inferior femaleness to a level of exemplary male humanity. Consequently, ancient Church Mothers strive to actualize their salvational equality with God-like men through ascetic defeminization, overcoming their sub-male femaleness by virginity or widowhood (Jensen, 1992). In fact, this transformation into perfect maleness remains a basic theme in early Christian and patristic texts concerning holy women, as well as in the few extant female writings from Late Antiquity.[5]

I find it essential to observe that such gender reversal is not reducible in terms of women's social advancement through androcentric promotion to honorary manhood. Their redeemed achievement of fully human religious capability by 'becoming male' in Christ is a necessary consequence of traditional Christology, where the divine Son is born and resurrected in perfect, male humanity.[6] During the Middle Ages, Christology makes an important shift to emphasize womanly vulnerability as instrumental for revealing divine mercy. In medieval perspective, female weakness can imitate God's lowering of himself through the incarnated and suffering Christ. In this sense of displaying divine power, feeble women can serve as God's chosen instruments by gifts of mystical grace and prophetic charisma. Starting with the traditional, although atypical use of female metaphors describing Christ's human nature, medieval Christology is therefore reshaped in terms of 'becoming female' (Børresen, 1982, 1983; Bynum, 1982, 1987). In contrast, creational gender hierarchy structures the institutional church so that cultic performance is restricted to a male priesthood. The resulting incoherence between ecclesiastical androcentricity and charismatic gynaecocentricity is particularly manifest in the lives and writings of *mulieres religiosae*, the women religious. These extraordinary women aptly exploit their God-given mystical charisma within the limits imposed by androcentric culture. Due to the church's dominance in medieval society, theological arguments are used to legitimate and strengthen man-centred social structures. Inversely, the doctrinal affirmation of equivalence in the order of redemption forces the church to tolerate female mystics and prophets, provided that they submit to clerical control of their activities and writings.

Female God-Language

In medieval matristics, the traditional stratagems of women 'becoming male' in Christ or claiming asexual God-likeness are relinquished. Perspicaciously challenging the correlated andromorphic or metasexual God-language, Hildegard von Bingen and Julian of Norwich seek to establish a model of female God-likeness at the divine level. Invoking God-given revelations in order to actualize their salvational empowerment, these innovative Church Mothers strive to remove the fundamental incoherence between Godhead and femaleness.

In Hildegard's main theological work, *Scivias* (1151) God's revelatory *Sapientia* appears as a female figure (Newman, 1987). The whole universe is visualized as being continuously upheld by this shaping *Creatrix*, permeating *Caritas* and providing *Scientia*. When Hildegard describes God's transcendence with male imagery and God's immanence with female imagery, she builds on early Christian tradition. Connected to I Cor. 1: 23–4, where God's incarnated, suffering Son and God's revealing Wisdom converge, medieval use of female metaphors to describe Christ's human nature elaborates previous Christology. Hildegard's vision is original in the sense that God's *Sapientia* provides a divine model of perfect female humanity, *feminea forma*. Hildegard's mariology is consequently rather subdued, although Mary as new Eve is the prime example of female human wholeness, realized through virginity.

Despite her validation of human femaleness as reflecting divine Wisdom, Hildegard considers creational gender hierarchy to be confirmed by women's bio-social inferiority. It is significant that this energetic abbess rejects women's ordination to the priesthood.

Combining male-centred gynaecology and traditional Adam-Christ typology, Hildegard argues that women's feebleness and receptive role in procreation make them incapable of performing sacramental consecration of bread and wine. In consequence, priestly office is defined as a male sex role, with Christ as the exemplary high priest. Nevertheless, Hildegard concludes with an innovative interpretation of traditional marriage imagery where the virgin or widow as bride of Christ assimilates his priestly eminence, just as the loving woman encloses her husband's body.[7]

Like Hildegard's divine *Sapientia*, Julian's concept of 'our Mother Christ' as 'our Mother God all Wisdom' starts from sapiential Christology in its patristic and medieval formulation of Christ's gynaecomorphic human nature. In the long version of her *Showings* (after 1393), Julian's God-language is original in the sense that she transposes Christ's motherhood to the pre-existent level of triune Godhead.[8]

It is important to observe that Julian's fundamental trust in universal salvation is strikingly opposed to Augustine's, and later Luther's, anguished seeking for a merciful God. In order to verbalize her visionary experience of God's recreating love 'that all things will be well', Julian elaborates her doctrine of divine Motherhood.[9]

> I saw and understood that the high might of the Trinity is our Father, and the deep wisdom of the Trinity is our Mother, and the great love of the Trinity is our Lord; and all these we have in nature and in our substantial creation. And furthermore I saw that the second person, who is our Mother, substantially the same beloved person, has now become our Mother sensually, because we are double by God's creating, that is to say substantial and sensual. Our substance is in the higher part, which we have in our Father, God almighty; and the second person of the Trinity is our Mother in nature and in our substantial creation, in whom we are founded and rooted, and he is our Mother of mercy in taking our sensuality. (Colledge and Walsh, 1978b, p. 294)[10]

Accordingly, Julian applies her concept of divine totality to the human level, since the initial creation and redemptive incarnation unify the spiritual and bodily elements of humanity. It is important to note that Julian's use of the terms *substannce* and *sensualyte* does not imply a dualistic anthropology. On the contrary, Julian's innovative discourse aims at healing the androcentric duality of traditional doctrine. In her *Showings* trinitiarian interaction is verbalized by means of human wholeness, in the sense that both male and female metaphors describing God correspond to both God-like women and men. Julian's consistent naming of Christ the Mother as 'he' points to this interchangeability.

Julian depicts Christ's maternal qualities in conformity with her culture's traditional female role where the mother is defined as protecting, nurturing and compassionate. Nevertheless, by placing Christ's metaphoric motherhood in his unified divine humanity, Julian overcomes the gender hierarchy of traditional typology, with Christ's church or Mary as subordinate new Eve. Focusing on God the Mother, Julian's mariology is consequently quite discreet. The main achievement of this learned anchoress and foremother of feminist theology is to provide a fully God-like, christomorphic and female role model for women.

Patristic Innovation, Matristic Achievement

The gradual inclusion of women in fully human God-likeness is based on Graeco-Roman patristic innovation and Northern European matristic achievement (Børresen, 1993). Starting from men's exclusive God-likeness and women's salvational 'becoming male' in Christ, the Church Fathers of Late Antiquity define women as asexually God-like already from creation in spite of their non-theomorphic femaleness. Metaphorically feminizing the Godhead, medieval Church Mothers provide a model of female God-likeness, thereby anticipating the holistic definition of *imago Dei* in twentieth century Western theology.

The contemporary collapse of androcentricity in European and North American civilization is already perceived as more threatening by Roman Catholic ecclesiastical institutions than the previous geocentric (Kepler) and anthropocentric (Darwin) breakdowns which left traditional doctrine and symbolism nearly intact. The insertion of female human beings into a fully God-like humanity is a radically new phenomenon in Christian history. This post-androcentric inculturation is incompatible with the traditional new Adam/new Eve typology which still structures Catholic and Orthodox christology, ecclesiology and mariology. In consequence, the non-Protestant majority of Christendom will have to rebuild its 'sacred canopy' in order to provide viable doctrine and symbolism. In the present situation of arrested *aggiornamento*, patristic innovation and matristic achievement are of exemplary value for this indispensable theological inculturation. Only when verbalized in terms of both women's and men's gendered experience does theology become a fully human God-language.

Conclusion

Women's studies of the Christian tradition can stimulate other fields of research by clarifying the fundamentally religious *rationale* of man-centred societies, where women's subordinate status is legitimated by their lack of a fully human, *in casu* God-like, capability. The androcentrism of all historically known, so-called higher civilizations, is no longer explored only in socio-economic terms. Even in the social sciences, religion is now understood as a quest for meaning and is considered as a basic human drive, essential to ensure human survival. Reciprocally, women's studies in religion are influenced by social anthropology, exploring the socio-cultural foundations of God-language and religious symbolism. The impact of hagiographical sources in women's studies of the Christian tradition is here significant. Of primary importance for comparative research is the use of bio-social genderedness as main analytical category in women's studies of religion. The manifestly androcentric character of Christian doctrine and symbolism provokes women's studies of this tradition to produce pioneering scholarship, thereby serving as hermeneutical model for humanistic and sociological women's studies. When human genderedness, both female and male, is fully integrated as an essential factor of interpretation in all types of research, women's studies will eventually become obsolete as a specialized academic task.

Notes

1 'Women's studies of the Christian tradition', in Børresen and Vogt (1993, pp. 13–127). Original version (covering 451 titles) in Fløistad (1990, pp. 901–1,001).

2 The gradual inclusion of women in fully human God-likeness, as realized through the interpretation of Scripture in the Christian tradition, is studied in Børresen (1991).

3 *Kvinden sk-ht i Guds Billede* (Woman created in God's image), Christiania 1878. Cf. Elizabeth Cady Stanton (ed.) *The Woman's Bible*, New York, 1895.

4   Kari Elisabeth Børresen, 'Image ajustée, typologie arrêtée. Analyse critique de 'Mulieris dignitatem' (in Børresen and Vogt, 1993, pp. 343–57).

5   Kari Vogt, 'Becoming male' A gnostic, early Christian and Islamic metaphor' (in Børresen and Vogt, 1993, pp. 217–42).

6   Kari Elisabeth Børresen, 'Ancient and medieval Church Mothers' (in Børresen and Vogt, 1993, pp. 245–75).

7   Scivias II, 6, 76–7. CCCM 43, pp. 290–1.

8   Børresen (1978) 'Julian of Norwich: a model of feminist theology' (in Børresen and Vogt, 1993, pp. 295–314).

9   *Showings* (short version) XV; Colledge and Walsh (1978a). The motherhood metaphor is found in *Showings* (long version) pp. 48, 52, 54, 57–63, 74, 83; *A Book of Showings* vol. 2, pp. 502, 546, 563, 580–616, 675, 724.

10   *Showings* (long version), 58. Cited from Colledge and Walsh (1978b).

References

Børresen, Kari Elisabeth 1978: Christ, notre Mère. La théologie de Julienne de Norwich. *Mitteilungen und Forschungsbeiträge der Cusanus-Gesellschaft*, 13, 320–9.

Børresen, Kari Elisabeth 1982: L'usage patristique de métaphores féminines dans le discours sur Dieu. *Revue théologique de Louvain*, 13, 205–20.

Børresen, Kari Elisabeth 1983: God's image, man's image? *Temenos*, 19, 17–32.

Børresen, Kari Elisabeth (ed.) 1991: *Image of God and Gender Models in Judaeo-Christian Tradition*. Oslo: Solum Forlag.

Børresen, Kari Elisabeth 1992: The ordination of women: to nurture tradition by continuing inculturation. *Studia Theologica*, 46, 3–13.

Børresen, Kari Elisabeth 1993: Discours sur Dieu: patristique et matristique. *Augustinus*, 38, 121–35.

Børresen, Kari Elisabeth and Vogt, Kari 1993: *Women's Studies of the Christian and Islamic Traditions: Ancient, Medieval and Renaissance Foremothers*. Dordrecht, Boston, London: Kluwer Academic Publishers.

Bynum, Caroline Walker 1982: *Jesus as Mother. Studies in the Spirituality of the High Middle Ages*. Berkeley, CA: University of California Press.

Bynum, Caroline Walker 1987: *Holy Feast and Holy Fast. The Religious Significance of Food to Medieval Women*. Berkeley, CA: University of California Press.

Colledge, Edmund and Walsh, James (eds) 1978a: *A Book of Showings* to the Anchoress *Julian of Norwich*. Toronto: Pontifical Institute of Mediaeval Studies.

Colledge, Edmund and Walsh, James (trs.) 1978b: *Julian of Norwich. Showings*. New York: Paulist Press.

Fløistad, Guttorm (ed.) 1990: *Contemporary Philosophy. A New Survey*, 6, Dordrecht, Boston, London: Kluwer Academic Publishers.

Jensen, Anne 1992: *Gottes selbstbewusste Töchter. Frauenemanzipation im frühen Christentum?* Freiburg, Br., Basel, Wien: Verlag Herder.

Newman, Barbara 1987: *Sister of Wisdom. St Hildegard's Theology of the Feminine*. Berkeley, CA: University of California Press.

12

Women and New Religious Movements in Africa

Rosalind I. J. Hackett

Africa, by virtue of its great size and diversity, serves to challenge even the humblest of generalizations. It has been generally noted that Africa's new religious movements, notably of the independent church variety, have, over the last seventy-five years in particular, provided important new roles for women, previously denied them in traditional religious cults or in the mission churches. Others have argued that women attain little more than ceremonial leadership and symbolic complementarity in these movements, being subject to ritual taboos and segregation and valued only for their nurturant capacities (Jules-Rosette, 1979, p. 6). It is my intention here to consider the roots, manifestations and explanations of these apparently paradoxical roles of women as founders, leaders and members in Africa's new religious movements.[1] By examining women's religious agency in its various manifestations in a particular context, I believe it is possible to discern patterns and interconnections of leadership and participation, as well as limitations on and perceptions and manifestations of women's spiritual power, ordinarily obscured. At very least, this essay, while sacrificing several of the historical and ethnographic details present in an earlier version (Hackett, 1990) points to the rich variety of creative religious options open to women in many parts of sub-Saharan Africa today. More generally, attention to women's religious roles and experience provides us with a fuller picture of the transformative capacity of religion in people's lives and throws new light on indigenous African attitudes to tradition and Western Christianity, as well as notions of power and authority.

My focus is on women's power in the African independent churches, as they are commonly called, but I do examine the implications for women of the development of the newer revivalist movements. While this is not written from a predominantly social-scientific perspective, the religious experiences of African women must be seen as embedded in particular historical, social and cultural contexts. Wherever possible and relevant, therefore, links will be drawn with external institutions and influences, although such differentiations are often contrived in the African context. At the outset it is necessary to emphasize the sheer complexity of this topic, not just in terms of regional, ethnic and cultural differences, but also in terms of the numbers and variety of religious movements themselves. They range from neo-traditional movements, which seek to revive and redefine traditional ideas and customs, to prayer-healing movements and spiritual churches, separatist churches, and now to a newer breed of Christian revivalist movement drawing on the repertoire of Western pentecostal and evangelical religion. In addition, there is a growing number of spiritual science movements, characterized by their predilection for things metaphysical, occult and Eastern. Despite the fact that women mystics have featured prominently in the history of this latter type of movement in the United States at least, in the African context they are virtually absent. Likewise, their involvement in the separatist or Ethiopian churches seems to be relatively muted.[2] A number of women were active in the prophetic movements in South Africa at the end of the nineteenth century which battled to preserve land and custom. I have excluded these movements from the ambit of this chapter, despite the fact that the prophecies of these young women were treated with the same seriousness as those of the Xhosa male. elders. There are also Islamic-related movements, but these are few and not well documented and generally involve women only as participants.

As stated above, my concern here is rather with the most widespread and rapidly growing of the new movements, namely the spiritual or independent churches (sometimes referred to as Zionist in the South African context or 'spiritual' or 'Aladura' ['praying-people'] in West Africa)[3] and the newer revivalist movements, which are more international in orientation and inspiration. The statistical information provided by the *World Christian Encyclopaedia* (Barrett, 1982, p. 782) on the African independent or indigenous churches from 1970 to 1980 shows a growth rate far in excess of the mission-related (notably Protestant) churches.[4] This is particularly the case for Ghana, Nigeria, Sierra Leone, Zaïre and Zimbabwe.[5] While Africa's independent churches are still in a minority, representing over 32 million or approximately 15 per cent of all Christians in sub-Saharan Africa, the numbers of those associated with this type of church in a more casual or unaffiliated way may be much higher.

So, contrary to many expectations and earlier theories, African independent churches did not decline in the post-colonial period with political independence and increased indigenization of the mission-related churches. While they have shown the capacity to transcend ethnic and national boundaries, and expand into the rural areas, these movements have remained an essentially urban phenomenon, pragmatically addressing the spiritual and material needs of migrant workers and urban dwellers. One of the reasons proffered for the persistence of new religious movements in more recent times is economic, in that they claim to offer (financial) enrichment or 'blessings' for their flocks. This is particularly the case for the newer revivalist movements whose 'gospel of prosperity' is central to their discourse and timely in periods of economic recession. As we shall see, the economic factor is not one of the major reasons for women's participation in these movements.[6]

It is more important and helpful, however, to attribute much of the persistence and dynamism of Africa's new religious movements to their social and cultural innovation, and transformation and (re)negotiations of the sacred and the secular and the old and the new (see, for example, Jules-Rosette, 1979, pp. 1, 12–14, 21; Fernandez, 1982; Comaroff, 1985). Women, in particular, have demonstrated their ambivalence toward tradition; they have called for the rejection of repressive institutions and practices while reaffirming others. The new movements have been instrumental in shaping new communities and new personal and collective values.

The appeal of these new religious communities for women, with their 'familial' structures based not on kinship or ethnicity but religious commitment, must be seen in the light of the alienation that many women feel in the urban context. For the most part they already have marginal status in their husband's family; their sense of rootlessness and loss of family support is aggravated in the towns and cities. They are further subject to ambivalent attitudes and stereotypes, being blamed by their menfolk and the press for marital instability, prostitution and economic failures (Obbo, 1980, pp. 4–9). These projections are related to fears and doubts about women changing their roles and their increasing participation in economic and political life. This, again, will help us to understand the place of women in these organizations. But we must not lose sight of the 'pragmatic spirituality' of these movements, the sheer appeal of their emphasis on health, spiritual protection, fertility, material well-being and recognition of dualistic theories of sickness and misfortune. By focusing on women as we are doing here, with their proximity to life and death and everyday concerns, we are unlikely to be seduced by explanations which explain away Africa's new religious movements as proto-political movements or as alternative forms of petty trading or more large-scale 'industry'.[7] It is fair to say, however, that the considerable amount of scholarly interest shown in these movements is in part linked to the fact that they are a barometer of important changes occurring at both individual and collective or institutional levels in contemporary Africa.[8] Theologically, they constitute a serious challenge to the mission-related churches in the quest for indigenization and inculturation (see Kailing, 1988).

Women's attitudes, behaviour and so on are too frequently studied (or ignored) as peripheral, invisible and non-interactional in the face of universal male dominance. Such simple reductionism and dichotomization would be a betrayal of the complexity of the context under discussion here. Men are not simply subjects and women objects. There are reciprocity and complementarity in the ritual sphere in many African movements as much as there are sexually exclusive or parallel ritual activities. Furthermore, there is commonly an overlap between the domestic/private and public domains – a framework adopted by many to describe and account for gender differences – in many African societies.[9] Informal or covert power may be considered to be more potent and subversive than overt power, so it is important to take account of the arbitrariness of meaning and indigenous notions of power (see MacCormack, 1980, p. 21). Likewise, we should be wary of imposing Western interpretations on segregation, marginality, menstruation, etc. From work done by anthropologists on menstruation, for example, ritual and domestic segregation may be a source of empowerment for women, a validation of their spiritual potency (see Buckley and Gottlieb, 1988).

Gender is not the only organizing category in these movements, it may be seniority, experience, spiritual gifts, wealth and so on, and we try to take account of the interplay between these factors. Put differently, gender is not just about men and women but about other things as well, such as prestige, success, orientation, etc. (Strathern, 1981, p. 177). However, it is none the less integral to any informed understanding and analysis of Africa's new religious movements and their way of structuring their world. For as Potash (1989, p. 189) rightly insists, 'we cannot continue to describe institutions as gender neutral when they are not'. In other words, gender, or more specifically the female gender, should not be studied in isolation, nor out of context. Male–female relations, gendered symbolism and the changing role of women may be regarded as significant indicators of innovation and symbolic reflections of wider social and political concerns and activities (Jules-Rosette, 1979, p. 3). To cite one example, Fabian (1979) maintains that male domination and female submission in certain religious movements symbolize the experience of colonial domination.

Strathern argues that cultural arrangements, such as gender, may be instrumental to the pursuit of particular personal or social (and let us add here, religious) interests, even though these can never be independently defined. This is reiterated by Potash (1989, p. 191) who emphasizes that social (here we may substitute 'religious') actors use systems to achieve ends, which both acknowledges human resourcefulness and suggests that men and women are not victims of social and economic trends. Strathern (1987, p. 5) goes on to state that cultural arrangements are certainly instrumental in respect of any analytical interests one might have in the issue of agency – that is, accounting for the sources of people's actions and for their being perceived as actors. This question of agency, i.e. the relationship between individual actors and society, culture or 'the system' and the extent to which an individual's actions are determined by 'the system' is of course of far wider import than is being discussed here (Strathern, 1987,

p. 22). Africa's new religious movements provide a rich and varied spectrum of women's agency. Religious symbols and practices shape women's perception of themselves, their relations with others, their ability to act, and provide strategies for survival and empower or disempower them within the context of their religious or wider communities.[10] Religion may serve to determine gender-related behaviour just as it may enable people to 'act independently of the stereotypes that define their gender' (Strathern, 1981, p. 184).

Women Founders: Renowned Yet Rare

Arguably the ultimate act of religious independency or self-determination is the founding of religious movements by women themselves. It is impossible to give exact figures on the number of new religious movements founded by women in Africa. Barrett, in his 1968 study, *Schism and Renewal in Africa*, suggests several hundreds over the last few decades out of six thousand (Christian-related) movements (p. 148). In a more recent and geographically focused study in the town of Calabar in south-eastern Nigeria, I identified six indigenous movements as having been founded by women – approximately 12 per cent of all religious institutions with indigenous origins (Hackett, 1987, p. 191). Several of the movements founded by women in sub-Saharan Africa once had large followings and some were seminal in terms of the history of religious independency in Africa. While we do not wish to restrict ourselves to the religious elite when examining the relationship between women and new religious movements in the African context, it is worth noting the distinctiveness and emphases of these women.

Women founders are not a recent phenomenon. One of the most legendary of African founders and prophetesses was a young Kongo woman, Dona Béatrice or Kimpa Vita, whose death and resurrection experience and belief that she was the reincarnation of Saint Anthony resulted in the formation of a movement known as the Antonians in the central African kingdom of the Kongo between 1704 and 1706.[11] This movement is reputedly the first recorded African new religious movement. Her attempt to organize an African church with black saints and an indigenous hierarchy presented a challenge to the hegemony of the Portuguese Roman Catholic Church. Part of the appeal of Dona Béatrice's message was its synthesis and reinterpretation of Kongo and Catholic beliefs and practices. Its messianic content was aimed at individuals as well as the Kongo people as a whole. Dona Béatrice's call for cultural nationalism, political unity and religious self-determination at a crucial time of social and political unrest was to serve as a foundation and inspiration for succeeding prophetic and messianic movements in the region.

Another religious movement founded by a woman in politically turbulent times was the Lumpa Church. Founded by Alice Mulenga Lenshina Lubusha in 1954, it grew to be one of the most successful churches in Northern Rhodesia until its violent clash with the newly created Zambian government in 1964. As in the case of Dona Béatrice, Lenshina professed formative religious experiences and was revered for her healing and witch-finding capabilities (for a detailed contemporary account see Robert Rotberg, 1961; see also Wilson, 1973, p. 94; Bond, 1979, pp. 142–3). Lenshina used the model of female chieftainship, although she was unable to establish an authority structure exclusively or even primarily for women. With Alice Lenshina we have once again the example of a woman revitalizing, reinterpreting and reforming both indigenous and exogenous traditions and establishing a new community which provided new values and new security in the midst of social, political and religious upheavals.

Two well-known West African women founders, Grace Thannie or Tani and Marie Lalou of the Church of the Twelve Apostles in Ghana and the Deima Cult in Côte d'Ivoire respectively, both experienced challenges to their authority. While the two women acknowledged their heritage from the great Liberian prophet, William Wade Harris, who led a movement of mass conversion to Christianity between 1910 and 1914, their rejection of many traditional values and customs and creativity in the realm of worship (notably a redirection towards healing) attest to their power and authority. Although Madam Tani's dual leadership with Kwesi 'John' Nackabah led to a de-emphasis of her real power, Marie Lalou's dreams, proclamations and healing activities brought about accusations of witchcraft and subversion.

Marie Lalou was able to nominate a female successor, Princesse Geniss, who was followed by an unapproved spiritual successor, Blé Nahi. It is interesting to note the similarities in their life experiences. They were arguably social misfits, since both were childless and both were accused of harming or killing their husbands. Their healing powers were viewed ambivalently until each eventually proved that their mission was to serve humanity (Walker, 1979a, p. 96). Both women transformed and legitimated their socially unacceptable circumstances through spiritual means. They claimed status and were valued as ideal, spiritual mothers, who had renounced their roles as traditional mothers for the good of the community. This was unprecedented in the traditional context (Paulme, 1962, p. 32).

The case of the Shona prophetess, Mai (Mother) Chaza, bears some relation to the above accounts.[12] A divorced woman with six children, she was thought to have died and returned to life following a chronic illness. Led by the spirit into the mountains of Chiwako which she called Mount Sinai, she claimed that God had chosen her as a new Moses. She became a ritual leader and miracle worker, focusing on sterile women, the blind and the infirm. People came from Rhodesia and neighbouring countries, and several 'Cities of God' (*Guta ra Jehova*) were established around Umtali. Although she tried to keep the movement within the Methodist Church, it became in 1955 a separate organization – the Church of Mai Chaza. She wrote the *Mai Chaza Book* and a hymnal. She was known as *Muponesi* (Healer) and *Gwayana* (Lamb) and drew on Shona traditional religion and history in her teachings. In order to achieve special ritual power, she had to separate herself from 'customarily accepted conceptions of women' and renounced all sexual relations and marriage, as well as the use of traditional medicines (Jules-Rosette, 1976, p. 75). She did however build upon the prominence of ritual women in Shona tradition, drawing upon the methods of a spirit medium and traditional healer (Jules-Rosette, 1987, p. 103). She died in 1960 and was accorded messianic honours, but her movement split until a male prophet, Mapaulos, was finally recognized in 1961.

The Cherubim and Seraphim movement in Nigeria has produced some remarkable women leaders. But let us discuss here the co-founder, Christianah Abiodun Akinsowon.[13] In June 1925, at the age of fifteen, Abiodun Akinsowon, who came from a very well-connected West African Christian family in Lagos, reportedly fell into a trance for several days after attending a Corpus Christi Day procession. While in this spiritual state, she was taken to celestial regions by an angel and subjected to spiritual tests. She was commanded to renounce traditional herbalism and was taught prayers for healing and the blessing of water. When Abiodun awoke from her trance, she found that her guardians had sent for the man who had been mentioned in her vision and whose prayers could save her from death. His name was Moses Orimolade (Baba Aladura) and he was already well-known for his praying activities. He declared that salvation had entered the house. The interpretations of these events vary widely and have been a source of subsequent dispute. Was Abiodun hallucinating, was she sick, insane or was she 'in spirit'? Abiodun claims to have already had a religious experience at the time of her confirmation in the Anglican Church and there was no doubt that Lagos was ripe for healings and visions, having suffered from the worldwide influenza epidemic (1918) and bubonic plague (1924–6), as well as a burgeoning population. Crowds flocked to the house because of the visions and very soon prayer meetings were started. The group was eventually organized into a prayer society known as the Seraphim Society and was intended as a supplement to church services. It was not until some years later that it became known as the Cherubim and Seraphim Society and adopted a more autonomous position. It is noteworthy that this name change as well as other important developments in the history of the movement were transmitted by women and young girls through visions (Omoyajowo, 1982a, p. 11).

Until Abiodun quarrelled with Orimolade in 1929 and organized her own independent faction, she was considered to be the most prominent and energetic evangelist in the movement. She was instrumental in establishing the Society throughout Yorubaland. The title of 'Captain' by which she is still widely known was awarded to her in 1927 following a successful evangelistic tour. She settled down to a married life in 1942 and still lives in her husband's modern building in Surulere, Lagos, surrounded by a loyal group of prophetesses (Omoyajowo, 1982a, pp. 40–1). Despite challenges to her authority and various legal battles, Captain Abiodun is still regarded as the founder of the movement in her section, and even in dissenting sections she is referred to as 'Mother'. More recently she has played an active leadership role in the movement as a whole, which will be discussed below (Omoyajowo, 1982a, pp. 200).

Gaudencia Aoko received a prophetic call in 1963 to reject traditional magic and divination. Together with another Luo Catholic, Simon Ondeto, they founded the Legio Maria (after the Catholic Legion of Mary). Aoko went on to conduct her own evangelistic campaign against witchcraft and sorcery and traditional religious objects. She, too, called for healing by faith and for the liberation of women from repressive structures and practices and from the constant threat of death and sickness to their children. While stories circulate of two or three of her children dying mysteriously one day, she credits her call to a vision from the Virgin Mary and Jesus. She was by all accounts an extremely captivating and successful preacher and evangelist.[14] Despite the important role that she played in the early development of the movement, today she is virtually forgotten, remembered as a small business woman who has two wives (Luo have hetero-sexual woman–woman marriage) and by outsiders as a woman who had her leadership wrested from her by men (Schwartz, 1989). The Communion Church later founded by Aoko was a deliberate attempt to have a Catholic Church with a less rigid hierarchy which would permit women to be priests.

I now turn to some lesser known movements and their women founders. Mother Christianah Mokotulima, a Ndebele woman from South Africa and reared in the Dutch Reformed Church, began to see visions in 1906. She eventually founded the St John's Apostolic Faith Mission of South Africa and was known as Mother or Ma Nku. She became renowned for her visions, prophecies and efficacious prayers. Her daughter, Dr Lydia August, who studied medical social work in the US, carries on the healing work of her mother whose life spanned nearly a century from 1894 to 1988. It is interesting to note that there have been at least six secessions from the church led by women.[15] In Kenya, Senaida Mary Akatsa, a Luhyia woman, has drawn thousands of people to her compound in the Muslim village of Kawangware, a poor suburb of Nairobi, where she conducts faith-healing sessions. Described by the press as a 'self-proclaimed Christian "prophetess" ', she hit the headlines in June 1988 due to a report that Jesus himself had attended one of her sessions, designating her as a true representative of the 'most high'.[16] Since then, and despite government investigations, Akatsa's Church of Bethlehem has gained a measure of respectability. A government minister attends regularly and healing miracles continue to be reported.[17] Another Kenyan (Kikuyu) woman, by the name of Margaret Wangare, also operates from her own compound, just outside Nairobi in the village of Banana Hill, Kiambu District. Her faith-healing activities also centre on a discourse of salvation and re-vivalism. She was initially associated with a local revival mission but then began to gain prominence and travel all over the country in the early 1980s.[18] Both women are considered to be simple, low-class women with special healing powers. In Nigeria, in the town of Calabar in the Cross River State, Ebele Eko, an Igbo professor of English, has for several years been an active evangelist on the University of Calabar campus. A member, with her husband, of the Assemblies of God, she has worked toward the creation of an independent organization on campus, known as the Evangelistic Church of the Redeemed. The Christ Holy Church or Odozi-Odobo, founded by another Igbo woman who, over eighty years old, now resides (in retirement) in Andoni, Rivers State, became popular after the Civil War in Nigeria. The church lays emphasis upon prayer, healing, problem-solving and a livelier, African-style worship with vigorous music and dance.[19] Yinka Olisa, a Nigerian woman widely known as Malaika, runs a fast-growing yet controversial church in Mushin, Lagos. She reportedly claims: 'I have the power to loosen or tie anything in this world. I am god, the father, god the son and god the holy spirit. I have given thousands of women pregnancies. I can wrought [sic] more miracles that would bring spark back to a miserable life.'[20]

There exist or have existed a number of semi-autonomous movements such as Mother Bloomer's Confidential Band, founded in Sierra Leone in 1910 by Martha Davies and nine other Creole women (Ndanema, 1961), but the importance of these movements in either stemming or nurturing religious independency on the part of women is beyond the purview of this chapter. Suffice it to say, however, that they provide contexts for women to express themselves freely, to take responsibility for their own affairs, to exercise leadership roles, to nurture group solidarity and above all to be in charge of their own religious destiny. The links between these semi-autonomous religious organizations for women and the independent churches is an area which merits further investigation.

Female Leadership in Africa's New Religious Movements: Reverence with Restrictions

Several observers have documented with enthusiasm the leadership opportunities available to women in the independent churches. We shall examine some of their accounts in this section. The positive value they see being (increasingly) attributed to women's leadership stems in part from the comparison they are making with the status of women in traditional religions or the mission-related churches. Other writers, by making more internal, structural comparisons with male roles and status, and on the basis of perceived political inequalities, are more critical of the limited authority that women achieve in these movements. They argue that ceremonial leadership may imply political subordination. (See, for example, Aquina, 1967; Jassy, 1971; Jules-Rosette, 1987, n.10.)

Bennetta Jules-Rosette, for example, in her various publications on this subject (Jules-Rosette, 1976, 1979, 1981, 1985, 1987), has focused on the failure or inability of Africa's women church founders to hand over their mantles of authority to succeeding women. This is indeed borne out by some of the cases we discussed above. In two of the movements founded and led by women in Calabar, Nigeria, where I conducted research, men were hovering in the wings, poised for a timely takeover. Jules-Rosette has also argued that this absence of political or institutionalized authority extends generally throughout the church hierarchies. Women are more readily given positions of ceremonial authority and symbolic privilege, and roles associated with their nurturant capacities. [21]

Let us now examine a number of examples to see whether a pattern of asymmetry or equal opportunity emerges and to what this may be attributed. The precedent of a woman founder seems to bode well in some cases for the emergence of other women leaders in the same movement. In the case of the Twelve Apostles Movement of Ghana, the dual leadership of Madame Grace Tani and Kwesi 'John' Nackabah (see above) is reflected in a marked ritual parallelism with very different roles for women and men. There are two very distinct services: the Friday healing service in the garden at which the prophetesses (*sofo*) preside and the Sunday 'Chapel' service, conducted by younger males who have been exposed to Western-style religion and education and literacy. Yet, the healing ritual is the central event of the week.

The Cherubim and Seraphim movement of Nigeria is a well-documented case which provides several examples of female leadership. Following in the footsteps of the charismatic Christianah Abiodun Akinsowon (see above), came Madam Christianah Olatunrinle from Ondo (Omoyajowo, 1982b). The daughter of a high-ranked Ondo chief, she travelled widely as a trader and was politically active. She was the *Iyalode* (senior female elder) of the

Anglican Church, and was also very involved with traditional religion. Following a vision in Lagos she converted to the movement, destroying all her traditional charms on return to Ondo and refusing to respect traditional mourning rites by attending a church outing after the death of her only daughter. This put an end to the practice in Ondo of long confinements following the death of a child. This great woman evangelist was renowned for her extensive and arduous evangelistic tours, conducted when she was in her late seventies. As the result of a number of grievances with her church in Ondo, St Stephen's Anglican Church (Cherubim and Seraphim was still only a prayer society at this stage), not least the fact that she was not allowed to speak in church, she broke away to found a separate church. In 1936 she became (though not without opposition) Mother Superintendent (*Iya Alokoso*) of the Western Conference of the Cherubim and Seraphim. This was a charismatic title rather than the actual chairmanship and averted a major split within the movement (Peel, 1968, p. 108). A woman of many visions, she presaged her own death and left behind a solid tradition of philanthropy and support for her own church.

In addition to Madam Olatunrinle, there have many other powerful female spiritual leaders in the Cherubim and Seraphim movement (C & S) (which incidentally is highly fissiparous): Akanke Igbalaolu, founder and leader of the Redemption Band of the C & S; Sarah Amope, founder and leader of the Oja-Igbo No. 1 (Ibadan); Mother-in-Israel Esther Mewaiyewon, the virtual founder of the first Onitsha branch and the present leader of the Mount Zion C & S branches in Warri and Sapele and Mrs Adebiyi, who pioneered the establishment of the Society in Northern Nigeria (Omoyajowo, 1982a, pp. 200–1). More generally within the organization, women may attain such high offices as Mother Cherub, Mother Seraph, Captain and Mother-in-Israel – ranks equivalent to Apostles and Senior Apostles. The High Spiritual Mother of the United Church of C & S is the female counterpart of the Archbishop of the Section and enjoys the same status as any Baba Aladura ('Praying Father'). Prophetesses have played major roles in facilitating the expansion of the movement and their sincerity as visioners and prophetesses is never questioned as it is for men (Omoyajowo, 1982a, pp. 200–1).

Despite the recognition of women's spiritual powers in the C & S movement and their predominance in terms of membership, there are none the less restrictions on and negative attitudes toward their leadership. These are particularly evident in the resistance shown in 1934 to Captain Abiodun's becoming leader of the whole Society. She was instead offered the post of Supreme Head of all women in the Society which she rejected. She disappeared into virtual political obscurity as head of her own section. In 1986, however, she emerged to reunite the majority of the many C & S schisms. This important act of leadership was necessitated by a loss of members to the stronger and more unified Aladura churches. Omoyajowo (1982a: 201; 1988, p. 83; see also Peel, 1968, p. 183 and n.4) maintains that Abiodun has constantly had to battle against male prejudice in the church. This 'traditional male superiority', as Omoyajowo calls it, in the Cherubim and Seraphim movement is reflected in the fewer openings for women leaders in the hierarchy (five as opposed to nine for men) and the limitations on women's 'spiritual services', because of menstrual and childbirth taboos (a woman cannot enter the house of prayer for forty days after the birth of a male child and for eighty days after the birth of a female child) (Omoyajowo, 1988, p. 201). The latter in itself is an important symbolic statement about perceived male primacy.

The case of the Legio Maria in Kenya does not demonstrate the continuity of a woman founder and female leadership. Women's roles in the church are restricted to those of 'mother' and 'sister', roles which do not offer overall leadership. It is possible that the movement's roots in the Roman Catholic Church may be significant here. A similar pattern may be observed in the Mai Chaza Church. While the founder is revered as the ancestral and spiritual mother, the increasing institutionalization of the movement has resulted in a loss of influence for women, as in the wider society.[22]

In his landmark study, *Bantu Prophets in South Africa* – the first scholarly study of religious independency in Africa which appeared in 1948 – Bengt Sundkler claims that it is the independent churches, particularly those of the Zionist type, that offer the most status to women. In traditional Zulu society, they were excluded from most ritual roles, except that of diviner. He states that in general Zulu women responded more favourably to mission Christianity and were to be found in greater numbers in both the churches and the schools. In the independent churches of the Ethiopian type (those that separated from the mission churches over questions of leadership), women's leadership runs on parallel lines to that of the men. He observes that they tend to show more energy and initiative than men in arranging prayer meetings, fund-raising, church visits, etc., and so wield great influence in the church as a whole.

Among the Zionist-type churches in Soweto, legal and charismatic authority are distinguished. Prophets stand outside the 'formal' hierarchy and are not therefore considered to be leaders of the churches. While both types of leadership are required for the successful growth of the church, they often exist in tension. In several churches this has led to the development of two separate hierarchies or streams of authority. In the Soweto independent (Zionist) churches most prophets are women and hence do not hold office in the formal hierarchy of the churches, nor do they pose any real threat to the male establishment. They are not without influence, however, since they are regarded as conduits or 'oracles' for the will of God through the Holy Spirit and will be heard and consulted on important matters pertaining to the church (West, 1975, p. 52). One small, independent church in Calabar, known as the Holy Face Healing Church, illustrated well this male/female division. I witnessed there regularly the tussle between male (bureaucratic) order and female (spiritual) disorder during services. As the founder told me, all the 'spiritual people' in the church were women.

Turner (1967, vol. II, pp. 36–41) has described the parallel hierarchies in the Church of the Lord (Aladura) as one concerned with 'visions, revelations and prophecies' and leading to the position of Apostle and the other stressing 'pastoral, preaching or administrative' gifts and leading to the position of Bishop. A similar structure obtains in the Celestial Church of Christ, another West African Aladura ('praying-people') church with headquarters in Nigeria. These are both good examples of variables other than gender providing the basis for the organizational structure.

What is interesting to note in the case of the Celestial Church is that up until fairly recently they permitted no societies or *egbe*, or any priesthood, for they see these as a source of factionalism. [23] Since women did not have separate (informal) associations as in some other churches they were therefore more integrated and prominent not just in terms of the prophetic hierarchy but also the administrative hierarchy. They still are not permitted to move to the highest echelons (the so-called ordained ranks) and are not allowed to preach (except at outdoor services), but their spiritual gifts, seniority, experience, wealth or talents are clearly recognized and drawn on by this movement and many women wield considerable influence. A case in point is Superior Senior Prophetess Rosaline Bola Sodeinde, who is widely known as the 'spiritual daughter' of the late founder of the church, Pastor S. B. J. Oschoffa, for the close relationship she enjoyed with him and the dynamic role she has played in the church, since joining in 1971.[24] Today she still speaks with gratitude of the cure she received in Celestial Church from a protracted and undiagnosed illness, following which she joined the church, becoming the Lady Chairman of the International Management Committee, Lady Vice Chairman of the Celestial Women's Council and Matron to many Celestial parishes throughout Nigeria and in Europe and the United States. Unquestionably the most powerful Celestial woman (she was reputedly called a 'man' by Pastor Oschoffa), she is credited with having supported and even facilitated Supreme Evangelist A. A. Bada in his difficult transition to the leadership of the church following the death of the founder.[25] In addition to her political skills, she has become one of the chief articulators of Celestial teachings, a function rarely attributed to women. Superior Senior Prophetess Sodeinde sees no limits to her real power in the church, even though she pays deference to the limitations on women's authority. She proudly declares how she and other women members of the National Women's Council have spearheaded the idea of having a basilica at Celestial City, Imeko (the burial place of the founder) and are raising the necessary funds. Women may also pioneer the founding of churches, sometimes donating valuable land as the result of their personal conversion.[26]

In contrast to the Celestial Church of Christ, the Church of the Lord has parallel positions for women right up to the top of the hierarchy. Women can found and head churches (Turner, 1967)[27] and theoretically, become Primate. The ministry of women, with certain limitations (exclusion from the sanctuary and silence in church, except in absence of minister or male lay leader), was confirmed by a proclamation of the Primate in 1959. Since that time internal debate has led to a fuller ministry for women. The difference in the Church of the Lord's attitude to women compared to the other Aladura churches may be attributed to the fact that it sees itself as a more progressive church and belongs to numerous church councils, including the World Council of Churches.[28]

The question of women's leadership in the independent churches is in a number of cases determined or facilitated by relationships of co-dependency. In those Zionist churches studied by West in

Soweto, he noted that even when a woman was the permanent head (in three out of 252 cases) – and titled 'Bishop Mrs' or 'Bishop Mrs Prophet' – there was a male head as nominal leader. In some cases it was husbands who became 'reluctant bishops' but generally left the running of the church to their wives (West, 1975, p. 52). Conversely, women may hold office (in their *manyanos* or associations) by virtue of the position of their husbands. In the Eglise Adaïste in the Côte d'Ivoire, the role of 'première dame' is held by the first wife of the prophet and two other principal roles are also played by prominent wives. Other women, not necessarily official wives, may also exert an important influence through their roles in the prophet's compound. The preparation of his food is regarded as a privileged activity and is subject to a number of ritual taboos (Holas, 1965, pp. 91–2). In the Holy Healing Church in Ghana, the four wives of the founding prophet, Daniel Nuba, are all ordained pastors and in fact, twenty-one out of the thirty-four pastors are women. Men recognize women's dominance in the life of the church in a number of symbolic ways, such as prostrating before women for prayers and blessing. They reportedly explain this by saying that the respect and honour is not due to the woman herself but to the Holy Spirit dwelling within her and of which she is the instrument (Nuakoh, 1986).

Another example of a symbolic figurehead is Mama Obu, the sole wife of the founder of the Brotherhood of the Cross and Star, one of the largest independent churches in eastern Nigeria. Her status is derived from her position as Obu's (sole) wife. She is known as 'Mama' to all members and functions primarily as a homemaker. She lives in separate quarters down the road from her husband. She is frequently represented with her husband on promotional items, emphasizing the family aspect of the church. In the last few years, she is taking on a more prominent role, perhaps to offset the pressures on her ageing husband of a large and growing religious organization. Another great mother of the church was Marie Mwilu, the wife of the renowned prophet, Simon Kimbangu, from Lower Zaïre. It is interesting that in the 1980s, her role became idealized through popular legends. Her chastity and fidelity were emphasized and she was described as the heavenly mediator and source of consolation (her husband died in 1951 after thirty years of imprisonment). Such themes seem to have been borrowed from Catholic models in order to counter the moral disintegration of the family (MacGaffey, 1983, p. 251).

Co-dependency may provide opportunities for independent activities. For example, the wife of Adejobi (late Primate of the Church of the Lord [Aladura]) as 'spiritual mother' of the church was able to make her own tours accompanied by other women. She also inaugurated women's prayer unions and women's local preachers' unions, and anointed their new members (Turner, 1967, vol. I, p. 169). In fact, several years ago, the church took steps to define the position, duties (delivering babies, conducting evening prayers, Friday clinics and preaching) and privileges of the minister's wife or 'Spiritual Mother' or 'Church Mother' (Turner, 1967, vol. II, pp. 47–8). This attempt to encourage women to be the professional partners of their husbands is in many ways revolutionary compared to many other churches. Along somewhat different lines, opportunities for leadership may come with the absence of the formal male leaders. For example, a branch of the Church of the Lord was founded in Ibadan, Nigeria in 1961 by a woman, known as the 'Lady Evangelist' while the bishop was away for some time (Turner, 1967, vol. I, pp. 57–8). Parallel organizations for women may also provide opportunities for leadership. In another case, the African Independent Churches' Association (AICA) in South Africa established in 1961 a parallel organization for women, known as the Women's Association of the African Independent Churches (WAAIC). The latter ran a number of successful programmes in literacy, sewing, child-care, cooking, hygiene and biblical knowledge and fund-raising drives to support widows and orphans. The men saw it as a daughter organization but, in general, the WAAIC was more successful than its male counterpart and the women were openly critical of AIC's financial mismanagement and ongoing disputes (West, 1975, pp. 164–5).

Another example of a parallel position, which is ceremonial and honorary, recognizing seniority and contribution to the community, is that of 'matron' or 'spiritual mother'. Although as Peel rightly indicates, for the Aladura churches, the position of *Iya Egbe* or *Iya Ijo* in the church (literally, 'mother of the society', or 'mother of the church') carries more power than its limited jurisdiction (i.e. over women) suggests. This is due to the predominance of women in the congregation, many of whom may be wealthy traders (Peel, 1968, p. 183). The same observation is made with regard to the *manyano* (women's services or movements) in Soweto independent churches (West, 1975, pp. 51–2).[29] There women enjoy direct authority and their wider influence is considerable, since they are numerically in the majority and are also the major fund-raisers in their churches. Their ability to stop raising funds, if necessary, puts them in a strong position to influence church leaders. A similar example may be drawn from the Church of the Apostles of John Maranke. Women are generally confined to the lower ranks of the church hierarchy and prevented from preaching. That does not prevent them from exerting their influence during sermons, for when they are tired or disagree, they start singing, and their voices rise gradually to such a volume that the preacher must stop (Aquina, 1967, p. 206). Lagerwerf notes that exclusion from the pulpit deprives women of the opportunity to enhance their status through oratorical skills (Lagerwerf, 1984, p. 80).

The newer revivalist (evangelical/pentecostal/charismatic) movements provide an interesting range of opportunities for women. The unstructured nature and unrestricted orientation of many of the movements (particularly those with pentecostalist leanings) allow women to take initiative, although this is tempered to varying degrees by an inherently conservative view of women's roles and nature (Hackett, 1993). These movements tend to predominate in Kenya, Ghana, Nigeria and South Africa. In Kenya, women may be seen organizing and leading, together with men, the popular lunchtime revivals which take place on Nairobi streets. In Nigeria, they have founded their own ministries (such as the Jesus Women Prayer Band Ministry in Benin City), associations (e.g. Nigerian Women for Christ) and newsletters (e.g. *The Virtuous Woman*). The perception of these movements as being more 'modern' and as having American links does not necessarily entail increased authority for women. The founder of the Emissaries Church in Madina, just outside of Accra in Ghana, studied at various theological colleges in the United States, but while women dominate in terms of membership in the church they enjoy positions of direct authority only in their own fellowship (see Sereboe, 1982). Men and women do, however, mix freely in the church.

We have considered a range of examples of women's leadership in the independent churches, ranging from regional superintendents to food supervisors. Some of these roles are defined through men or created by men as token positions, often with responsibility limited to other women and children. It is common for the ministry of women to be limited to those who have passed the menopause. In other cases, women have created separate spheres of activity for themselves, establishing peripheral authority (which, as we have seen may, in fact, play a central role). In general, however, it appears that women do not benefit from the charisma of office, in other words they rarely get promoted to high office from within the organization. It is rather through secession and their own initiative that they enjoy elevated status. The charismatic (usually prophetic) and traditional (in terms of seniority, as matriarchs) authority of women is recognized, but often subject to rational-legal authority. To put it another way, women *qua* spirits and women *qua* men are accorded respect, prestige and authority, but not in their own right.

Public leadership in the church is generally seen as a male domain by both men and women. The line is nearly always drawn at women heading whole organizations and dominating the men as a group (Peel, 1968, p. 183). But is the explanation that child-production and child-rearing are considered to be a woman's primary responsibilities sufficient? There is rather a configuration of forces, both local and global, historical and contemporary at work here. There are the structures of traditional society which generally are patrilineal and patriarchal, despite the great respect and economic independence that many women enjoy. Mission Christianity promoted the rights of women, but at the same time prepared them for domestic and supportive roles in society. Westernization has generally served to weaken women's roles, by favouring male-oriented education and professions. There is, however, an increasing number of professional women in many African societies. In her study of women in independent churches in Botswana, Lagerwerf (1984, p. 79) identifies three factors which appear to influence the presence of women in local leadership structures, namely the numerical strength of women in a particular area, fewer 'strong' women than in the 1960s, and a church's position on the 'traditional-Christian' continuum, i.e. there are fewer opportunities for women in Western-style churches. More generally there is an abiding conviction that women possess great spiritual powers and that these are somehow linked to their life-giving capabilities. Such powers are viewed ambivalently and controlled by men through taboos and ritual restrictions (see Hackett, 1993). In other words there is a dialectic operating between social and religious forces and competing types of authority.

While social, cultural, economic and political forces may combine to restrict women's leadership roles in the independent churches, the subverting and empowering influence of the spirit is a potential and latent reality. We have seen in the previous section how charismatic women, empowered by spiritual experiences and often suffering from marginality or misfortune, may rise up to challenge the status quo both religiously and politically and call for the reform of existing structures for the salvation of individuals and community, whether church or nation. There would seem to be significant, but not necessary, links between the movements founded by these women and the more general opportunities for leadership. The question of participation and appeal of the independent churches for women will be treated in the next section.

Membership and Participation of Women in the New Movements: Repression or Recognition?

It is readily apparent and well documented that the independent churches are very popular with women, and that they tend to dominate the majority of congregations.[30] Is it the increased leadership opportunities, discussed in the previous section, which draw women in the first place or are there more prevailing considerations? In my survey of membership in the Celestial Church of Christ I made a distinction between reasons people gave for coming to the church in the first place and those they adduced for staying (Hackett, forthcoming; see also Jules-Rosette, 1987, pp. 110–11). The former were generally more critical in nature, i.e. related to sickness or problems while the latter pertained to more long-term issues such as preference for the liturgy, greater participation, heightened spirituality, increased spiritual power, or sense of greater protection. In other words, women are unlikely to cite lack of political power, but rather spiritual frustrations or material problems as a reason for changing their religious affiliation. The fact that they are given greater responsibility, at whatever level, once in an independent church will for the most part induce them to stay, but not draw them initially.

Healing is undoubtedly what attracts many women in the first place to the independent churches and the promise of ongoing protection which retains them (Turner, 1967, vol. II, pp. 151–4). Healing must be understood in its more holistic sense, as not just dealing with the physical, but also the psychological, spiritual and material. Women (not necessarily church members) constitute the majority of the clientele availing themselves of the services of prophets and spiritual healers.[31] Some of the reasons for this have been alluded to earlier, notably the primary responsibility of women for child production and child care. Callaway (1987, p. 327) sees an important continuity between Yoruba traditional healers (*babalawo*) and the Cherubim and Seraphim Society in the attention and causal explanations they give to the special health care problems of women and children.[32] Claims to have had a child through the ministry of these churches are very common. Instead of being subject to the impersonal and often inadequate treatment of government hospitals or being unable to afford private treatment, women may enjoy the round-the-clock pastoral care and personal attention which is characteristic of the independent churches, the Brotherhood of the Cross and Star in Nigeria being a good example of this with their maternity homes, often being asked for no more than a freewill offering or a testimony during a service or at most some commitment to membership (Callaway, 1980, p. 329). In addition, women supplicants may identify with the experience of their female founders and prophets, many of whom underwent some form of suffering before embarking on their spiritual careers.[33]

More generally, many of the independent churches offer practical help for women in a number of respects. For example, the Kimbanguist Church in Zaïre, offers literacy and French language courses and intensive courses in 'housewifery and child care' (Martin, 1975, p. 139). Many of Africa's independent churches both symbolically and structurally resemble families. As suggested earlier, in the rapidly changing and rootless urban context, these communities offer important support (both moral and logistic) for women and men. In the absence of traditional family structures, women may benefit from the company of female peers and the advice of senior women. In other words, they may learn strategies for urban survival.

It has often been said that the liturgy and style of worship of the independent churches are more attuned to women's needs which are more expressive, fluid, and spontaneous (receptive to the vagaries of the Spirit). Women may feel that their spirituality is not devalued or repressed as it was in many mission-related churches.[34] In many independent churches the great majority of those possessed during services are women (see, for example, Turner, 1967, vol. II, p. 127). In the Brotherhood of the Cross and Star, the testimonies of female members receive as much, if not greater, prominence (through the church's publications) than those of their male counterparts. Women are also able to show initiative in the area of music, as composers, choir leaders and conductors. They have gained fame as hymn composers in the Wanga independent churches in East Africa (Barrett, 1968, p. 150). Prophetesses in the Brotherhood of the Cross and Star in Calabar, south-eastern Nigeria, often compose songs 'in spirit'. The services of Alice Lenshina's Lumpa Church were mainly devoted to the singing of the distinctive songs that Lenshina herself had taught, set to old Bemba tunes and expressing a simple evangelical faith (Rotberg, 1961, p. 74; Wilson, 1973, p. 97). The blind Kenyan (Luo) evangelist, Mary Atieno, is nationally renowned for her gospel compositions, musical productions and broadcast performances. There is every evidence that women enjoy the more active roles that they may play in the life of their churches, even though responsibilities may vary from church to church. Within Zionist churches, for example, women serve as 'front-line recruiters of Zion' as they are able to mix more freely with their co-workers and neighbours than the men, who are subject to much more pronounced moral exclusiveness (Kiernan, 1974, p. 87).

Women do not have the same social outlets as men, even though in some contexts they may enjoy greater freedom as co-wives; socializing in the church compound and dancing at the services may be the main sources of entertainment for many women. This is readily observable by visiting the compounds which are active day and night, with women just sitting around talking, praying, performing personal rituals or looking after children. A number of Celestial women stated that the fact that the church was close to their homes and accessible at all times had influenced their conversion. This solidarity is particularly evident in the South African churches where the women are left to run homes and families as their husbands work away from home.

Mobility within the independent church hierarchies is often not determined by literacy but rather by spiritual gifts, seniority, and experience. In this way, a woman may have received little (Western) education and have limited economic means and a lowly social status, yet within the ritual context, her role and status may be heightened, even reversed. This negotiation and transformation of identity is apparent on a much wider scale. As noted by Leny Lagerwerf (1975, pp. 48–9): 'The African independent churches with their small communities, offer then another social group in which they are known and accepted as persons, in which they become full citizens of the Kingdom of God, in which they can take initiatives and responsibilities, and in which they can acquire a social position independently from their situation at home.' It should be added, however, that in the larger, rapidly expanding churches such as the Celestial Church of Christ, women (and men) with particular professional skills or significant wealth, will most likely be given accelerated promotion or be placed on, or in charge of, various committees.[35] This also serves to affirm in passing that, in West Africa in particular, these churches are by no means 'churches of the dispossessed'.

It is characteristic of many African independent churches to have a number of rituals and taboos surrounding menstruation and childbirth. Many of these rites of purification are performed by men. The churches claim that they are biblically (Old Testament) based. The affinities with traditional customs and beliefs about the dangers of menstrual blood are apparent. The women themselves do not always see their exclusion and purification in negative terms. Some enjoy the break from domestic duties and church attendance, others see it as a recognition of their mystical powers, others claim that it gives them a sense of identity and helps define their sphere of operation. In the Church of the Lord (Aladura), the churching rite serves rather as a thanksgiving to God for victory over the perils of childbirth and as a dedication and blessing of the child. There appears to be no idea of purification of uncleanness of the woman (Turner, 1967, vol. II, p. 188). Among the Zionists, women are viewed by the men as more open to defilement and contamination not because of their biological functions but because they are more socially involved in the lives of other women and constitute the frontline of recruitment (Kiernan, 1974, pp. 86–8). In general, though, this is an area which deserves further research.

Having examined some of the reasons why women join and remain members of Africa's independent churches, let us now consider the range of male opinions in this regard. Joining the independent churches independently of their husbands in many cases and breaking with the tradition of a wife adopting the denomination of her husband (if different) have created fears of insecurity among men. Popular fears voiced by men both privately and in the media are that the late-night services and special prayers by the prophet are a cover for illicit relationships and an explanation for the high fertility rate of these churches. They also may feel threatened by the strict moral injunctions that their wives may bring home from church. Some churches caution the women not to cause rifts or initiate strife in this regard and to make compromises in order to protect the family unit, hoping that the husband will eventually be persuaded to convert of his own volition.

Male attitudes are far from always negative. One of the tenets of the Women's Council of the Celestial Church of Christ is 'to instil and maintain discipline within the Celestial women'.[36] For this reason also, it was popularly said that many young men came to the church to find a 'good wife'.[37] Much attention is paid to the modesty of women's dress, with detailed requirements concerning covered heads, necklines and sleeves. Virginity and marital fidelity receive emphasis in many churches. Obbo reports that Luo men were able to control and manipulate their wives through the machinations of prayer leaders in the Legio Maria church in Uganda. These leaders/mediums would induce the women to confess publicly in church on Sundays in front of their husbands about misdemeanours, frustrations or desires which the leaders had learnt of through gossip and while out preaching in people's houses (Obbo, 1980, pp. 112–13).

In contrast to such manipulation, the Bwiti religion of Gabon, so thoroughly and insightfully researched by James Fernandez, provides a striking example of ritual complementarity (Fernandez, 1982, pp. 424–8).[38] Through their dances, rituals, architecture and even a tug of war between men and women (the latter often win), harmonious relations between the sexes are of paramount importance (and reflected in the Bwiti claim that their divorce rate is much lower than the rest of Fang society). This is in striking contrast with traditional Fang rituals which are mainly exclusive to one sex or the other (Fabian, 1979, p. 335).

Conclusion

In many respects this chapter is a survey of materials and case studies on women and their association with new religious movements in Africa. Naturally such a synthesis seems to generate more diversity than unity, given the very different historical, geographical, social, religious and cultural contexts. Certain themes, however, have emerged. The first is the recognition of women's mystical and spiritual powers, even if sometimes this recognition is indirectly manifest in ritual control rather than affirmation.

Secondly, there is a tendency by women founders to reject oppressive practices for women, notably those involving witchcraft and sorcery accusations and to protest against male domination and suppression of female expression and action. In the absence of formal cultic roles for women, the belief in spirit possession (whether in the traditional context or in a spiritual church) facilitates and legitimates women's (spiritual) voices and actions.

Thirdly, while there is arguably an affinity between women's traditional religious activities and their roles in the newer movements, there is a general ambivalence toward tradition. Groups that appear to reject tradition periodically restore aspects of it (Jules-Rosette, 1979, p. 228). Jules-Rosette suggests that this represents the attempt by such religious groups to maintain their boundaries and identities as they creatively manipulate local and global forces. She also notes the occurrence of a conservative nostalgia in the face of rapid social change where women become idealized as symbols of motherhood, family, unity and an idyllic past (Jules-Rosette, 1979, p. 228). In other words, an 'increasing liberalism in sex-role expectations' is not necessarily concomitant with religious independency and self-determination.

Fourthly, it is my contention that, overall, women may enjoy greater participation and leadership within the new religious movements. But why is full equality generally beyond their reach and why do they not hold on to power? Women manifest those same gifts of charismatic authority such as preaching, evangelizing, diagnosing, healing, speaking in tongues. In several cases, women may have the charismatic authority in the early stages but for a movement to survive it has to develop certain institutional structures. In traditional society, women's primary responsibility was the family. As mentioned above, they were often denied access to Western education or were given training to prepare them for supportive roles either in the home or the workplace. It is therefore not surprising that women are either unskilled, unprepared or unwilling to take on the managerial role of church leader. In many independent churches we see them rather assuming traditional roles by virtue of age, experience and seniority like their male counterparts.

On a similar note, one might point to the belief that women have lost ground in the colonial and post-colonial periods. They are often confined to the rural areas, while the men work in the towns and cities. Or, if they move to town, they may not have the skills for urban employment. In other words, women are disadvantaged in comparison to men when it comes to assuming leadership roles in the churches, as well as having to deal with the prejudices and insecurities of men regarding the changing roles of women.

Fifthly, as emphasized earlier, we must never lose sight of the complexity of this whole issue – not just the sheer variety of roles performed by women in the new movements, but also the configurations of forces which have shaped these diverse roles in different historical periods. Women's roles, therefore, are not just simply the survival of traditional forms or the result of the impact of mission churches. In the post-colonial period, movements must be seen as part of an emerging popular culture in all its complexity. The newer revivalist movements perpetuate many of the ambiguities and paradoxes of the earlier movements (Fabian, 1979, p. 170).

In viewing religion as a primary vehicle of cultural creativity, expression, interpretation and transformation, it is possible to see how women may negotiate their wider identities and roles through the more adaptive medium of the newer movements. It has not been possible to do justice in the present context to the mobilizing potential of these movements for women's lives in general. In fact, many avenues have been left unexplored. There is a need for more work on male–female relations in the new movements as well as in individual movements. In this way we may gain a better understanding of the links between leadership and participation. In particular, we must hear from the women themselves as they account for and interpret their own power (or access to power), experiences and responsibilities. There is also a call for more detailed biographies of individual women founders and leaders. It is a full agenda and the field of Africa's new religious movements is constantly growing, but such challenges are surely a researcher's dream!

Notes

I would like to thank all those who have made helpful comments and criticisms on this essay. Various versions of it were presented at a seminar at the Center of African Studies, University of Florida, Gainesville in the summer of 1990, the IAHR Congress in Rome in September 1990, and the Institute of African Studies, University of Ghana in February 1991. I am particularly grateful to the library staff and Center of African Studies at the University of Florida for facilitating the research for this essay.

1   This chapter is both a development and extension of my previous publications in this area (Hackett, 1985, pp. 247–71; 1987, pp. 191–208). I have also drawn up a proposal for an edited work on *Women and New Religious Movements in Africa*.

2   This is mainly due to the fact that these churches are largely modelled on the parent mission bodies from which they seceded, but this is an important area for future research.

3   In Kenya there has been a move to refer to all independent African churches as 'African-instituted churches'.

4   Note that many of the revivalist movements would not be included in these statistics, since they are interdenominational, of recent creation, often unstructured and neither clearly independent nor affiliated.

5   Barrett (1982, pp. 323, 432, 610, 758, 768). Selection made by Kailing (1988, p. 41, n.12).

6   Nor is it the reason why women migrate to urban areas; rather, they cite family problems and dissatisfaction with rural conditions. See Little (1973, ch. 2).

7   I am here reminded of the popular references to Calabar in southeastern Nigeria as a 'city of church industry' because of its plethora of religious institutions, many of them independent and Ibibio in origin. See Hackett (1989).

8   It is impossible even to summarize the wealth of publications here, but see Turner (1979). Terence Ranger's (1986) important survey of 'Religious movements and politics in sub-Saharan Africa' makes no reference to gender.

9   Niara Sudarkasa (1987, pp. 32–4) argues in this respect against Rosaldo, who sees the public/private domains as corresponding to the distinctions between male and female. See Rosaldo (1974).

10 Bennetta Jules-Rosette (1987, pp. 114–15) maintains that participation in their own sub-groupings in the Church of the Apostles of John Maranke leads women 'to have a sense of their own efficacy and to use collective interactions to redefine their positions in the religious community'. She advocates the use of such data together with information about household structure, the economic autonomy of women, child-rearing practices, traditional ideals to examine women's leadership and self-assertiveness in other contexts.

11 The following account is based on Goncalves (1985) and Jadin (1961). This lengthy (213 pages) article contains many details (from

first-hand accounts) on the life of Dona Béatrice, reactions to her prophetic activities and development and impact of the Antoniens following her death. See also Jadin (1968).

12 This account draws on the short biography of Mai Chaza in ' ... And some fell on good ground', *Risk*, 3 (1971) (a special edition on African independent churches).

13 This account of Abiodun's life is taken from Omoyajowo (1982a, pp. 5–12, 39–41) and Peel (1968, pp. 71–3).

14 'African women and the independent churches', *Risk* (1971) p. 50.

15 I am grateful to Professor G. Oosthuizen for sharing with me an unpublished paper that he wrote on Mother Nku. See also Omoyajowo (1988, p. 81).

16 *The Weekly Review* (Nairobi), 1 July 1988, p. 12. I am grateful to Peter Wanyande for bringing this information to my attention.

17 *The Weekly Review*, 26 January, 27 April 1990.

18 Hezron Nyangito, personal communication, 16 August 1990.

19 *The African Guardian* (Lagos), 11 December 1989, pp. 13, 14, 15.

20 *The African Guardian* (Lagos), 11 December 1989, pp. 13, 14, 15.

21 Inus Daneel observes that this may be the case for the Apostolic churches in Southern Africa, but it is less so for the Zionist churches, where women sit on church councils and are involved in the decision-making process. Personal communication, 29 September 1992.

22 Herbert Chimhundu, personal communication, 12 June 1990.

23 Shortly before his death in 1985, the founder, Rev. S. B. J. Oschoffa, instituted the Women's Council, as well as a number of other councils, in part because of the growing size of the church.

24 This information is taken from personal interviews with Mrs Sodeinde in Lagos in August, 1987 and 'Interview: face-to-face with Superior Snr. Prophetess Rosaline Bola Sodeinde', *The Cross* 2, 4 (December 1985) pp. 12–13, and Obafemi (1985/6, pp. 6, 12).

25 Deirdre Crumbley, personal communication, 14 June 1990.

26 Such is the case of Superior Senior Elder Sister Mrs Otumba Fadeke Otegbeye, a longstanding member of Celestial Church, who has built a parish church at Ikeja, Lagos. See Obafemi (1985/6, p. 5).

27 Turner (1967, pp. 65, 75, 90, 190). One of the earliest female students accepted for training in the ministry went on to become the 'Spiritual Mother' of the Liberian church (p. 145).

28 I am grateful to Deirdre Crumbley for making this comparison. Personal communication, 14 June 1990.

29 For a detailed description of the *manyanos*, see Brandel-Syrier (1962).

30 See, for example, Comaroff (1985, p. 258) and Little (1973, p. 61); Obbo (1980, p. 112), notes that membership was balanced in terms of sex ratio in the ten churches she studied in Kampala, except for the Legio Maria with its woman founder/leader Gaudencia Aoko

where men were more numerous than women. I have observed in my own field work on the Celestial Church of Christ that it is fairly balanced, although may fluctuate according to branches and services.

31   For example, just under two-thirds of the patients who consulted a senior prophetess in the Bantu Bethlehem Christian Apostolic Church of South Africa were women (West, 1975, p. 104). West provides some useful and detailed case histories of female prophets (pp. 99–118); Helen Callaway (1980, pp. 323–6) also includes a portrait of a woman spiritual worker or *elemi* in the Cherubim and Seraphim Society.

32   See also Bennetta Jules-Rosette, 'Women as Ceremonial Leaders in an African Church: the Apostles of John Maranke', in Jules-Rosette (1979, pp. 136–9) for a discussion of illness and curing.

33   See, for example, West (1975, p. 104), who notes that most prophets in the independent churches in Soweto that he studied are female and have a long and early history of illness. Western medicine was unable to cure them and they sought the help of diviners or prophets. Their sickness was interpreted as a spiritual calling and their cure was predicated upon purification and initiation.

34   See Enang (1986, p. 205), who notes in his study of more than thirty independent churches among the Annang of eastern Nigeria, that women are the most frequently possessed during worship.

35   See the case of Superior Senior Prophetess Sodeinde described above.

36   'Interview: face-to-face with Superior Senior Prophetess Rosaline Bola Sodeinde', *The Cross* 2, 4 (December 1985) p. 11.

37   See, for example, the detailed analysis of the marriage service and prescriptions in the Church of the Lord (Turner, 1967, vol. II, pp. 237–52).

38   See also Fabian (1979, p. 179), who writes of the basic value of complementarity being reflected in structures of organization and leadership in the Jamaa movement. He does note, however, that the leading roles of women do not necessarily entail a significant predominance of women.

References

Aquina, Sister Mary 1967: The people of the spirit: an independent church in Rhodesia. *Africa*, 37, 2, 203–19.

Barrett, David B. 1968: *Schism and Renewal in Africa: An Analysis of Six Thousand Contemporary Religious Movements*. Nairobi: Oxford University Press.

Barrett, David B. 1982: *World Christian Encyclopaedia: A Comparative*

Study of Churches and Religions in the Modern World, AD 1900–2000. New York: Oxford University Press.

Bond, George C. 1979: A prophecy that failed: the Lumpa Church of Uyombe, Zambia. In George C. Bond et al. (eds), *African Christianity: Patterns of Religious Continuity*. New York: Academic Press, 137–60.

Brandel-Syrier, Mia 1962: *Black Woman in Search of God*. London: Lutterworth.

Buckley, Thomas and Gottlieb, Alma 1988: *Blood Magic: The Anthropology of Menstruation*. Berkeley and Los Angeles: University of California Press.

Callaway, Helen 1980: Women in Yoruba Tradition and in the-Cherubim and Seraphim Society. In O. U. Kalu (ed.), *The History of Christianity in West Africa*, London: Longman.

Comaroff, Jean 1985: *Body of Power: Spirit of Resistance*. Chicago: University of Chicago Press.

Enang, Kenneth 1986: *The African Experience of Salvation*. London: M&C Publishing.

Fabian, Johannes, 1979: Man and woman in the teachings of the Jamaa movement. In Bennetta Jules-Rosette (ed.), *The New Religions of Africa*, Norwood, NJ: Ablex Publishing, 169–84.

Fernandez, James W. 1982: *Bwiti: An Ethnography of the Religious Imagination in Africa*. Princeton, NJ: Princeton University Press.

Goncalves, Antonio C. 1985: Approche sociologique du mouvement des 'Antoniens' au Kongo: essai du modèle actantiel de A.-J. Greimas. *Anthropos* 80, 555–68.

Hackett, Rosalind I. J. 1985: Sacred paradoxes: Women and religious plurality in Nigeria. In Y. Haddad and E. Findly (eds), *Women, Religion and Social Change*, Albany, NY: State University of New York Press, 247–71.

Hackett, Rosalind I. J. 1987: Women as leaders and participants in the spiritual churches. In Rosalind I. J. Hackett (ed.), *New Religious Movements in Nigeria*, Lewiston, NY: Edwin Mellen Press, 191–208.

Hackett, Rosalind I. J. 1989: *Religion in Calabar: The Religious Life and History of a Nigerian Town*. Berlin: Mouton de Gruyter.

Hackett, Rosalind I. J. 1990: 'Women No Saby Book?' Women and new religious movements in Africa. Paper presented at the XVIth Congress of the International Association for the History of Religions, Rome, 3–9 September.

Hackett, Rosalind I. J. 1993: From exclusion to inclusion: women and Bible use in Southern Nigeria. In I. Wollaston and J. Davis (eds), *The Sociology of Sacred Texts*, Sheffield: Sheffield Academic Press, 142–55.

Hackett, Rosalind I. J. 1993: Women in African Religions. In Arvind

Sharma (ed.), *Religion and Women*, Albany, NY: State University of New York Press, 61–92.

Hackett, Rosalind I. J. forthcoming: *Oschoffa and the Celestial Church of Christ*. Ibadan: Spectrum Books.

Holas, B. 1965: *Le Séparatisme Religieux en Afrique Noire: L'Exemple de la Côte d'Ivoire*. Paris: Presses Universitaires de France.

Jadin, Louis 1961: Le Congo et la secte des Antoniens: Restauration du Royaume sous Pedro IV et la 'Sainte Antoine' Congolaise (1694–1718). *Bulletin de l'Institut Historique Belge de Rome*, 33, 411–614.

Jadin, Louis 1968: Les sectes religieuses secrètes des antoniens au congo (1703–1709). *Cahiers des Religions Africaines*, 2, 109–20.

Jassy, Marie-France Perrin 1971: Women in the independent churches, *Risk*, 7, 3, 46–9.

Jules-Rosette, Bennetta 1976: Sources of women's leadership in an indigenous African church. *Sociological Symposium*, 17, 69–89.

Jules-Rosette, Bennetta (ed.) 1979: *The New Religions of Africa*. Norwood, NJ: Ablex Publishing.

Jules-Rosette, Bennetta 1981: Women in indigenous African cults and churches. In Filomina Chioma Steady (ed.), *The Black Woman Cross-Culturally*, Cambridge, MA: Schenkman, 185–207.

Jules-Rosette, Bennetta 1985: Cultural ambivalence and ceremonial leadership: the role of women in Africa's new religions. In J. C. B. Webster and E. L. Webster (eds), *The Church and Women in the Third World*, Philadelphia: Westminster Press, 88–104.

Jules-Rosette, Bennetta 1987: Privilege without power: women in African cults and churches. In Rosalyn Terborg-Penn et al. (eds), *Women in Africa and the African Diaspora*, Washington, DC: Howard University Press, 17–42.

Kailing, Joel B. 1988: Inside, outside, upside down: in relationship with African independent churches. *International Review of Mission*, 77, 305.

Kiernan, J. P. 1974: Where Zionists draw the line: a study of religious exclusiveness in an African township. *African Studies*, 33, 2, 79–90.

Lagerwerf, Leny 1975: Women in the church. *Exchange*, 12, 2–79.

Lagerwerf, Leny 1984: *'They Pray for You': Independent Churches and Women in Botswana*. Leiden: Interuniversitair Instituut voor Missiologie en Oecumenica.

Little, Kenneth 1973: *African Women in Towns: An Aspect of Africa's Social Revolution*. Cambridge: Cambridge University Press.

MacCormack, Carol P. 1980: Nature, culture and gender: a critique. In Carol P. MacCormack and Marilyn Strathern (eds), *Nature, Culture and Gender*, Cambridge, UK: Cambridge University Press, 1–24.

MacGaffey, Wyatt 1983: *Modern Kongo Prophets: Religion in a Plural Society*. Bloomington, IN: Indiana University Press.

Martin, Marie-Louise 1975: *Kimbangu: An African Prophet and his Church*. Oxford: Basil Blackwell.

Ndanema, I. M. 1961: The Martha Davies Confidential Benevolent Association. *Sierra Leone Bulletin of Religion*, 3, 2, 64–7.

Nuakoh, Charles Wilberforce 1986: Independent religious movements in West Africa: the case of the Holy Healing Church of Ghana. University of Cape Coast long essay in Religious Studies, June.

Obafemi, Olu (ed.) 1985/6: He delivered the complete contract of God. In *Life and Times of Papa Oschoffa: 1909–1985*, Lagos: Mission Publications.

Obbo, Christine 1980: *African Women: Their Struggle for Economic Independence*. London: Zed Press.

Omoyajowo, J. A. 1982a: *Cherubim and Seraphim: The History of an Independent Church*. New York: Nok.

Omoyajowo, J. A. 1982b: Mother in Israel: Christianah Olatunrinle in Ondo (c. 1855–1941). In Elizabeth Isichei (ed.), *Varieties of Christian Experience in Nigeria*, London: Macmillan, 142–8.

Omoyajowo, J. A. 1988: The role of women in traditional African religions and independent church movements. *Dialogue and Alliance*, 2, 3, 77–87.

Paulme, Denise 1962: Une religion syncrétique en Côte d'Ivoire: le culte deima. *Cahiers d'Etudes Africaines*, 31, 5–90.

Peel, John D. Y. 1968: *Aladura: A Religious Movement Among the Yoruba*. London: Oxford University Press for the International African Institute.

Potash, Betty 1989: Gender relations in sub-Saharan Africa. In Sandra Morgen (ed.), *Gender and Anthropology*, Washington, DC: American Anthropological Association.

Ranger, Terence 1986: Religious movements and politics in sub-Saharan Africa. *African Studies Review*, 29, 1–70.

Rosaldo, Michelle Z. 1974: Woman, culture, and society: a theoretical overview. In Michelle Z. Rosaldo and Louise Lamphere (eds), *Woman, Culture and Society*, Stanford: Stanford University Press, 17–42.

Rotberg, Robert 1961: The Lenshina movement of Northern Rhodesia. *The Rhodes-Livingstone Journal*, 29, 64–78.

Schwartz, Nancy L. 1989: World without end: the meanings and movements in the history narratives and 'tongue-speech' of Legio of African Church Mission among Luo of Kenya. PhD dissertation, Princeton University.

Sereboe, Edward Kofi 1982: The spiritual churches in Ghana: A survey of Emissaries Church in Madina at Accra. University of Cape Coast long essay in Religious Studies, September.

Strathern, Marilyn 1981: Self-interest and the social good: some implications of hagen gender imagery. In Sherry B. Ortner and Harriet

Whitehead (eds), *Sexual Meanings: The Cultural Construction of Gender and Sexuality*, Cambridge, UK: Cambridge University Press, 166–91.

Strathern, Marilyn (ed.) 1987: *Dealing with Inequality: Analyzing Gender Relations in Melanesia and Beyond*. Cambridge, UK: Cambridge University Press.

Sudarkasa, Niara 1987: The 'status of women' in indigenous African Societies. In Rosalyn Terborg-Penn et al. (eds), *Women in Africa and the African Diaspora*, Washington, DC: Howard University Press.

Sundkler, Bengt G. M. 1961 (1948): *Bantu Prophets in South Africa*, Second edn. Oxford: Oxford University Press.

Turner, Harold W. 1967: *African Independent Church*, 2 vols. Oxford: Clarendon Press.

Turner, Harold W. 1979: *New Religious Movements: A Bibliography*, 2 vols. Boston, MA: G. K. Hall.

Walker, Sheila S. 1979a: Women in the Harrist Movement. In B. Jules-Rosette (ed.), *The New Religions of Africa*, Norwood, NJ: Ablex Publishing, 87–97.

Walker, Sheila S. 1979b: The message as the medium: the Harrist Churches of the Ivory Coast and Ghana. In G. C. Bond et al. (eds), *African Christianity: Patterns of Religious Continuity*. New York: Academic Press, 9–64.

West, Martin 1975: *Bishops and Prophets in a Black City: African Independent Churches in Soweto, Johannesburg*. Cape Town: David Philip.

Wilson, Bryan R. 1973: *Magic and the Millenium*. London: Heinemann.

13

Liberator or Pacifier: Religion and Women in Japan

Marilyn F. Nefsky

'Historically, Japanese religions have offered only pacifiers to the frustrated women who have been boxed in by traditional family structures ...' (Nakamura, 1980, p. 143) That Japanese religions held women in low regard is evident from the advent of Buddhism in Japan in the sixth century. The pacifiers they offered women served several pragmatic purposes but ultimately reflected a view of Japanese women as both subordinate and inferior to men. Although interest in Japanese religion has increased since World War II, interest in women's studies has been evident in Japan only since the 1970s.[1] As for research on women and Japanese religion, the scholarship is still sparse, primarily scattered in periodicals and edited volumes (Uchino, 1983; Hoshino and Takeda, 1987; Nakamura, 1980). This chapter will consider not the numerous reasons for this dearth of material, but rather the role religion has played and currently plays in the lives of Japanese women.

The History of Japanese Religions
Buddhism

In the first six centuries in Japan (sixth to twelve centuries CE) Buddhism contained unmistakable misogynist elements. These elements were rooted in two contrary notions of woman. The first notion perceived woman as a sensual being, close to nature, and destructive; the second perceived her as a wise, maternal, and compassionate being. The expressions of the first notion ranged from mild misogynist claims to the calumny that women were inherently evil. Woman was evil incarnate, 'the daughter of evil', 'the emissary of hell'.[2] She was 'born as woman to prevent man from following the way of the Buddha' (Ackroyd, 1959, p. 55; see Paul, 1979, p. 175). This view regarded the female personality as rife with jealousy, desire and animalistic lust (Paul, 1979, pp. 9, 309). The second notion of woman considered procreation a mysterious process in which women became the source of life. In this regard, she was the 'veritable image of becoming and all forces of ... growth and productivity which Buddhism knew as *samsara*' (Falk, 1974; Nakamura, 1973). Attached to home and children, woman was inextricably bound up with the world of suffering and was to be avoided if liberation were to be possible.

The texts of Mahayana Buddhism depicted three typologies for woman's access to enlightenment: she was (1) denied entrance into Buddhaland; (2) given limited acceptance; or (3) accepted as an advanced bodhisattva (a saint-like figure) and imminent Buddha (Paul, 1979, p. 169).[3] The majority of Mahayana sutras fall into the second category, but even limited acceptance required a woman to disdain her own female nature. In some of these sutras a woman achieves enlightenment only after rebirth as a male; in others she attains enlightenment within her lifetime but only after sexual transformation.

The most liberal portraits of women's spiritual attainments are found in an extremely small portion of sutras, which represent some of the most popular and influential Mahayana passages. Instead of using sexual transformation as the motif for spiritual growth, these passages represent asexuality: 'If all phenomena are impermanent and insubstantial, then there are no self-existent entities which have inalienable and unchanging characteristics such as "maleness" or "femaleness"' (Paul, 1979, p. 217; see also pp. 220, 307). The most significant and pervasive theme of the popular sutras was that of promoting the welfare of all human beings without prejudice or favour (Paul, 1979, pp. 309–10).

The Mahayana tendency in Japan has been to present somewhat sympathetic portrayals of women; the most popular and appealing sutras usually admitted the spiritual potential of women. Buddhism offered the symbol of motherly love for Buddha's boundless compassion: 'As a mother at risk of her life watches over her own child, so also let everyone cultivate a boundless (friendly) mind toward all beings' (*Suttanipata*: 148, cited in Nakamura, 1973, pp. 75–76; see also p. 175).

Until the Kamakura period (1192–1333) no school of Japanese Buddhism accorded woman equal social status. During the Heian period (794–1160), when Buddhism was beginning to take root in the Japanese soil, the Tendai sect became one of the most important schools in terms of its impact on later developments of Japanese Buddhism (Earhart, 1982, p. 83). Brought to Japan from China by the monk Saichō, Tendai maintained many of the basic tenets of the Chinese school. The esoteric teachings of Tendai advocated the equality of all humankind (Ogata, 1958); yet Tendai also taught that women suffered from the 'Five Obstacles' (*goshō*): desire, anger, drowsiness, restlessness and remorse, and doubt. The earlier Indian notion of the 'Five Impediments' (*nīrvarana*) had been fundamental to Mahayana Buddhism,[4] affecting both men and women, by hindering them from attaining enlightenment.

In Tendai, however, these impediments became obstacles from which women innately suffered; they did not hinder women but actually incapacitated them from attaining enlightenment or any of the five states of spiritual existence accessible to men.[5] Saichō further reinforced the earlier Buddhist notions of women when he prohibited women from coming 'near the temple and certainly [they] may not enter its sacred precincts' (Grover, 1984, pp. 158–9). In restricting his monks from leaving the precincts of the mountain temple for twelve years, Saichō imposed stricter rules than had previously been observed.

With the advent of the Kamakura period there arose a few Buddhist leaders who considered women capable of attaining enlightenment. One of these leaders was Nichiren, who argued against the prevalent notion of woman's sinfulness. Although Buddhist sutras tended to deny women, the wicked and the ordinary people the capacity of enlightenment, Nichiren maintained that the Lotus Sutra alone was their salvation. In the Kamakura period Buddhist schools of faith believed in the notion of the three declining stages of the Buddhist Dharma (Dobbins, 1989, p. 36). The Kamakura period was in the final stage, the period of the decline of the Dharma (*mappō*), a time when evil flourished throughout this world. During this time it was precisely those who were most disadvantaged – women, the wicked, the ordinary people – who would achieve enlightenment, for they alone were egoless enough to turn to another power, the Lotus Sutra, for salvation (Hardacre, 1984, p. 205; cf. Dobbins, 1989, pp. 53–4, 70–1).

Nichiren fully believed, as the Lotus Sutra taught, that the Buddha nature was inherent in every human being, female and male alike. Although he never denied the traditional notions of female defilement, he deemed it unnecessary for women to be precautious of the effects of pollution and counselled them to continue to recite the Lotus Sutra as usual, irrespective of their physical state. So sensitive was he to the prevailing norms that he advised a woman, reluctant to hold the sutra during her menstrual period, at least to pronounce its sacred name.[6] Nevertheless, the teachings of Nichiren were not perpetuated by the school bearing his name.

Dōgen, the founder of the Sōtō sect of Zen Buddhism, initially affirmed women's potential for Buddhahood. When discussing the nature of the Buddha Dharma, Dōgen maintained that 'there must be no distinction between men and women, high and low ... It is simply a question of whether the will is there or not' (Waddell and Abe, 1971, pp. 148–9). At one time he protested against restricting women from entering some of the holy sites, for such places, he noted, already welcomed kings, premiers, ministers and officials of this corrupted world.[7] However, after Dōgen moved to Echizen in 1243, he revised his position: only monks were capable of practising Zen and of achieving genuine enlightenment. Although this revision may have been the result of a change in rhetoric to suit the audience, these later comments had considerable impact on women. As Sōtō Zen developed, his earlier affirmation of women was effectively displaced.[8]

Eisai, the founder of the Rinzai sect of Zen, reinforced Dōgen's apparent change of heart; he believed nothing and no one should be allowed to disturb the equanimity of monks in residence. Emphasizing the importance of walled cloisters to protect the monks, Eisai maintained that 'Nuns, women or evil people should on no account be permitted to stay over night' (Collcutt, 1981, pp. 188–89; see Kraft, 1992, p. 107). The Rinzai monk Genko, on the other hand, reinforced Dōgen's earlier views, insisting that 'there is no difference whether man, woman, old, young, wise, foolish, human [or] animal'; all were equally capable of attaining enlightenment (Cleary, 1978, p. 78). Such occasional support did little to improve the status of women in Zen Buddhism.

Hōnen, the founder of one of the most popular forms of Japanese Buddhism, Jōdo-shū (Pure Land Sect), viewed women disparagingly. Legend has it that the monk Hōnen had encouraged his disciple Shinran to marry a certain princess in order 'to show openly that [Buddha] Amida's all embracing Compassion shall lead a monk with absolute faith to Enlightenment though he should *commit the sin of association with women*' (Fujikawa, 1964, p. 18, italics added). In reality, of course, Shinran did marry, for quite different reasons.

Shinran became the founder of the Jōdo Shinshū (True Pure Land) school of Buddhism. So totally did he believe in the absolute compassion of the Buddha that the precepts of traditional Buddhism became meaningless to him. After he was forced to leave the monastery on Mt Hiei, he decided to marry and work among the ordinary people. Convinced that he was living in the period of *mappō*, Shinran believed, as did Nichiren, that the most disadvantaged – the wicked, the destitute and women – were more worthy of salvation than others (*akunin shōki*). Because women were naturally disadvantaged by the defilements of menstruation and childbirth, they were all the more the recipients of Amida's absolute compassion (*akunin jōbutsu*).[9]

Still, many Buddhists believed women had little chance for attaining enlightenment unless they were first reborn as men. The Buddhist poet Kenkō reflected the attitudes typical of the Kamakura and subsequent periods when he wrote: 'In fact, women are all perverse by nature. They are deeply self-centred, grasping in the extreme, devoid of all susceptibility to reason, quick to indulge in superstitious practices ... Only when a man enslaved by his infatuation is courting a woman does she seem charming and amusing' (Keene, 1967, p. 90).

The status of women in Japan was not influenced by Buddhist scripture alone. The prevailing patriarchal views had immense impact. By the Kamakura period the common view placed the woman in the home, bearing children and serving her family. Within this context Buddhism tended to view woman not as religious devotee but as wife and mother, serving her husband and family. In Buddhism wife and mother was considered a commodity supreme, 'for through her future bodhisattvas and noble rulers would take birth' (Talim, 1972, pp. 121, 133, 136, 144). Extensive training in Buddhism was considered detrimental to the innate virtues of Japanese womanhood. Concerned with the disintegration of the family, textual passages criticized the nun's path, implying that a woman's rejection of the standard norms threatened the very fabric of Japanese society (Kondō, 1915, pp. 1–2; Kuga, 1916, pp. 18–19; Paul, 1979, p. 305). As a dissuasion from entering the orders, Buddhist nuns were restricted from ordaining disciples, holding high ecclesiastical posts or visiting holy sites such as Mt Hiei or Mt Koya (Uchino, 1983, pp. 183–4, 187; Kraft, 1992, p. 23).

The ideal norm for woman was that of *ryōsai-kenbo* – 'good wife and wise mother', the paragon of virtue. Though the phrase was a Meiji creation, the notion long preceded its conceptual articulation (see Takamure, 1966, vol. 5, pp. 544–52; see also Smith, 1983; Hardacre, 1984, p. 194). Reinforcing this norm, Buddhism emphasized such attributes as obedience, patience, modesty and non-resistance. It taught that a woman's present and future lives had to do with the law of karma (*innen*), especially with the concept of karmic hindrances (*goshō ga fukai*), considered much deeper in women than in men. This tenet conveyed a sense of fatalism (Heine, 1991, p. 398), encouraging women not to improve their lot in life but to accept it with resignation. Even where the tenet itself was rejected, the attribute of resignation – *shikata ga nai* ('It can't be helped') – was successfully inculcated.

Confucianism

The text most influential in defining the role and status of women was the *Li Chi* (Book of Rites) (trs. Legge, 1967), which held a high place of honour among the Confucian Classics (Ch'ü, 1972, pp. x, lxxiv, lxxviii). This text portrayed most aspects of Confucian life in pairs: heaven and earth, male and female, music and ceremony, east and west, honour and love. These pairs were considered complementary in nature, for 'by their interdependence they fulfil their functions' (Legge, 1967, xvii:103–5, xxi:219; xxix:341; quotation xli:434). The rite of marriage was the greatest ongoing rite of Confucian society (Legge, 1967,

xli:430, xxiv:264). Through this rite the interdependency and interaction of the complementary equivalents of husband and wife
produced 'the harmony of all under the sky' (Legge, 1967,
xxi:219). The basic values of marital union – love and respect
– were seen as extending to the very foundation of good government (Legge, 1967, xxiv:261). Given the requisite participation
of both males and females in the 'Great Way' of the Confucian
cosmos, neither male nor female was seen as having greater
inherent value (Legge, vii:36).

From the ninth century Confucianism in China began allying
itself with Buddhism, thereby developing a more metaphysical
understanding of the world and humanity. In Neo-Confucianism
marriage remained 'the most fundamental of all human relationships' (Tu, 1985, p. 142). In the conjugal relationship genuine
reciprocity and mutual responsibility were necessary to maintain
domestic harmony and, by extension, social stability. The governing virtue between husband and wife was respect based not only
on the division of labour but also on mutual appreciation. In
marriage the relationship between women and men, though functionally differentiated, was at the same time substantively unified.
The Neo-Confucian vision required women and men to participate
actively in shaping the moral character of society. Underlying this
vision was the belief that every human being, male and female,
had the potential to perfect their human-relatedness (*jen*) and
thereby 'form a unity with heaven, earth and the myriad things'
(Tu, 1985, p. 144–5; Fingarette, 1972, pp. 1–17, esp. p. 16;
Tucker, 1989, p. 9). This was not only an intellectual assertion
but also a spiritual commitment.

This new form of Confucianism began to make its mark in
medieval Japan. After unifying the nation in the early seventeenth
century, the Tokugawa shogunate (1603–1868) sought to stabilize
the social order and maintain the *status quo*. It formally adopted
the Neo-Confucianism of the Shushigaku (Chu Hsi) school, which
defined the human being in terms of interpersonal relations. By
reinforcing the household as the basic social unit, Shushigaku
stressed the obligations incumbent on a person as a member of a
family. In the subsequent Meiji period (1868–1912) this emphasis
on duty was extended to include absolute loyalty to the emperor
and applied to each person as a member of the state – the family
writ large.

Interpersonal relations in Confucian society were oriented vertically: there could not be two suns in the sky nor two kings in

the land (Legge, 1967, xxvii:285). Emphasis was placed on five basic social relationships (*gorin*), hierarchically ordered and obligation bound. One of these was the husband–wife relationship, the wife maintaining the subordinate role. In the Confucian Classics there were frequent references to sexual discrimination, of both a spatial and functional nature. Spatially, the *Li Chi* insisted that girls and boys, both within and beyond the family, were to keep a discreet distance (Legge, 1967, i:77, x:478). Functionally, *Shih Ching* (Book of Poetry) (trs. Waley, 1960), an early Confucian Classic, demonstrated the different roles expected of the son and daughter from the time of birth:

> So he bears a son,
> And puts him to sleep upon a bed,
> Clothes him in fine robes,
> Then he bears a daughter,
> And he puts her upon the ground,
> Clothes her in swaddling clothes. (Waley, 1960, pp. 283–4)

The female's domain was the inner world of the household; the male's domain, the outer world of society. According to the *Li Chi* a woman's duty in life was to defer: 'In this way when the deferential obedience of the wife was complete, the internal harmony was secured' (Legge, 1967, vii:365; quotation x:232).

Schools teaching Neo-Confucian notions proliferated under the Tokugawa regime. By 1868 literacy had spread throughout almost 40 per cent of the population, including the highest levels of villagers. However, in the patriarchal society of Tokugawa Japan Neo-Confucianism continued to be interpreted in androcentric terms. A woman's function was specifically to provide the male heir for the husband's lineage and thereby maintain the all-important continuity between the ancestors and their descendants. Aphorisms such as 'the wife is the main pillar of the family' (*Nyōbō wa ie no daikoku-bashira*) illustrate high regard expressed for women in this role. However, women not in this role were paralleled with 'small men that are difficult to deal with. If you let them get too close, they become insolent. If you keep them at a distance, they complain' (Lau, 1979, xviii:25, 148).[10] Inculcated with the doctrine of the Three Obediences (*Sanjū*), a woman was expected to 'obey her father in her youth, her husband after marriage and her son in her old age'.[11]

Central to Confucianism was the metaphysical theory of *yin* and *yang*, two complementary principles whose interaction brought about the universe: *yang* – the positive, bright, male principle; *yin* – the negative, dark, female principle. In marriage a wife and husband symbolized *yin* and *yang* in dynamic interplay. In the 'Wisdom literature' circulated to teach women their proper place in Neo-Confucian metaphysics, such as the seventeenth century *Onna Daigaku* (Greater Learning for Women), there was little doubt that *yin* and *yang* were also vertically oriented:

> A woman regards her husband as heaven ... Woman has the quality of *yin* (passiveness). *Yin* is of the nature of night and is dark. Hence, because compared to man, she is foolish, she does not understand her obvious duties. ... Therefore, since she is foolish, in everything she must submit to her husband. (Takamure, 1948, pp. 172–3)

After the first liberal decade of the Meiji Restoration, the authorities sought to renew 'stability and order' by reverting more stringently to Neo-Confucian values. The Meiji Constitution (1889), the Imperial Rescript of Education (1890) and the revised Civil Code (1898), based primarily on Neo-Confucian teachings, served to instill in the Japanese an ethic extolling loyalty, filial piety, obedience, and righteousness – an ethic that endorsed absolute authority in the head of the family and absolute loyalty to the head of state. The further this ethic was instilled, the lower fell the status of Japanese women.

Shinto

Long preceding the formal introduction of Buddhism, the ancient tradition of Japan supported a positive notion of woman. In this early period the Japanese believed that *kami* (deities), ancestors and human beings were tied together through a powerful bond, and Japanese women, through the act of procreation, were perceived as mediators of this bond (Okane, 1976, pp. 207, 211–12). Through woman came forth life and humanity; even the mythological progenitor of Japan, Amaterasu, was a woman. The arrival of Buddhism gradually modified this belief but could not eradicate it, for Shinto, a religion of celebration and gratitude, was too deeply rooted to succumb to 'the demoralizing creed of Buddhism that taught that woman's salvation is impossible until she becomes reincarnated as a man (Mason, 1935, p. 201).

Much of Japanese religious thought was bound up with pollution. The greatest source of defilement (*kegare*) was death, but there were other types as well. Diseases, wounds and blood, especially those connected with female bodily functions, were likewise considered polluting. It was not merely those suffering these defilements who were considered taboo, but also those who had any contact with these sources of pollution. In other words, both men and women were at times restricted from participating in sacred rituals or visiting sacred sites.[12]

As Buddhism made headway in Japan, both Shinto and Buddhism began to accommodate one another. Shinto ameliorated Buddhism's other-worldly character while Buddhism provided Shinto with a world-view beyond the here-and-now. So closely entwined did the two become that Buddhist temples were occasionally found in the precincts of Shinto shrines. In the late Tokugawa and early Meiji periods, however, authorities attempted to separate Buddhism from Shinto and to purge Shinto of all 'superstitious' elements in order to promote the 'enlightenment' of the people.

Among these attempts was the prohibition on the activities of female shamans who posed a threat to the power structure. The role of the female shaman was rooted in the ancient tradition which conceived of such women as emulating the sun deity Amaterasu. With the power of tradition behind such a conception, the authorities perceived the threat as very real. Despite the legal prohibitions, many of these women continued to practise their calling, though furtively, long after the defeat in 1945. That they were able to survive at all bears witness to the powerful role they played in prewar Japan (see Blacker, 1975).

In the early Showa period (1930–45) almost all aspects of organized religion, including participation in public rituals, were supervised or controlled by government officials. Restrictions applied to all the people, but particularly to women. Women, reputedly more deeply religious and more keenly sensitive to the supernatural, were excluded from any real participation. The only exceptions were the *miko* (young female shrine attendants)[13] who, as daughters of priests or local residents, played a supplementary role, which they had to relinquish upon marriage (Ono, 1962, p. 43).

New Religions

Emphasis on women's shamanistic power was particularly evident in the New Religions. Significant among the founders of new religious movements were female shamans. Though these women were able to rise above certain social norms through their revelatory experiences, they were unable to transcend fully the beliefs and values of the underlying ideology prevalent in Japan. They never advocated dramatic change in the sex roles or the power relations between men and women. Even though they conducted their own lives outside the normative pale, they tended to reflect and reinforce the traditional world-view (Nakamura, 1980, pp. 134; Hardacre, 1984, pp. 41, 119; Earhart, 1989, pp. 189, 193).

These female founders, regarded as either living *kami* (*ikigami*) or mediums delivering a divine message, had emerged from a life of spiritual and physical oppression. Their charisma as well as their message attracted a following. As the sect organization expanded, however, it required increasing managerial expertise. Women, with less education and training in the public sphere, were ill-equipped to direct a growing movement; consequently, key administrative positions went to men. Living under improved social conditions, the founder's successors tended to be less charismatic, less dynamic in personality, relying more heavily on the message and other techniques to attract members. The pattern of strong female leadership naturally lapsed shortly after the founder's death (Nakamura, 1980, pp. 134, 142–3).

The slow rate of change in organized religion is best epitomized by the new religious movements which began to flourish immediately after World War II. Although the rapid growth of the New Religions has subsided since the late 1960s, one striking feature remains: women 'are a good deal more numerous than men' both as founders and adherents of the new religious movements (Offner and Straelen, 1963, pp. 37, 244–45; Hardacre, 1986, pp. 121–2, 92; Earhart, 1989, pp. 186, 193, 255 fn.18; Nakamura, 1981, p. 187).[14]

The New Religions provide an outlet for women to utilize their potential energies, offering opportunities for leadership at various levels of the organization. The New Religions also offer women compassion and fellowship not found in their families or social environments (Hardacre, 1986, pp 192–93; Offner and Straelen, 1963, p. 255; Earhart, 1989, pp. 157, 193). But while the horizontal bond among believers creates this supportive fellowship, the vertical relation between leader and believer reinforces the traditional *oyako* (parent–child) relation. In this way, the New Religions reinforce and strengthen many of the traditional norms and values of Japanese society.

Popular religion

Excluded from formal public ritual, Japanese women participated in lay activities. The most fundamental of these religious activities were conducted within the household. Placing high priority on ancestor veneration as a means of ideological control, the Meiji government encouraged the Japanese to make daily offerings at family altars. The responsibility of ancestor veneration was shared by both males and females; the household head was responsible for the care of the ancestral tablets, and his wife, for the daily offerings of food and drink. The preparation of food offerings was a crucial part of the routine duties of women in the the prewar household.

In present-day Japan women continue to share the responsibility of caring for the ancestral tablets and preparing the offerings for the ancestral rites. A study of ancestor worship conducted in the 1960s and mid-1970s found that women's role in these rites had not changed radically since the prewar period. Surveys conducted in the mid-1980s indicated that ancestor veneration, though not as prevalent as in the prewar period, had not declined as anticipated.[15] As an extension of their participation in ancestral rituals, an increasing number of women are resorting to memorial services to overcome the anguish of abortions, miscarriages or still-births (*misuko kuyō*) (Hoshino and Takeda, 1987; Smith, 1988). Developed as a memorial service only in the last two or three decades, the practice of *misuko kuyō* suggests a profound religious consciousness that is not waning but accommodating to new and unique circumstances.

Among the other lay activities they have engaged in, Japanese women have resorted to diviners, curing priests and other religious practitioners and frequented local temples and shrines to make personal petitions for easy childbirth, health for families and 'exorcism of spirits placed in their bodies by witches' (Embree, 1982, p. 49; see also Smith and Wisell, 1982, pp. 23–31, 48–57, 93). In the mid-1930s anthropologists Ella and John Embree found that the women of Suye Mura got their greatest pleasure from pilgrimages to nearby shrines and temples. In other words, popular religion played an important role in the lives of Japanese women.

There were other family rituals in which women participated freely. Since it was thought that the child received his or her soul from *kami*, a naming ceremony was conducted at the household *kamidana* (*kami* shelf) with offerings prepared by the women. On the thirty-first or thirty-third day after birth, mothers went to the local shrine to introduce their child to the guardian *kami* (*ujigami*) under whose aegis the child was born and survived the dangerous first month of life. When their children reached the age of three, five or seven years, mothers once again took them to the local shrine for renewed blessing by the *ujigami*.

The religious activities in which the Japanese woman could actively participate had important personal significance: (a) she attended shrines and temples and engaged religious practitioners for practical benefits as well as for solace and comfort; (b) within the household she prepared offerings for the ancestors and guardian *kami*, considered her contribution to the ongoing family relations with the sacred; and (c) psychologically, her participation in religious associations and communal festivals offered stability and security she could find nowhere else. The religious preoccupation of Japanese women had to do with the joy and suffering of the here-and-now – with birth, life and death – not with a hereafter. Maintaining relations with the ancestors was perceived as having its greatest impact on this life.

Discussion

In one sense the postwar constitution profoundly altered the relation between women and religion in Japan; in another sense it had little effect. The disestablishment of State Shinto (Shinto Directive), the constitutional separation of religion and the state (Article 20) and the right to freedom of religion (Article 89) removed the ideological support and institutional framework for the subordination of women in Japanese society. No longer were Japanese women subjugated by an ethic embodied in the Confucian *Onna Daigaku*, in the misogynist texts of the Buddhist tradition, or in the repressive demands of the Meiji Rescript on Education and the Meiji Civil Code. No longer were organized Buddhism, Shinto and Confucianism subsidized by the state or overtly incorporated into a religio-political ideology. The disestablishment of these religions as state-supported institutions contributed to considerable changes in the status of Japanese women. The postwar constitution and subsequent legislation guaranteed to Japanese women numerous rights and freedoms, among the most liberal in the world.

However, institutionalized religion in prewar Japan had power not only because it was supported by the state but also because it had been motivated by the patriarchal beliefs and values of a society directed toward the goal of stability and security – a goal present-day Japan seeks to maintain. Beneath the surface of contemporary Japanese society remains a strongly patriarchal ideology. The deinstitutionalization of religion was neither an act of self-determination nor a grass roots movement; it was forced on Japan by the occupation powers, who succeeded in eliminating the prewar manifestations of the patriarchal ideology but left intact the underpinnings of a value system which continues to have power to manipulate.

The position of Japanese women is not unique; there are numerous parallels with women in other countries.[16] In Japan patriarchal forces manipulated Shinto, Buddhism and Confucianism to reinforce a perception of woman's role as subordinate and her nature as inferior. The culmination of this manipulation became the ideal norm which placed the Japanese woman inside the home (*kanai*), striving to be a 'good wife and wise mother'. Though social change is evident in present-day Japan, pressures still abound for a woman to maintain this ideal.

Yet, these patriarchal forces were only quasi-successful. Shinto stood in their way. Unmarked by a highly developed system of philosophy or metaphysics, Shinto has always been intimately associated with the daily life of the Japanese people. Despite the impact of the institutionalization of religion, the view of woman as compassionate and life-sustaining continues to flow in the background as a strong undercurrent. The negative view of women which emerged under the aegis of Tokugawa Neo-Confucianism could not wholly prevail.

Although Shinto abhorred anything having to do with blood, disease or death, especially in its view of menstruating and childbearing women, Shinto has another side, evident in neither Confucianism nor Buddhism. This is an affirmative perception of this world; a world 'progressing from chaos to order, from confusion ... to harmony and unity' (Ono, 1962, p. 102). Optimistic and this-worldly in nature, Shinto does not speculate on another realm. The world of the *kami* and this world are closely interlaced; the Shinto reality includes human beings, nature and *kami*.

Elizabeth Schüssler Fiorenza (1983) insists that there is more to women's religious experience than the oppression they suffer from social institutions. If one look only at the oppression, one will miss the creative response women make to their cultural environments (Miles, 1985, p. 3). From this context it is imperative to note that Japanese religion has always been less a matter of religious doctrines than of religious practice. Doctrinal 'truth' is far less important to the Japanese than religious feelings and aspirations expressed in the many rituals that touch human life (Swyngedouw, 1986). In this way, Japanese women have not been wholly bound by the patriarchal forces of institutionalized Shinto, Buddhism and Confucianism – the latter two which took root in Japanese soil only after centuries of accommodation to its cultural climate.

Rituals and festivals involve the whole person; they appeal to the senses and emotions as well as the intellect (Kalven, 1984, pp. 363–4). For Japanese women the act of participating in the communal experience reaffirms their faith in the value of this life and the part they play in it. Their prominent participation in festivals and rites of passage throughout the year – the New Year (*Shōgatsu*), the mid-summer Feast for the Dead (*O'Bon*) or the 'Three-Five-Seven' (*Shichi-go-san*) Festival (e.g. Sakura, 1971, pp. 146, 148, 150; Hori et al., 1972, p. 65) to name but a few – attests to the important role religious ritual plays in their lives. These festivals and rites of passage allow women to express their religious feelings through a celebration of life inherent in which is an affirmation of both human nature and this world as essentially positive and good.[17] In so far as they share in these rituals and festivals, Japanese women participate in religion at a most profound level. It is this level of Japanese religion that nourishes their religious consciousness; it is this dimension that is all too often neglected in any discussion of women and religion in Japan.

Conclusions

This chapter considered the images of woman portrayed by traditional religions and the realities of women's social experiences. To what extent were the traditional images informed by the social realities? To what extent were these images merely a reflection? It took over three centuries for Buddhism to set deep roots in the Japanese soil and for Shinto to accommodate to Buddhism's success. In the period immediately following World War II Japan suffered from religious anomie. Buddhism,

Confucianism, even Shinto failed to avert the disaster of defeat: they lost their credibility. No longer enjoying their state-induced patronage, no longer able to turn to the family or community for moral and financial support, temples and shrines were forced by want of survival to adapt to the changing environment. In the three decades following Japan's defeat Shinto and Buddhism made considerable strides in accommodating the changing needs of a postwar society; temples and shrines made efforts to appeal to individuals, offering such opportunities as study sessions, personal counselling, classes in the arts, and providing child-care facilities.

As the social climate continues to change, perhaps Japanese religions will once again realize that their survival depends on accommodating the norms and values of a post-industrial society. Perhaps, Japanese religions will direct their appeals to Japanese women in ways more meaningful than in the past. As we have seen, Buddhism, Shinto and Neo-Confucianism have within them the seeds for mutual appreciation and human liberation. It was the patriarchal forces of historical Japan that infected Japanese religions, thereby bringing about the traditional structures that boxed in Japanese women for over a millenium. As the patriarchal forces diminish, the seeds of true liberation may bear fruit. Although it may be slow to blossom, the fruit will no doubt be sweet.

Notes

1   The first bibliography for the study of women in Japan was compiled by Uchino Kumiko (Uchino, 1981), *Nihon josei kenkyū kiso bunken mokuroku* (Bibliography of essential Japanese works for the study of women).

2   *Nihon Kyōiku Bunka*, pp. 62–3; *Onna jitsugo kyō*, from Takamura Itsue's *Nihon josei shakaishi*, p. 165, both cited in Ackroyd (1959, p. 55).

3   See Paul (1979, p. 106) where she defines bodhisattva as 'the hallmark of Mahayana Buddhism, exemplifying the state of spiritual perfection in which social and sexual distinctions between living beings have been removed through the universal practice of compassion for all beings'.

4   A. K. Warder discusses the five impediments (*nīrvarana*) as: (i) will to pleasure (*kāmacchandas*), (ii) malevolence (*vyāpāda*), (iii)

stupidity (*styānamiddha*), (iv) vanity (*auddhatyakaukrtya*), (v) uncertainty (*vicikitsā*).

5 *Bukkyō Daijiten*, cited in Ackroyd (1959, p. 54). The five states of spiritual existence are Brahma, Indra, Mara, a 'Wheel-Rolling King', and a Buddha, according to Smyers (1983); *Bukkyō Jiten* (1977, p. 278).

6 Kasahara (1975); *Nichiren's Works* (ed.) Katō, Tokyo, 1904, pp. 477–85, cited in Masaharu (1966, pp. 47, 81–2). See also Ishimoto (1935, pp. 341–2).

7 'Raihai Tikuzui', Shōbō Genzō, in *Dōgen zenji zenshū, (ed.) Okubo Dōshū, Tokyo: Shunjusha, 1930, pp. 44–51, cited in Nakamura (1969, pp. 69–70).*

8 *Shōbōgenzō sanjushichihon bodaibunpō*, in *Dōgen zenji zenshū* (Tokyo: Chikuma Shobo, 1969–70, pp. 511–13); Kraft (1992, p. 104). For the contemporary attitude of Sōtō Zen toward women, see Uchino (1981, p. 178).

9 By implication see Dobbins (1989, pp. 37, 53–4, 70–1, 75); also Hardacre (1984, pp. 204–5).

10 See also Legge (1967, xvii:ii:25, 330): 'We hardly expect such an utterance, through correct in itself from Confucious.' [!]

11 The Sanju doctrine first appeared in the *Gempeiseisuiki*, vol. 47; cited in Ackroyd (1959, p. 57); also Nakamura (1969, p. 60).

12 *Kokushi-taikei*, vol. 13: 156, cited in Kato (1988, p. 139).

13 For the various roles of the *miko*, see Okane (1976, pp. 210–12).

14 Offner and Straelen (1963: 37), where they claim that there is 'an obviously new respect for women seen in both the number of women founders and the large proportion of women preachers, teachers and believers.'

15 For the 1960s and 1970s data, see Smith (1974, pp. 118–19). For the 1980s data see, for example, Ernest E. Best's (1980) research; also see the National Character Study, published by the Japanese government every five years since 1953.

16 Marilyn Frye (1983, p. 9) comments: 'There is a women's place, a sector, which is inhabited by all women of all classes and races, and it is not defined by geographical boundaries but by function. The function is the service of men and men's interests as men define them ...'

17 Reischauer (1980, p. 6) refers to it as the 'joyful acceptance of life'. See also Ono (1962, p. 3), Hori et al. (1972, p. 16).

References

Ackroyd, Joyce 1959: Women in feudal Japan. *Transactions of the Asiatic Society of Japan*, 7, 55, 31–68.

Best, Ernest E. 1980: Self and society in post-war Japanese religiousity. Paper delivered at conference on The Value of Individualism in Modern Japan. University of Toronto, Canada.

Blacker, Carmen 1975: *The Catalpa Bow.*. London: George Allen & Unwin.

Bukkyō Jiten 1977: Tokyo: Isseido.

Ch'ü, Li-fu 1972: *Han Social Structure*. Ed. Jack Dull. Seattle: University of Washington Press.

Cleary, Thomas (trs.) 1978: *The Original Face: An Anthology of Rinzai Zen*. New York: Grove Press.

Collcutt, Martin 1981: *Five Mountains: The Rinzai Zen Monastic Institution in Medieval Japan*. Cambridge: Harvard University Press.

Dobbins, James C. 1989: *Jōdo Shinshū, Shin Buddhism in Medieval Japan*. Bloomington: Indiana University Press.

Earhart, H. Byron 1982: *Japanese Religion: Unity and Diversity*. Belmont: Wadsworth.

Earhart, H. Byron 1989: *Gedatsu-kai and Religion in Contemporary Japan*. Bloomington: Indiana University Press.

Embree, John F. 1982: *Suye Mura*. Chicago: University of Chicago Press.

Falk, Nancy A. 1974: An image of women in old Buddhist literature: the daughters of Mara. In Judith Plaskow and Joan Arnold (eds), *Women and Religion*, Missoula: Scholars Press, 105–12.

Fingarette, Herbert 1972: *Confucius – The Secular and the Sacred*. New York: Harper & Row.

Fiorenza, Elisabeth Schüssler 1983: *In Memory of Her: A Feminist Theological Reconstruction of Christian Origins*. New York: Crossroad.

Frye, Marilyn, 1983: Oppression. *The Politics of Reality: Essays in Feminist Theory*. Trumansburg, NY: The Crossing Press.

Fujikawa, Asako 1964: *Daughter of Shinran*. Tokyo: Hokuseido Press.

Grover, Paul 1984: *Saichō, The Establishment of the Japanese Tendai School*. Berkeley, CA: Berkeley Buddhist Studies Series.

Hardacre, Helen 1984: *Lay Buddhism in Contemporary Japan: Reiyūkai Kyōdan*. Princeton: Princeton University Press.

Hardacre, Helen 1986: *Kurozumikyō*. Princeton: Princeton University Press.

Heine, Steven, 1991: From rice cultivation to mind cultivation: the meaning of impermanence in Japanese religion. *History of Religions*, 30, 4, 373–403.

Hori, Ichirō et al. (eds) 1971: *Japanese Religions*. Tokyo: Kodansha International.

Hoshino, Eiki and Takeda, Dōsho 1987: Indebtedness and comfort: the undercurrents of Mizu Kuyō in contemporary Japan. *Japanese Journal of Religious Studies*, 14, 4, 305–20.

Ishimoto, Shidzué 1935: *Facing Two Ways*. New York: Farrar & Rinehart.

Kalven, Janet 1984: Epilogue. In Janet Kalven and Mary I. Buckley (eds), *Women's Spirit Bonding*. New York: Pilgrim Press, 357–72.

Kasahara, Kazuo 1975: *Nyonin ōjō shisō no keifu*. Tokyo: Yoshikawa kōbunkan, 197–220.

Kato, Genchi 1988 (1973): *A Historical Study of the Religious Development of Shinto*. New York: Greenwood.

Keene, Donald (trs.) 1967: *Essays in Idleness: The Tsurezuregusa of Kendo*. New York: Columbia University Press.

Kondō, Soken 1915: Kansai Nigakuin seito ni shimesu. *Jōrin*, 4.

Kraft, Kenneth 1992: *Eloquent Zen*. Honolulu: University of Hawaii Press.

Kuga, Kanshu 1916: Atte tsumarazu. *Jōrin*, 5.

Lau, D. C. (trs.) 1979: *Confucius, The Analects*. Middlesex: Penguin.

Legge, James (trs.) 1967: *Li Chi, The Book of Rites*. New Hyde Park, NY: New York University Books.

Legge, James (trs.) 1971: *Confucius* (1893). New York: Dover.

Li Chi, The Book of Rites. Trs. James Legge, 1967. New Hyde Park, NY: New York University Books.

Masaharu, Anesaki 1966: *Nichiren, The Buddhist Prophet*. Gloucester, MA: Peter Smith.

Mason, J. W. T. 1967 (1935): *The Meaning of Shinto*. Port Washington, NY: Kennikat Press.

Miles, Margaret R. 1985: Introduction. In Clarissa W. Atkinson, Constance H. Buchanan and Margaret R. Miles (eds), *Immaculate and Powerful*. Boston, MA: Beacon Press, 1–14.

Nakamura, Hajime 1969: *A History of the Development of Japanese Thought*, vol. 2. Tokyo: Kokusai bunka shinkokai.

Nakamura, Kyoko (trs. and annot.) 1973: *Miraculous Stories from the Japanese Buddhist Tradition*. Cambridge: Harvard University Press.

Nakamura, Kyoko Motomochi 1980: No women's liberation: the heritage of a woman prophet in modern Japan. In Nancy A. Falk and Rita M. Gross (eds), *Unspoken Worlds, Women's Religious Lives in Non-Western Cultures*, San Francisco; Harper & Row, 174–90.

Nakamura, Kyoko 1981: Revelatory experience in the female life cycle. *Japanese Journal of Religious Studies*, 8, 3–4, 187–205.

Offner, Clark B. and van Straelen, Henry 1963: *Modern Japanese Religions*. New York: Twayne.

Ogata, Doken 1958: Kuden homon no jissen rinri. *Nippon Bukkyo*, 2, 41–9.

Okane, Haruko 1976: *Die Stellung der Frau im Shinto*. Wiesbaden: Otto Harrassowitz.

Ono, Sokyo 1962: *Shinto, The Kami Way*. Rutland: Charles E. Tuttle.

Paul, Diana Y. 1979: *Women in Buddhism*. Berkeley, CA: Lancaster-Miller/Asian Humanities Press.

Reischauer, Edwin O. 1980: Introduction. In Stuart Picken, *Shinto, Japan's Spiritual Roots*. Tokyo, NY: Kodansha International, 6–8.

Sakura, Tokutarō 1971: *Minkan Shinko to Gendai Shakai*. Tokyo: Hyōronsha.

Shih Ching, *The Book of Songs*. Trs. Arthur Waley, 1960. New York: Grove Press.

Smith, Bardwell 1988: Buddhism and abortion in contemporary Japan: Mizuko Kuyō and the confrontation with death. *Japanese Journal of Religious Studies*, 15, 1, 3–24.

Smith, Robert J. 1974: *Ancestor Worship in Contemporary Japan*. Stanford: Stanford University Press.

Smith, Robert J. 1983: Making village women into 'good wives and wise mothers' in prewar Japan. *Journal of Family History*, 70–84.

Smith, Robert J. and Wisell, Ella Lury 1982: *The Women of Suye Mura*. Chicago: University of Chicago Press.

Smyers, Karen A. 1983: Women and Shinto: the relation between purity and pollution. *Japanese Religions*, 12, 4, 48–9.

Swyngedouw, Jan 1986: Religion in contemporary Japanese society. *The Japan Foundation Newsletter*, 13, 4, 1–14.

Takamure, Itsue 1948: *Nihon josei shakaishi*. Osaka: Nihonsha.

Takamure, Itsue 1966: *Takamura Itsue zenshū*. Tokyo: Rironsha.

Talim, Muna 1972: *Women in Early Buddhist Literature*. Bombay: University of Bombay.

Tu, Wei-ming 1985: *Confucian Thought, Selfhood as Creative Transformation*. Albany, NY: State University of New York Press.

Tucker, Mary Evelyn 1989: *Moral and Spiritual Cultivation in Japanese Neo-Confucianism*. Albany, NY: State University of New York Press.

Uchino, Kumiko 1981: *Nihon josei kenkyū kiso bunken mokuroko*. Tokyo: Gakuyo Shobo.

Uchino, Kumiko 1983: The status elevation process of Sōtō Sect nuns in modern Japan. *Japanese Journal of Religious Studies*, 10, 2–3, 177–94.

Waddell, Norman and Abe, Masao (trs.) 1971: Dōgen's bendowa. *The Eastern Buddhist*, 4, 1.

Waley, Arthur (trs.) 1960: *Shih Ching, The Book of Songs*. New York: Grove Press.

Warder. A. K. 1970: *Indian Buddhism*. Delhi: Motilal Banarsidass.

Index

Compiled by Mrs M. Davies (Society of Indexers)